Endorsements

The debate on Singapore's political economy has been too narrow, pitting an establishment defence of the status quo against a vaguely European-style social-democratic alternative. This book lays out an alternative: a limited government, free-market worldview of the classical liberal tradition. This view hardly figures in Singapore's debate. It is time it did.

> — Prof. Razeen Sally, Lee Kuan Yew School of Public Policy. Director of the European Centre for International Political Economy, Member of the Mont Pelerin Society and Ex-Chair of World Economic Forum's Global Agenda Council on Competitiveness.

This splendid book offers in a short space not only an intelligent critical discussion of issues of policy and institutional design in contemporary Singapore but also a tour of the economic and philosophical literature that guides the analysis. Classical liberals as well as their critics will learn much from this clear, thoughtful, and learned work.

> — Prof. Chandran Kukathas, Dean, School of Social Sciences & Lee Kong Chian Chair Professor of Political Science, Singapore Management University. Ex-Head of Department of Government at London School of Economics, author of *The Liberal Archipelago: A Theory of Diversity and Freedom* (OUP).

I highly recommend Bryan Cheang and Donovan Choy's fresh take on Singaporean policy discourse. They put forward a new classical liberal perspective that challenges both the establishment "Singapore consensus" and its progressive liberal critics. Engaging with themes such as social inequality, environmentalism, and media freedom, this book argues that classical liberalism offers a new "third way" for the future, one that moves beyond the ideas and tactics of top-down technocracy and that embraces a more diverse economy and society.

— **Prof. Christine Henderson,**
Associate Professor of Political Science,
Singapore Management University.

Bryan Cheang and Donovan Choy have produced a brilliant and useful book. They describe how Singapore's path forward is contested between "conservatives", who support continued state power over society, and "democratic socialists", who seek state control over the economy. Instead, they chart a "classical liberal" course for Singapore, emphasizing freedom, economic and social. They show how and why this improves the human condition. Importantly, they also show liberalism is not a "western" concept, but a universal one that recognizes the dignity of all individuals to make their own choices. This book should have a huge impact on the thinking of Singapore's future!

— **Fred McMahon,**
Dr. Michael A. Walker Chair of Economic Freedom Research,
Fraser Institute.

Moving away from polarized positions and emphasizing a perspective that starts from the complexity of the social order, the limits to knowledge and the need to foster institutions to promote competition, this book is a rich vein for an open and fertile discussion for

Singaporean society. Bryan Cheang and Donovan Choy make a strong case for Singapore to evolve to greater stages of prosperity, which only comes through freedom. The proposal: governance rooted in the political philosophy of epistemic liberalism.

— Prof. Sary Levy-Carciente,
Full Professor at Universidad Central de Venezuela,
Board Member of the International Institute of
Advanced Economic and Social Studies in Italy and
Lead Author of the International Property Rights Index.

Singapore has long shown the rest of the world how a country with few natural resources other than its people can become innovative, prosperous and functional. Singapore stands at a junction, with increasing pressure to head down a social democratic path. The authors convincingly demonstrate the dangers of this route and how classical liberalism provides a convincing alternative.

— Philip Stevens,
Executive Director,
Geneva Network.

Singapore is a development success story because it embraced the free market. But there is plenty of scope for reform. Contrary to the arguments of the establishment's defenders and of much of its critics, the authors of this book make the compelling case for a classical liberal program that maintains economic freedom but does away with technocratic paternalism, thus increasing choice and diversity in the lives of Singaporeans. In short, the book explains why a greater appreciation of freedom in all its dimensions holds the most promise among the competing alternatives facing Singapore today.

— Ian Vasquez,
Director,
Center for Global Liberty and Prosperity,
Cato Institute.

"Friedrich Hayek's book *The Fatal Conceit: Errors of Socialism* expressed with clarity and authority what I had long felt but was unable to express, namely the unwisdom of powerful intellects, including Albert Einstein, when they believed that a powerful brain can devise a better system and bring about more "social justice" than what historical evolution, or economic Darwinism, has been able to work out over the centuries." — Lee Kuan Yew, as quoted in Han et al. (1998), *Lee Kuan Yew, the Man and His Ideas*, p. 158.

LIBERALISM UNVEILED

FORGING A NEW THIRD WAY IN SINGAPORE

LIBERALISM UNVEILED

FORGING A NEW THIRD WAY IN SINGAPORE

Bryan Cheang

Adam Smith Centre, Singapore
King's College London

Donovan Choy

Adam Smith Centre, Singapore

W **World Scientific**

V JERSEY · LONDON · SINGAPORE · BEIJING · SHANGHAI · HONG KONG · TAIPEI · CHENNAI · TOKYO

Published by

World Scientific Publishing Co. Pte. Ltd.

5 Toh Tuck Link, Singapore 596224

USA office: 27 Warren Street, Suite 401-402, Hackensack, NJ 07601

UK office: 57 Shelton Street, Covent Garden, London WC2H 9HE

Library of Congress Cataloging-in-Publication Data

Names: Cheang, Bryan, author. | Choy, Donovan, author.

Title: Liberalism unveiled : forging a new third way in Singapore /
    Bryan Cheang, Donovan Choy.

Description: Singapore : World Scientific Publishing Co. Pte. Ltd., [2021] |
    Includes bibliographical references and index.

Identifiers: LCCN 2020028470 | ISBN 9789811220746 (hardcover) |
    ISBN 9789811220753 (ebook) | ISBN 9789811220760 (ebook other)

Subjects: LCSH: Liberalism--Singapore. | Singapore--Politics and government--Philosophy. |
    Singapore--Politics and government--21st century.

Classification: LCC JC574.2.S5 C47 2021 | DDC 320.51/2095957--dc23

LC record available at https://lccn.loc.gov/2020028470

British Library Cataloguing-in-Publication Data

A catalogue record for this book is available from the British Library.

For any available supplementary material, please visit
https://www.worldscientific.com/worldscibooks/10.1142/11841#t=suppl

Desk Editor: Ong Shi Min Nicole

Typeset by Stallion Press
Email: enquiries@stallionpress.com

About the Authors

Bryan Cheang is the Founder of the Adam Smith Center, Singapore's only organisation promoting research & education in the classical liberal tradition. Founded in 2018, it is part of the Atlas Network, and has since collaborated with government institutions, schools, and student societies to communicate its unique message of an open society.

Bryan is also a graduate of the National University of Singapore and King's College London, where he is completing his PhD in Political Economy. He is also a Humane Studies Fellow with the Institute for Humane Studies and an Adam Smith Fellow with the Mercatus Center. His academic research interests revolve around the political economy of development and applied economic policy, and his current focus is on state-market relations in the East Asian developmental state tradition. Bryan combines his academic interests with his previous policymaking experience with the Singapore civil service, where he worked on human capital policies for small-medium enterprises. Bryan is also the author of an upcoming book *Optimist's Guide to the Future*, published by Beard and Balloon.

Donovan Choy is a Visiting Research Fellow at the Adam Smith Center, Singapore. He is a graduate of the CEVRO Institute where he obtained a Masters in Philosophy, Politics, and Economics (PPE) with a specialisation in Institutional, Behavioural, and Austrian Economics. He was also

previously a Visiting Scholar at the American Institute for Economic Research (AIER). He is also an alumnus of the Institute for Humane Studies and a Young Affiliate at the European-based Network for Constitutional Economics and Social Philosophy (NOUS). His research interests revolve around the political economy of immigration and cultural political economy.

Foreword

Singapore has a hybrid political economy, a distinctive mix of "state" and "market". External observers tend to have a selective, indeed distorted, take on it, all the better to fit it into their worldviews.

For free-market types, Singapore is a global beacon of free trade, low taxes, business-friendly regulations, and a smallish government with low public expenditure and, by Western standards, a basic safety net. Hence the "Singapore-on-Thames" fantasies of liberal Brexiteers. For adherents of a state-guided market economy, Singapore is an exemplary "developmental state": the government plays a leading direct and indirect role in the economy, politics, and society. State-owned companies dominate the domestic economy in goods, services, and capital markets; the Central Provident Fund (CPF) dominates local savings; the Government Investment Corporation plays a major role in capital markets; industrial policy targets selected sectors and companies with tax breaks and other instruments; and powerful statutory boards like the Housing Development Board (HDB), Urban Redevelopment Authority (URA), and Jurong Town Corporation (JTC) give the government further means of control. In short, the government makes myriad interventions to nudge the economy and society in desired directions. Hence, in this telling, the Singapore state, like its counterparts in other East Asian tiger economies, "governs the market" to deliver economic success.

In reality, Singapore's political economy has evolved pragmatically under the leadership of Lee Kuan Yew, his People's Action Party (PAP) contemporaries and successors, combining a small, highly open economy with extensive domestic intervention to take advantage of unprecedented economic globalisation in the last half-century. "Pragmatism" is the governing elite's non-ideology, and its self-image. It is this peculiar mix that both free marketeers and developmental statists do not really grasp.

Domestically, the debate on Singapore's political economy has changed, particularly since the 2011 general election. The government and its sympathisers — the PAP state and its adherents — defend the status quo, more or less. To them the "model" is a proven success. It needs tweaking, pragmatically, to adapt to changing circumstances. What it does not need is radical surgery. Dissonance comes from a mix of local academics, civil-society activists, and media professionals, some clearly distant from the governing elite, others part of a comfortable semi-establishment elite tolerated, even indulged, by the state (a testament to the PAP state's extraordinary and enduring success in co-option).

These dissidents have a broadly centre-left, social-democratic orientation. European-style social democracy seems to be their lodestar; many idealise the mixed economies and welfare states of Western Europe. They focus on widening inequalities in "global-city" Singapore; what they see as excessive immigration; economic and social deprivation among the underclass; middle-class anxieties; and even the lack of civic and political space. They tend to favour political and social liberalism, but are also economic interventionists. They advocate a bigger, more active and redistributive state to make society "fairer". It is said that some dissident views resonate in parts of the PAP state.

These views are certainly influential on campus, as I have noticed among Singaporean colleagues and students at NUS. They prevail among the Singaporean students I have taught at the Lee Kuan Yew School. They will join Singapore's elite, particularly its administrative elite, and march through Singapore's institutions. Would this worry modern Singapore's founding father, gazing down at the public-policy school to which he gave his name? Would they endanger, and ultimately dismantle, his legacy? Might they eventually turn Singapore into an East Asian version of an economically sclerotic and socially decadent European state? I wonder.

Like the authors of this book, I find the debate on Singapore's political economy too narrow. It pits an establishment defence of the status quo against a vaguely European-style social-democratic alternative. That omits a different take on Singapore's political economy: a limited government, free-market worldview that comes from the classical-liberal tradition, starting with the Scottish Enlightenment of Adam Smith and David Hume, running through the 19th-century English classical economists, to 20th-century luminaries such as Friedrich Hayek and Milton Friedman. This tradition has been influential in the West, most recently and powerfully in Margaret Thatcher's UK and Ronald Reagan's USA, and in some developing countries and ex-command economies that have undergone radical market reforms. But it has never take hold in Singapore, despite the free-market features of its hybrid political economy. The governing ideology of pragmatism — an aversion to ideology itself — may have something to do with this. And so does the nearest thing to classical liberalism's categorical imperative: the primacy of individual liberty in all its forms, civic, political, social, and economic.

This book lays out such an alternative view, theoretically, institutionally, and programmatically. It looks at the Singapore state, and its role in the economy, polity and society, from a different angle: one of a normatively limited state that continues to exercise strong regulatory functions, but which leaves much more room for an entrepreneurial, bottom-up market economy, as well as a more open and diverse society. This is far from the minimal "night-watchman" state and anarcho-capitalism of popular caricature; rather it is a more nuanced calibration of how the state, economy, and society interact. The book also addresses pressing issues such as inequality and environmental protection from a different angle. It emphasises market-based instruments, and it is wary of the power-seeking and rent-seeking entanglements and sundry unintended consequences that accompany unchecked government intervention. Such views hardly figure in Singapore's debate. It is time they did. They would subject prevailing views, both pro-establishment and pro-social democratic reform, to much needed scrutiny.

Singapore needs to build on the successes of the last half-century and adapt flexibly to challenging times ahead. I think this book's classical-liberal vision and programme will help to clarify and widen the range of options open to Singapore. Finally, what happens in Singapore matters to the rest of the world — as a model of good governance and successful economic and social development, especially for other small states, and indeed for cities and city-regions. A classical liberal vision is most relevant for them.

Professor Razeen Sally
**Associate Professor, the Lee Kuan Yew School of Public Policy,
Chairman, the Institute of Policy Studies, Sri Lanka,
Director, the European Centre for International Political Economy.**

Contents

Classical Liberalism as A New Third Way

Singapore today is regarded as one of the most prosperous and successful nations in the world, with high material living standards relative to our neighbours, a peaceful and stable society, and a highly acclaimed public service. That this was achieved within a single generation is even more impressive. Singapore's governance today remains a model attracting the emulation of others on the world stage.

The Singapore system is one that stems from particular principles and institutions. On a philosophical level, there is a strong belief in competitive meritocracy, which translates into an aversion to universally-provided welfare in favour of merit-based human resource practices. That its economic success has been built on a system of technocratic elitism has led to public acceptance of the concentration of power into the hands of technocrats who are specially selected to helm the apparatus of government. On the whole, Singapore's system may be understood as a semi-democratic, developmental state capitalist model.

This "Singapore Consensus", crafted, shaped, and maintained by the People's Action Party (PAP) is, of course, not without its critics and detractors. Anti-establishmentarianism in Singapore arguably reached its high point in the watershed election of 2011, which saw, for the first time, the ruling PAP losing a Group Representative Constituency (GRC), for the first time in history (Singh, 2019, ch. 6). The recent elections in 2020 confirm the increasingly contested nature of the political space.

Beyond the electoral stage, political discourse today is also increasingly diverse. This may be due to a more vocal and globalised citizenry, and a civil society that desires higher post-material values. In this broader context, a new paradigm challenging the political establishment has emerged. Led by academic figures, media personalities, and civil society activists, Singapore has witnessed an emergence of what may reasonably be labelled as a new generation of progressive, social democratic voices.

This new chorus of voices shares several vital convictions. First, Singapore's political system can and should be reformed in a left-liberal direction. This involves higher levels of inter-party electoral competition, stronger protections of civil liberties, and personal lifestyle freedoms. On a closely related note, this group also emphasises the importance of social justice as a political value. It makes criticisms against the political status quo that is said to give too much emphasis to economic growth, material benefits, and large corporations. Motivated by the concern over economic inequality and environmentalism, these progressives call for a more sustainable and equitable economic system.

This perspective is best captured by the authors Donald Low and Sudhir Vadaketh in their bestselling 2014 book *Hard Choices: Challenging the Singapore Consensus.* According to the authors, the political status quo, which they label "the Singapore Consensus", is under challenge and should be reconsidered. Low and Vadaketh (2014, pp. 9–11) specifically aimed to "reframe" policy discourse in Singapore, to help steer the narrative away from the dominant framing of the ruling PAP. Their compilation of essays "question and interrogate many of the PAP government's long-standing beliefs", and consequently "examines a wide range of policies that should be rethought and reformulate" (Low & Vadaketh, 2014, pp. 11–12).

It should be made clear that the authors provide not just any random set of policy alternatives, but rather, a conscious "liberal agenda for the Singapore state" (see Low & Vadaketh, 2014, ch. 15). In response to the long-standing practice of political authoritarianism, Low and Vadaketh explore the possibilities and merits of political liberalisation (see ch. 15), and in response to the government's market-based policymaking, recommend the use of universal entitlements-based welfare provisions (see chs. 1, 9, and 10).

The arguments made by Low and Vadaketh do not stand alone. They are also supported, echoed, and advanced by other like-minded scholars and public figures who exhibit a distinct leftist political orientation. Professor Teo You Yenn is one such prominent figure, having written the bestselling *This is What Inequality Looks like*, which captured public attention with her ethnographic study of low-income families in Singapore and her recommendations of Scandinavian style welfare systems. The ex-GIC economist Yeoh Lam Keong has also emerged as a prominent critic of the PAP state, denouncing its neoliberal policies in favour of greater redistribution and comprehensive welfare schemes (Rahim & Yeoh, 2019). These social-democratic scholars in Singapore have called for a "new social compact", with a "larger state" (p. 20) that engages in more comprehensive social welfare programmes (Yeoh *et al.*, 2012)

Aside from scholars, other non-academic public figures have coalesced on the political left. Tommy Koh, a Singaporean lawyer, ambassador, and diplomat, has also made similar criticisms of the political establishment. In one revealing incident, he not only advocated for a national minimum wage — which is anathema to the pro-business orientation of the PAP — he also criticised the PAP for using "fake" ideological arguments to resist it.[1] The Straits Times Roundtable that he participated in is indeed reflective of the growing contestation in policymaking circles over the future of Singapore public policy.

We endorse the increasing plurality of voices on Singapore's governance and how it should move forward. When policies are questioned, debated, and questioned, new ideas might emerge to help us face an increasingly uncertain future. Our book participates in this ongoing effort to reframe political discourse in Singapore in a new direction.

We do so, however, from a new classical liberal perspective that has been little considered until now. Just as the "Singapore Consensus" has been challenged from the political left, which emphasises the principles of social democratic liberalism, we challenge the current discourse from a classical liberal lens, emphasising the importance of limited state

---

[1] Ang, M. (2018, December 4). *Straits Times panel on minimum wage is extension of Tommy Koh's FB post on debate with Lim Boon Heng*. Retrieved from: https://mothership.sg/2018/12/minimum-wage-tommy-koh-roundtable-discussion/.

intervention in society, individual self-responsibility, and decentralisation. Various thinkers have developed these principles throughout history, but they feature here for the first time concerning local, Singaporean political debate.

Transcending a Dichotomy

Classical liberalism offers a new third way in policy discourse in Singapore because the current narrative has settled into a binary left-right dichotomy typical of politics in many developed democratic countries.

The dynamics of political competition in many Western democratic countries typically follow a left-right pattern. On the right-wing of the spectrum are conservatives who are guided by notions of "order and community", and who believe in a strong state to stabilise an otherwise fragile social order (Brennan, 2016, pp. 14–15; Kling, 2017, ch. 1). These conservatives typically, though not always, favour policies that conform to traditional moral values, which are, in turn, believed to underpin stable or virtuous social order. Conservative positions also usually, though not by logical necessity, emphasise pro-business policies. The Republican Party in the USA and the Conservative Party in the U.K. are the best examples of this, combining socially conservative policies with economic policies that are fiscally conservative and which emphasise market forces.

Consequently, one may characterise the ruling People's Action Party (PAP) as "conservative" and thus occupying the right-wing of the political spectrum. We acknowledge that the PAP, its supporters, and intellectual defenders, may not subscribe to this label. It has defined itself precisely in rejection of ideological labels, in favour of what is considered as a form of non-ideological pragmatism. That much is true.

However, the rhetoric and policies of the PAP are not a random mass of inchoate opinions, but conform to clear patterns. The policies and style of governance created by the PAP do map somewhat coherently to an identifiable set of values. The policies implemented also bear a high level of consistency. The pro-business, fiscally conservative, economic growth orientation puts the PAP in the same camp as numerous other conservative parties worldwide, as the PAP's harshest critics contend. Its maintenance of strict legal restrictions on personal lifestyle choices is evident to every Singaporean and may rightly be described as socially conservative.

In the world of politics today; however, the political left is in the ascendancy. These "progressives", or "liberals"[2] emphasise the value of social justice, and thus solidarity with the oppressed, minorities, the poor, and those of lower social-economic class. While they are socially liberal, progressives tend to advocate government intervention into the market economy for fairness. In the current social context, some of these individuals take up the label of "democratic socialism" and oppose the excesses of global capitalism in favour of equitable regulation and redistribution of wealth.

The increasing influence of the political left is recognised all over the world. It has led to the prominence of figures such as Bernie Sanders, Jeremy Corbyn, and Alexandria Ocasio-Cortez, and the mass youth following they command. The Economist Magazine has explored this "rise of millennial socialism" in the developed world.[3] This is arguably also associated with the current state of higher education, where it is found that a vast majority of university academics are leftists (Langbert *et al.*, 2016; Langbert, 2018). They not only influence what students learn in class but key media platforms and social institutions (Cofnas *et al.*, 2018; Selepak, 2018).

It is thus unsurprising, given the global influence of left-wing ideas, that Singapore politics is also impacted. The PAP is challenged by a range of opposition parties in Singapore, such as the Workers Party, the Singapore Democratic Party, and the National Solidarity Party. However, many of these parties are relatively small. They do not pose a substantial challenge to the PAP, and that, more often than not, they mirror the PAP rather than produce substantially different platforms (Abdullah, 2017).

This caveat aside, it cannot be denied that there are general points of agreement that unify opposition politics in Singapore. Generally, opposition figures question the ongoing authoritarianism of the Singapore

---

[2] There are many labels used for this group, including "democratic socialists", "liberals", "modern liberals", "progressives", and "social democrats". For ease of reference, we use these terms interchangably.

[3] Economist. (2019, February 14). The Rise of Millennial Socialism. *The Economist*. Retrieved from: https://www.economist.com/leaders/2019/02/14/millennial-socialism.

government and call for reform in economic policy to become more generous to help the least well-off. The Singapore Democratic Party is arguably the party most diametrically opposed to the PAP, and it has a clear and consistent platform that features leftist policies such as the minimum wage, universal entitlements, and more significant redistribution.

It should be acknowledged, of course, that terms like "right-wing", "left-wing" are very much contested, and in fact, make more sense in relative terms. It may be said, for instance, that the former U.S. Vice President and current presidential candidate Joe Biden is to the "left" of Republicans, while still being on the "right" of the radical, self-declared democratic socialist Senator Bernie Sanders from Vermont. One should also rightly acknowledge that at times, policy recommendations may cross party and ideological lines. The non-interventionist instinct of the incumbent U.S. President Donald Trump is often at odds with the more common hawkish foreign policy penchant of the Republican establishment.

Thus, we confess that terms like "conservatives" and "progressives" are imperfect labels that obscure much of political reality. Political coalitions and alliances do not always fit neatly demarcated boxes. Yet, one may still use these terms as "ideal types", to better organise the otherwise confusing plurality of voices in social discourse. Just as a map necessarily simplifies geographical reality to make navigation easier, a "political map" may assist us in better conceptualising political reality with the use of simplifying ideal types.

Accordingly, we attempt to map out policy discourse in Singapore at the current moment, and what we view as its bifurcated nature along a left-right spectrum. We believe that the political establishment is now confronted by a range of critics who oppose them on numerous fronts, in academia, elections, media, and civil society. This dichotomy is split between the PAP's "Singapore Consensus", which is increasingly criticised by those on the political left.

The table below lays out the bifurcated nature of policy discourse in Singapore. The right-hand side of the table features the "Singapore Consensus" in Singapore, which has dominated local politics for decades. This is generally based on the governing philosophy of the PAP, with its emphasis on firm state control of society, aversion to Western-style democratic norms and human rights, a pro-business economic orientation,

Table 1:   Map of bifurcated policy discourse

New Progressive-Liberal Consensus	Conservative Consensus (Singapore Consensus)[4]
Academic Thought Leaders / Intellectual Advocates	
Scholars writing on socio-economic matters: Yeoh Lam Keong,[5] Donald Low,[6] Teo You Yenn[7] Political Scientists critical of PAP: Garry Rodan, Michael Barr, Kenneth Paul Tan[8] Revisionist historians[9] Lysa Hong, Tan Tai Yong, P.J. Thum.	Lee Kuan Yew Kishore Mahbubani?[10]

(Continued)

---

[4] Donald Low and Sudhir Vadaketh (2014, p. xiii) calls this the "Singapore Consensus".

[5] Together with his co-author, the ex-GIC economist Yeoh Lam Keong has argued that "to avoid the inequality trap, we need not just expanded social safety nets, but also more inclusive, even universal, ones" (Low & Vadaketh, 2014, p. 119).

[6] Donald Low is perhaps the most prominent anti-establishment academic in present-day policy discourse, not only because of his strong advocacy of progressive-liberal alternative policy principles, but also due, in part, to his public confrontations with the PAP ministers. Refer to: The Straits Times (2017, April 27). K. Shanmugam rebukes academic Donald Low over remarks misrepresenting his comments on criminal sentencing. *The Straits Times*. Retrieved from: https://www.straitstimes.com/singapore/k-shanmugam-rebukes-academic-donald-low-over-remarks-misrepresenting-his-comments-on.

[7] While her leading book *This is What Inequality Looks Like* is primarily an ethnographic study on inequality in Singapore, rather than a set of policy proposals, she nonetheless commended the Nordic universal entitlements welfare state system in Europe as worth following for Singapore.

[8] The political scientist from the Lee Kuan School of Public Policy has been critical, both in his academic and popular writings, of the PAP's system of governance, which he has explained, adheres to an ideology of neoliberalism and which has fostered income inequality and "systematic elitism". See his article: Tan, K. P. (2018, October 14). *S'pore's income inequality is made worse by elitist values & systematic elitism*. Retrieved from: https://mothership.sg/2018/10/kenneth-paul-tan-income-inequality-sg-elitism/.

[9] A new wave of revisionist Singaporean historians have made penetrating criticisms of what has been called "The Singapore Story", which is the official state-constructed narrative emphasising the indispensable role of the PAP leadership in transforming Singapore into the success it is today; refer to Barr (2019, ch. 1) and Hack (2012) for useful reviews of these new perspectives.

[10] He is placed here largely because of his consistent defence of Asian values, which we might interpret as conservative.

Table 1: (*Continued*)

New Progressive-Liberal Consensus	Conservative Consensus (Singapore Consensus)
Political Parties	
Singapore Democratic Party (SDP)[11] Reform Party[12] Workers Party[13]	People's Action Party (PAP)
Policy proposals / initiatives / recommendations	
A more expansive role for the state in redistribution and social welfare: implementation of minimum wage law, the establishment of European-style universal entitlements welfare system, increased social spending[14] Political liberalisation, increased competition in civic space, relaxation of censorship, increased protection of human rights.	A more circumscribed role for the state in redistribution and social welfare, insistence on the primacy of self-responsibility, co-payments principle in the provision of social welfare, maintenance on incentives to work Paternalistic and restrictive policies towards individual lifestyle choices, such as resistance to reform on LGBT issues & severe penalties on drug consumption and trafficking. Censorship and restrictions on civil liberties, civil society activists, and independent media activities.

[11] The SDP and its leader, Chee Soon Juan, has clearly on multiple occasions promoted policies that resembling progressive-leftist parties elsewhere, such as higher taxes on the rich, minimum wage law, and higher social spending. See the article: Yong, C. (2016, January 19). SDP calls for minimum wage, abolishing CPF minimum sum in its economic plan. *The Straits Times*. Retrieved from: https://www.straitstimes.com/singapore/sdp-calls-for-minimum-wage-abolishing-cpf-minimum-sum-in-its-economic-plan. Their manifesto also clearly lists the implementation of a minimum wage as a key policy goal and increased social spending and taxes on high-income earners. Retrieved from: https://yoursdp.org/news/sdp_lays_out_comprehensive_economic_measures_to_take_singapore_forward

[12] See manifesto of the Reform Party, Minimum Wage. (2010, September 28). Retrieved from: http://reform.sg/minimum-wage/.

[13] The Workers Party has supported a national minimum wage, more progressive taxation, and also more pro-active social welfare for the needy. In GE2020, Dr Jamus Lim also popularised the minimum wage. Retrieved from: http://www.wp.sg/wp-content/uploads/2015/08/Manifesto-2015-Official-online-version.pdf. See also article: Lee, A. (2015, September 6). Minimum wage viable, says WP's Gerard Giam. *TODAY Online*. Retrieved from: https://www.todayonline.com/ge2015/minimum-wage-viable-says-wps-gerald-giam.

[14] Low, D. (2019, February 14). The Curious Case of Missing Wealth Taxes in Singapore. *TODAY Online*. Retrieved from: https://www.todayonline.com/commentary/curious-case-missing-wealth-taxes-singapore.

and also a resistance to European style welfare states in favour of individual self-responsibility and targeted means-tested subsidies. An interesting point to note is that this perspective is heavily and singularly shaped by the personal worldview of Lee Kuan Yew himself (see Barr, 2000a for a comprehensive breakdown of Lee Kuan Yew's outlook), whose intellectual vision continues to cast a long shadow over the PAP's policies, and thus Singapore society.

For numerous decades since Singapore's independence, this consensus was mostly unquestioned, until now. But as Low and Vadaketh (2014, p. xi) have rightly pointed out, "the 'Singapore Consensus' that the PAP government has constructed and maintained in the last five decades is fraying". The 2011 watershed election brought to light the increasingly contested nature of Singapore policy discourse, featuring more vocal civil society activists and prominent thought leaders propagating alternative ideas for Singapore. We have grouped them in the left-hand side as the "New Progressive-Liberal Consensus", which generally favours greater liberalisation of the hitherto restricted political space in Singapore, and also a re-orientation of economic policy to consider the problem of socio-economic disparities, which are deemed to be increasingly urgent.

A revealing sign that this left-right dichotomy is coalescing is the results of the recent GE2020, which saw the PAP achieve one of its lowest ever vote shares, but also significantly, the strong showing of the Workers' Party. The breakthrough of the Workers' Party in Sengkang GRC featured the economist Dr Jamus Lim who championed the minimum wage, and also a civil society activist Ms Raeesah Khan who has cited a radical Marxist political philosopher, Angela Davis, as her political inspiration.[15] Their surprising performance, coupled with their youth following, arguably marks a clear shift of Singaporean politics towards the left.[16]

---

[15] Lee, S. (2020, July 6). *Left voices in Singapore's election*. Workers' Liberty. https://www.workersliberty.org/story/2020-07-06/left-voices-singapores-election

[16] This has also caused the PAP establishment to be worried about a "generational shift". Geddie, J., & Aravindan, A. (2020, July 16). *Singapore's rulers fret over generational shift in big election win*. Reuters. https://www.reuters.com/article/us-singapore-election-youth/singapores-rulers-fret-over-generational-shift-in-big-election-win-idUSKCN24H1D4

What Table 1 shows is also the critical role of intellectual opinion-makers, rather than just political figures. Anti-establishment figures have greater freedom to voice their criticism of the government beyond the confines of electoral politics. Unsurprisingly, numerous academics on the political left champion social democratic ideas, comprising prominent figures like Donald Low, Teo You Yenn, and Yeoh Lam Keong, as well as other political scientists and revisionist historians.

We acknowledge that there is much more diversity within this group than what has been outlined above. It is useful to identify several distinct sub-groups here. First, there are prominent thought leaders who have criticised the establishment for paying insufficient attention to economic disparities and who have promoted a more generous, universal, and redistributive social system, with prominent individuals such as Donald Low, the ex-GIC economist Yeoh Lam Keong, and sociologist Teo You Yenn coming to mind. The criticisms they make of the PAP's economic policy mirror the long-standing criticisms that political scientists have made about the PAP's governance and political authoritarianism. Additionally, they are accompanied by a new wave of revisionist historians critical of the state-constructed national historical narrative (Hack, 2012).

In addition to these academics, civil society activists have also increased their vocal activism in public, agitating for progressive causes such as the abolishment of the death penalty, media liberalisation, and human rights (see Vincent, 2018 for useful profiles of such activists). We do not, in any way, assume that their views are homogenous. But what this group has in common is their critical attitude towards either the political principles of the PAP or their defining policies.

It is also acknowledged that not all the critics of the pro-PAP establishment actively promulgate policy alternatives, as some may only be providing descriptive, albeit critical analyses of Singapore's economy, history, or society. However, it is reasonable to identify a distinct set of policy alternatives that conforms to progressive-liberal political philosophy and which resembles the proposals made by political parties and politicians under this banner elsewhere.

We thus come back to Donald Low and Sudhir Vadaketh's (2014) *Hard Choice: Challenging the Singapore Consensus*, which we take very seriously in our account. Written consciously in opposition to the traditional belief that what Singapore requires is a "competitive meritocracy accompanied by relatively little income or wealth redistribution", this book goes on to promote a progressive, liberal agenda for Singapore, which features two policy thrusts, first, a move to a more proactive universal entitlements based welfare system and away from the current model of limited provision, and second, greater political liberalisation and thus a move away from PAP's authoritarianism.

Our book challenges the defining features of the existing status quo dominated by the PAP and also the nascent progressive-liberal consensus that has emerged to criticise it.

Classical Liberalism's Distinctiveness

Classical liberalism is a distinct political perspective that has never featured in any prominent way in Singapore society. It has never been propagated by any leading academic, politician, or media personality in Singapore. To better understand its unique contributions, it is necessary to define it.

What is Classical Liberalism?

Classical liberalism is a political philosophy that generally emphasises the importance of civil and economic freedoms. As with any other political philosophy, it is contested and interpreted by a variety of its advocates. What unites its advocates, however, is the conviction that the role of the state should be circumscribed to preserve a private sphere for the individual. Societies, as much as possible, should be governed by voluntary associations forged between friends, families, and civil society groups, or in the form of market transactions. This is not to say, as some of its critics have alleged, that the government should simply "do nothing". Instead, classical liberals argue that state action should be limited, or minimal, and bounded by general constitutional rules, akin to a "traffic light" system that provides a legal framework for individuals to otherwise act freely according to their separate plans (Epstein, 1995).

Classical liberalism is not a new political philosophy but has roots in the Western Enlightenment of the 18th century, with luminaries such as John Locke, David Hume, and Adam Smith. While it has experienced upturns and downturns of popularity, classical liberal voices have existed in each generation, with the most prominent standard-bearers in the 20th century being the political economists Milton Friedman and Friedrich Hayek (Brennan & Schmidtz, 2009).

At this point in the characterisation so far, it would be understandable for the reader to associate classical liberalism so described with an extreme form of free-market advocacy, otherwise referred to as the "neoliberalism" of the Washington Consensus, which is said to have failed in countries that adopted it (Stiglitz, 2002). We reject this characterisation. The classical liberalism we introduce does not refer to any fixed or specific policy bundle, let alone the "privatization, deregulation and market liberalization" of the Washington Consensus, even though classical liberals generally favour these policies (Boettke & Nicoara, 2015).

Instead, by classical liberalism, we refer to an *intellectual tradition* comprising of a whole cast of thinkers who have propounded and developed different political programmes, but which generally endorse an *institutional* regime of polycentricity, decentralisation, and a plurality of rules. In other words, we mean that classical liberalism is not defined by one single, fixed, unchanging set of dictums that are commanded from the high altar of neoliberalism: "the market shalt make all things right". Classical liberal thinkers have always acknowledged the role of state action and have varying degrees of political-economic stances. Even the so-called 'high priest' of 20th century neoliberalism Friedrich von Hayek endorsed a range of social provisions, including the increasingly popular universal basic income (Burczak, 2013).

Classical liberalism is, however, a *tradition* that takes seriously the prevailing institutions, or the rules of the game that operate in any given society, since they determine the incentive and epistemic environment of human action. Classical liberals engage in comparative institutional analysis to ascertain the cases where markets may perform better than state action, by considering the very real problem of limited human rationality (we can't possibly know everything there is to know) and limited benevolence (humans are not angels) (Pennington, 2011). What classical liberals tend to conclude from this analysis is that when there are competing, decentralised sets of rules, rather than centralised control, people live better lives (Kukathas, 2003; Sabetti & Castiglion, 2016; Boettke *et al.*, 2019).

The focus on the prevailing institutional rules of the game by classical liberals highlights the vital contribution classical liberalism brings to Singaporean policy discourse. The bifurcated nature of discourse today, as mapped out above, has mostly revolved around a "political level of analysis" which assumes much more than we care to realise. Both conservatives and the new generation of progressive-liberals in Singapore do not question fundamental assumptions about the proper extent of the state in society, and in fact, take for granted the underlying necessity of central planning by the state as a locus of authority. The PAP state believes it ought to maintain the decision-making power to restrict lifestyle choices, censor the media and the Internet, maintain the death penalty, etc. Many on the left, however, if given their way, would similarly empower the state to intervene more heavily into the economic life of citizens through an array of tax and redistributive policies. Classical liberals contest the specific areas of how, *but also whether if at all*, the state should be involved.

We thus challenge the new progressive-liberal agenda for being guilty of the same planning bias that they criticise the Singapore Consensus of being guilty of. We recommend a higher level of "institutional analysis", which goes beyond a left-right dichotomy and which explores the fundamental question of the extent to which the state should be involved in shaping economic, social, and political life.

Classical Liberalism Challenges the Single Power Principle, which Most Take for Granted

Classical liberalism is worth considering because it offers a distinct worldview that transcends what we currently have available. This is because it challenges the single power principle, which most other worldviews, political proponents, and scholars take for granted. Rather than reformulating what the state ought to be doing, classical liberals question whether many of the existing functions of the state should be subject to centralisation in the first place.

Classical liberalism as a unique worldview in the world

On a larger level, classical liberalism is a unique worldview that challenges the preconceived notions taken for granted in all other competing philosophies. Specifically, it questions the very idea of political authority and whether it is legitimate, just, and even necessary (Huemer, 2013). All philosophies, including the dominant conservative and progressive positions, are guilty of the "single power principle", which Georgetown University legal scholar Randy Barnett defines as:

> "The *Single Power Principle* specifies that there must exist somewhere in society (a) a single institution per unit of geography (a "monopoly"), (b) that is charged with authorizing the use of force ("power"), and that (c) the monopoly itself must be preserved by force ("coercively"). In sum, the Single Power Principle involves a belief in the need for a *coercive monopoly of power*" (2014, p. 240).

Most politicians, political parties, and other prominent political philosophies subscribe to this principle. Randy Barnett has shown that both left and right philosophies are motivated by a central fear, which in their view, justifies a strong role for the state to avert a certain calamitous future. Both conclude that "there must be a boss" in charge.

We have decided to reprint the relevant passages from Barnett (2014, p. 240–243) and display them in a table here. The reader will notice that these words bear a striking resemblance to much of the current day political rhetoric both in local discourse and globally.

	Left ("Progressive liberals")	Right (Conservatives)
The fear	The Left believes in the Single Power Principle to ensure some positive conception of "social" justice. According to this view, resources must be distributed among individuals in society according to some formula or, to use Robert Nozick's term, a "pattern."	The Right believes that a coercive monopoly of power is needed to preserve "civilisation" and prevent social chaos; that without a coercive monopoly of power, people will give in to their animalistic side and engage in a Hobbesian social "war of all against all."
The dark future	The image that best describes the world that the Left sees as resulting from the absence of a coercive monopoly of power is one in which unreconstructed Scrooge-like characters enslave or exploit helpless Cratchets and Tiny Tims at below subsistence wages in small, cold (or hot, depending on the imagery), dark rooms.[17]	The image that best describes the world the Right sees as ultimately resulting from the absence of a coercive monopoly of power is one in which people are fornicating in public places with heroin needles hanging from their arms.[18]
The necessity of state intervention	Resources must be held, for example, according to some criteria of need, desert, or desires, or all holdings must be "equal" or "efficient" — that is distributed to their highest-valued use. It is argued that without a coercive monopoly of power, actual distributions of resources will not be in accordance with the mandated pattern or principle. Thus, in addition to prohibiting the forcible	Thus, it is argued that to avoid such social degeneration, a central authority must outlaw certain kinds of conduct: the forcible interference with person and possessions should be prohibited, to be sure, but also included should be sexual conduct, such as prostitution, pornography, homosexuality,[19] and extramarital sexual relations;

[17] This is precisely the same fear that motivates the work of non-governmental organisations in Singapore promoting the rights of migrant workers, who are seen to be severely exploited. See article: Silvam, P. (2019, April 7). In rich Singapore, why must migrant workers go hungry?. *South China Morning Post*. Retrieved from: https://www.scmp.com/week-asia/health-environment/article/3004901/rich-singapore-why-must-migrant-workers-go-hungry.

[18] This fear is precisely what animates the PAP's policy on drugs in Singapore, which according to international standards is one of the most punitive and antithetical to human rights.

[19] Singapore is on the ever-smaller list of countries that maintains a criminal law against private homosexual activity.

Left ("Progressive liberals")	Right (Conservatives)
interference by some with the person and possessions of others, a central authority is needed to "regulate" (usually a euphemism for prohibit) economic transfers between individuals by such measures as labour regulations,[20] antitrust regulations, price or rent controls, and licensing schemes in various occupations; to regulate other social interactions by such measures as quotas and preferences; and to regulate consumptive activity, by such measures as food and drug regulation and the regulation of automobile design. Above all, we must redistribute income by tax and "welfare" laws.[21]	or conduct that encourages "antisocial" beliefs, such as religious "cults," unacceptable books and music, manners of dress, Internet communication,[22] and public assembly;[23] or behavior that is "destructive of values," such as drug and alcohol consumption, gambling, pool rooms, video arcades, and rock and roll.[24]

[20] There are increasing calls for greater worker protections for transient migrant workers in Singapore. Myths and Facts: Migrant Workers in Singapore. 2017, September 9. Retrieved from: https://newnaratif.com/research/myths-and-facts-migrant-workers-in-singapore/. There are also calls for the minimum wage.

[21] The advocacy of redistributive and expansive welfare policies by centre-left politicians and public figures is clear. The Deputy Prime Minister Tharman Shanmugaratnam himself acknowledged this shift to the left. See article: Chang, R. (2016, January 19). Govt made shift well before 2011 election: Tharman. *The Straits Times*. Retrieved from: https://www.straitstimes.com/singapore/govt-made-shift-well-before-2011-election-tharman.

[22] The PAP state has put in place numerous measures to shape, define, and restrict the use of the Internet as a medium of communication, with the Protection from Online Falsehoods and Manipulation Act (POFMA) as the latest intervention in this regard. For an academic review of the Internet being subject to state control, see https://www.jstor.org/stable/2657651?seq=1.

[23] Every Singaporean would be aware that public assemblies are highly regulated in Singapore and require permissions if they are to be held at Speakers Corner. Singapore: Restrictions on Freedom of Expression (2005, August 5). Retrieved from: http://www.thinkcentre.org/article.php?id=2623.

[24] The Singapore PAP government, only very recently in 2019, controversially banned the rock and roll group, Watain, from performing, due to concerns about the offensiveness of their lyrics. See article: Channel NewsAsia (2019, March 14). 'I can't see how we could have agreed to it': Shanmugam on Watain performing in Singapore. *Channel NewsAsia*. Retrieved from: https://www.channelnewsasia.com/news/singapore/shanmugam-watain-singapore-concert-cancelled-11327984.

At this point, one may assert that this "single power principle" is an inevitable necessity in society. If the state did not exist, then how would there be law and order? It is intuitive to think that social order, stability, and law are creations of the state, and would evaporate in its absence. This is where classical liberals offer unique insights by exploring the concept of spontaneous order, which is that order can, and has often, arisen through "human action, but not of human design". Classical liberal historians of law and governance have shown how legal systems have spontaneously emerged outside of the state sector (Benson, 2011; Leeson, 2014). This does not imply that anarchy always works or is always desirable, but that human beings have an underappreciated capacity for self-governance. These include not only public governance but also private forms of governance that allow people to live harmoniously (Stringham, 2015).

We do not argue for the abolishment of all state authority. Indeed, we are not calling for the total abolition of the Singapore state. Yet, we do advocate for it to be circumscribed, certainly much more than currently envisioned by leading participants in local policy discourse. This implies not lawlessness, but a strong rule of law that governs an otherwise private realm of action. The unique contributions of classical liberal political economy, emphasising the need for institutional rules to facilitate bottom-up experimentation in the private and civil society sectors, has been found in the wider fields of public administration (Boettke *et al.*, 2019), environmental policy (Ostrom, 2009), development studies (Coyne, 2013), regulatory studies (Thierer, 2016), and more.

These classical liberal ideas, elsewhere applied to real-world concrete policy concerns, have never been considered in relation to local Singapore issues. The PAP state finds top-down, command-control mechanisms very amenable to its style of governance. Not only has it maintained authoritarian controls in politics, but it also has, on various occasions, engaged in stringent regulations on personal choice. While it does accord a high degree of market freedoms, the economy is nonetheless subject to national economic plans, which are formulated by the Singapore economic agencies. The economy is shaped, steered, and directed by a range of incentives and also the leadership of numerous government-linked corporations (Barr, 2019, ch. 7).

Critics of the PAP style of governance have rightly criticised its authoritarian nature, advocating for greater protection of human rights and civil liberties. However, most of the PAP critics are still subject to the same single power principle that the PAP has been guilty of. While the new progressive-liberals criticise PAP government policies, they do not question the very necessity of state action, but merely ask for other forms of intervention that they favour. If their signature policies like the minimum wage, state redistribution, and labour regulations are consistently pursued, state power in society will be greatly heightened. From a classical liberal viewpoint, they seek to replace political authoritarianism with economic authoritarianism.

We present arguments throughout this book to be sceptical of the increased advocacy for universal entitlements, welfare states and generous social previsions that a large chorus of local academics are calling for, including but not exclusive to Donald Low, Sudhir Vadaketh, Teo You Yenn, and Yeoh Lam Keong. We maintain that economic freedom and minimal government regulation not only is the best means to achieve mass prosperity for people but is a necessary component of any effort to liberalise Singapore politics.

Thus, our book cannot be construed as a conservative defence of the PAP political establishment, which has engaged in illiberal practices both in the political and economic realm. If anything, our account represents a more profound critique of the Singapore model of governance than what others have offered.

Structure of the Book

At this point, we clarify what this book is *not* trying to achieve. We are not attempting to make a knock-down argument for the superiority of classical liberalism as a philosophy and to present it as necessarily the best of all possible worlds. Rather, we wish to offer, for the first time, a good case to consider its principles in relation to significant policy concerns in Singapore.

Part 1: Challenging Technocratic Governance

We focus, in the first part, on the realm of political philosophy. We specifically investigate the philosophical tenets that underpin the Singapore system of governance as constructed by the PAP, which are the concepts of

Asian values, meritocracy, and also the belief in technocratic elitism. These three major principles not only undergird the current status quo but justify an aversion to liberalism. We dedicate a chapter to each of these concepts, thereby allowing us to more clearly delineate the account of classical liberalism we defend.

The concept of "Asian values", which prizes communitarian political principles over individualist ones, is perhaps the primary theoretical justification *against* liberalism in Singapore. We address this in **Chapter 2**, which discusses classical liberal philosophy in relation to the long-running debate over Asian values and human rights. While the Asian values thesis may have been used as a smokescreen for authoritarianism in some countries, it still possesses intellectual pedigree and has been developed by various scholars (Bauer & Bell, 1999). In the Singapore context, it has been advanced by public figures like Lee Kuan Yew, Kishore Mahbubani, Tommy Koh, and Bilahari Kausikan (Barr, 2000b). Any discussion of liberalism in Singapore cannot escape the persistent idea that it is a Western ideology that has no basis in a communitarian, Asian society.

Classical liberal philosophy should be understood with reference to what the political economist Fredrich Hayek called the "knowledge problem", which emphasises the complexity of social order and the limits of the human mind. The moral case for classical liberalism does not necessarily rest on any particular set of cultural values, like Western notions of individualism or autonomy, but rather, the recognition that no one is necessarily in a position to know what is best for others, and that central planning of society runs into inevitable problems that occur in *any* human context. This has been called "epistemic liberalism", by various scholars (Tebble, 2016; Gaus, 2017).

We note that many criticisms of Western liberalism by advocates of Asian values are based on arguments made off empirical grounds, and not just on moral grounds. These critics of liberalism insist that Western liberal democracies like the United States and other European ones suffer from serious economic, social, and political problems that Singaporeans should be very happy to avoid. It is also said that Western countries have been hypocritical and hubristic in their advocacy of human rights around the world.

Our account takes both the moral arguments in favour of East Asian cultural particularism and the more practical arguments about Western failures seriously. We conclude that these very legitimate concerns are best resolved once we conceive liberalism in a classical sense. The unique form of classical liberalism we outline, that of epistemic liberalism, is best placed to cope with the particularistic demands of specific cultural groups in a diverse world. Additionally, many of the problems in Western society may themselves be traced back to the deviation from its classical liberal heritage.

East Asian political theory not only emphasises cultural particularism but the superiority of political meritocracy over Western liberal democracy. This is why the Singapore model of political meritocracy has been held up as an exemplar. Yet, the new progressive-liberal consensus has criticised this system for promoting elitism and social disparities. With this in mind, *Chapter 3* examines the philosophy of meritocracy in Singapore's system of governance and responds to this criticism. We refer to the leading perspective on this issue made by Professor Kenneth Paul Tan (2008) and present a classical liberal analysis. We mostly agree that the problem of elitism that is prevalent in Singapore's system of meritocracy but argue that this is an inevitable and unavoidable result of the state's role in shaping the parameters of meritocracy. Consequently, we suggest that much of this problem will be alleviated through a more organic, market-driven discovery of "merit" that is necessarily bottom-up.

The third major pillar of Singapore's governance is the belief in technocratic elitism, which is the basic idea that some individuals in society are necessary more intellectually endowed to rule over the rest of society. This practice has previously been criticised for being anti-democratic, for abusing the civil liberties of people, and for being intellectually arrogant (Rajah, 2012; Barr & Rahim, 2019; Barr, 2020). In our chapter, we add to the literature by showing how this technocratic attitude has not waned over the years but has *accelerated* in recent years due to the rise of the discipline of behavioural economics and new big data tools.

In *Chapter 4*, we analyse the limits of behavioural economics and big data technologies as tools of governance. We engage with the text by Donald Low (2011) titled *Behavioural Economics and Policy Design: Examples from Singapore*, which provides a theoretical justification for and empirical evidence of how behavioural nudging is used locally. We also investigate the widespread use of big data technologies and scenario planning, best explained by Peter Ho, a former top civil servant in Singapore. The approach of "behavioural paternalism" in Singapore is based on excessive confidence in the ability of central planners to aggregate complex information. This paradigm ignores the problem of bounded rationality and dispersed knowledge and thus excludes the necessity of competition as a discovery procedure.

The concept of Asian values, meritocracy, and technocratic elitism together form the philosophical underpinnings of Singapore's governance. It is a system that has strict regulations on political competition and free expression. This is an open secret that needs no further elaboration. *Chapter 5* turns to this aspect by focusing on the media landscape. We not only affirm the criticisms made by liberals in Singapore of the incumbent government's restrictive stance on the media landscape, but we also provide a classical liberal analysis for why media liberalisation is desirable. If we wish to achieve a society that is socially and economically progressive, we need to have one that allows people to learn from best practices and correct their errors. A free media is essential.

Part 2: Challenging Emerging Progressive, Leftist Advocacy

In the second part of the book, we turn our attention to the critics of the "Singapore Consensus". These are largely voices that not only advocate for greater political liberalisation but also vast changes to the PAP's economic policies. Being progressive-liberals, these critics condemn what they deem as the excessive faith placed in neoliberalism in Singapore. Professor Teo You Yenn, for example, has written extensively about how neoliberal values guide moral thinking in Singapore (Teo, 2012). They argue that the severity of economic inequality requires the PAP to abandon its market-leaning orientation in favour of greater redistribution.

We investigate this by engaging with the two leading progressive-liberal academics in Singapore, Mr. Donald Low, and Professor Teo You Yenn. We do so in part because their works have captured public attention in recent years, and also because we find it constructive to juxtapose the classical liberal perspective we put forward against leading alternatives. We believe that this conscious use of the dialectical method will allow the reader to discern the differences between various philosophies and draw out the implications for themselves, and hopefully to see our position as a unique "third way".

After which, we move onto the topic of inequality, which has been the chief source of consternation of progressive-liberals in Singapore, many of whom have criticised the sustainability of the PAP's welfare policy, or lack thereof. Here we examine the topic from a political economy perspective and ask whether the state is best placed to solve market problems. We examine the arguments from leading proponents of the liberal welfare state in Singapore.

We also decided to engage with the arguments of Donald Low and Teo You Yenn for disciplinary reasons, since we wish to demonstrate the versatility of classical liberalism as a research paradigm. In *Hard Choices*, the authors present arguments from a more traditional *economics and public policy* perspective, and Teo You Yenn's work, from a rather different *sociological* perspective. Coupled with the philosophical approach in the first part of the book, this selection allows us to demonstrate the methodological versatility of *classical liberal PPE (philosophy, politics, and economics)*.

Accordingly, we continue our account with **Chapter 6**, which applies the insights of political economy to the challenge of inequality. We question whether inequality per se merits state intervention, particularly the minimum wage, income, and wealth redistribution that leading social democrats in Singapore favour. We also refer to the "four myths of inequality" that the PAP government is accused of perpetuating (see Low & Vadaketh, 2014, ch. 1), and with that, build the case against more generous universal welfare provisions, a proposal in vogue in policy discourse all around the world.

In **Chapter 7**, we expand our methodological toolkit by engaging with the unique, sociological, and ethnographic method presented by Professor Teo You Yenn in her bestselling book. *This is What Inequality Looks Like*. We commend the attempt to explore poverty and inequality beyond traditional economics and public policy approaches, which all too often reduce these trends to mere statistics to be fixed by technocrats. A sociological, ethnographic approach restores dignity to the subject under investigation: ordinary people.

Our analysis draws on the insights of interpretive political economy, which blends economics and sociology. We show that numerous culturally-sensitive political economists have gone beyond the confines of positivist, mainstream economics and incorporated ethnography, cultural methods, and sociology into their research. This has been called humanomics (Wilson & Smith, 2019), humane economics (High, 2017), humane liberalism (McCloskey, 2019), or Austrian social economics (Chamlee-Wright & Storr, 2015), all of which emphasise the positive interlinkages between markets and human welfare.

It is with this larger understanding in mind that we examine Professor Teo's book. We argue that her ethnographic approach is fundamentally neutral to any specific policy conclusion and can, in fact, be employed in favour of different prescriptions. While Teo recommends progressive liberal policies, her investigation of human inequality may easily lead one to an opposite conclusion: which is to expand economic freedom to generate prosperity. We also extend our analysis by presenting original interviews. Inspired by Teo's methodological lead to go up close and personal with her research subjects, we have done likewise. While we did not conduct a comprehensive ethnography, which would go beyond the scope and feasibility of this project, we conducted a series of personal interviews with individual Singaporeans. We show from these conversations that while Singapore's meritocracy has flaws, it has facilitated social mobility for many.

We conclude by engaging with a relatively new policy issue that has burst into the mainstream: environmental protection and climate change. *Chapter 8* allows us to compare and contrast the incumbent PAP government's approach to the environment, which has mainly been based on economic growth, and also the new progressive-liberal critiques levelled against it, which call for the state to be more interventionist, legislating carbon taxation, 'net zero emissions' policies, etc.

Our classical liberal perspective allows us to synthesise both dominant approaches by showing that the PAP's commitment to economic growth may be achieved at the same time as the new proposals for environmental conservation. The cause of environmentalism in Singapore is best served through a framework of bottom-up adaptation rather than outright mitigation. This involves an ongoing process of experimentation involving the public, private, and civil society sectors in Singapore, rather than through a single national blueprint.

Classical liberalism is a political philosophy, but we do not assume that philosophy alone is the only factor that should guide policy. Policymaking cannot, and should not, proceed linearly from the ivory tower, but must indeed take into account real-world constraints, trade-offs, and potential unintended consequences. This is why while this book is cast through the lens of classical liberal philosophy, we also adopt an eclectic methodological approach that blends insights from political philosophy as well as political economy. Both work in tandem with one another, and in fact, the most robust analyses combine both elements (Badhwar, 2016; Levy, 2016; Schmidtz, 2016). Any discussion of what is just, moral, and desirable in politics — the realm of political philosophy — should be considered with how political & economic institutions function in the real world in conjunction with human action — the realm of political economy. It is in this spirit that we make a preliminary case for why classical liberalism provides better moral and practical guidance for understanding how to improve governance in Singapore.

Asian Values and Classical Liberalism

Singapore, Asian Values, and the Aversion to Liberalism

One source of criticism against the political philosophy of liberalism stems from the ideological contentions with "Asian values." Associated with East Asian societies' rise to global prominence in the late 20th century, the essence of Asian values, which include consensus and community, flies in the face of Western liberalism. Given their fundamental differences, scholars have argued that Western models of governance do not hold universal applicability, both on a normative and descriptive level. Normatively, Western-style liberalism is not necessarily desirable. It may not take into account legitimate cultural values that non-Western societies prize and may even lead to harm if practiced excessively. Descriptively, there have been many societies, most dramatically Asian ones, that have achieved success and prosperity by deviating from liberal prescriptions (Amsden, 2000).

The "Asian values" argument is a school of thought that emerged from the rising global prominence of the non-Western world and the exposure of the contemporary problems that plague Western societies. The Western triumphalism at the end of the Cold War was short-lived and gave way to a global financial crisis in 2008, undermining the confidence in the Western world and, to some extent, global financial institutions. Today, Western societies experience rising populist pressures driven by fears of economic uncertainty, anti-globalisation sentiments, and a range of socio-economic challenges. In such an atmosphere, it is only logical to question: what is so great about Western liberalism?

Singapore has been the site of this major debate. The founding father of Singapore, Lee Kuan Yew, had famously remarked that "westerners value the freedoms and liberties of the individual. As an Asian of Chinese cultural background, my values are for a government which is honest, effective and efficient" (Lee, 1992). While some have denounced this as reactionary justification for authoritarian rule, there is a distinct "Singapore school" of thought which has emerged, led by prominent diplomats and foreign service professionals, namely, Tommy Koh, Bilahari Kausikan, and Kishore Mahbubani (see Barr, 2000b).

Within the Singapore context, there exists the argument that on a practical level, the West has been hubristic and hypocritical in their promotion of liberal values; even as they preach the gospel of freedom worldwide, they have themselves engaged in unsavoury practices. This is best captured in the seminal essay[1] by Kishore Mahbubani, which pointed out what he called "heresies" that the Western liberal establishment has failed to acknowledge, amongst which the fact that Western governments have "worked with genocidal rulers when it serves their interests", and that they will "happily sacrifice the human rights of third world societies when it suits Western interests" (Mahbubani, 2018a, pp. 122–127). The question therefore is: how dare Western societies lecture others about human rights and democracy when they have done so much to the contrary of these principles?

Not only does this undermine their moral authority, but the failed policies of the West have also diminished their global standing and security. Kishore Mahbubani specifically criticises how "the West has sought to impose its ideology on the world", and concludes that "it must stop seeking to intervene, politically and militarily, in the affairs of other nations" (Mahbubani, 2018b). Given the concurrent rise of new powers like China and India, global institutions should also be reformed to account for this shift.

The Asian values thesis has, to some extent, influenced policymaking on the part of the People's Action Party (PAP) government. It is well-known

---

[1] This essay was initially presented at a 1993 symposium, and which has been republished in the latest edition of *Can Asians Think?*

that Singapore performs poorly on press freedom, civil liberties, and political competition, maintains criminal laws on LGBT (lesbian, gay, bisexual and transgender) individuals, and has a death penalty on drug offenders (Freedom House, 2019). On this note, PAP policymakers have resisted what they perceive as inappropriate calls by global Western organisations, politicians, and media for Singapore to liberalise these domestic policies. In a revealing interview with the BBC, Prime Minister Lee Hsien Loong insisted that "the world is a diverse place, nobody has a monopoly on virtue or wisdom", and that "I would not presume to tell you how your Press Council should operate. Why should you presume to tell me how my country should run?" (BBC, 2017). The implication is that Singapore has its own set of values and practices, which are working very well, thank you very much.

Singapore's relative socio-economic success and political stability mean that this argument must be taken seriously, even if others reject it. Indeed, Singapore has consciously forged its own path of governance, at times adhering to Western practices, but many times deviating from them. The leading socialist intellectual in Singapore, Chua Beng Huat, has aptly written that Singapore has "disavowed liberalism"; this is true not only on a political level but also in the way Singapore has constructed its brand of state capitalism, which diverges from laissez-faire economics (Chua, 2017). Singapore's pragmatic policymaking seems to have brought much success. In the face of such success, it sounds almost hollow even to consider that the West may have something better to offer.

This issue being discussed is no mere academic exercise but has policy implications. The Singapore school advocates believe that considering the problems in Western societies today, it would be harmful if one emulates them. The leading proponent of this worldview, Kishore Mahbubani, articulates that the excessive individualism of the West has led to "results (that) have been disastrous", with an increase in violent crime, divorce rates, and the percentage of children living in single-parent homes (Mahbubani, 2018a, p. 111). This is "massive social decay" that other countries would be wise to avoid. On the economic front, it is argued that "Western societies are trying to defy the economic laws of gravity", with the fact that "budgetary discipline is disappearing, expensive social programs and pork-barrel projects multiply with little heed to costs" (Mahbubani, 2018a, p. 111).

As such, it is fair to summarise the "Singapore school thesis" as comprising the following claims:

1. The West has been hubristic and hypocritical in its promotion of liberal values, i.e., they don't practice what they preach. They have no moral authority to advocate liberalism worldwide.
2. Western liberalism has problems of its own, i.e., it's not that good a model to follow after all. Deviations from Western prescriptions of liberalism, human rights, and democracy are appropriate, even desirable, for securing good social outcomes.

One might easily dismiss the "Singapore school thesis" as simply borne out of short-term political interests, rather than possessing any form of academic rigor. We choose, however, to take these concerns seriously. We also engage the wider literature on Asian values, specifically, how East Asian societies are said to possess cultural, historical, and social values that are very distinct from the West, which in turn suggests that Western liberal universalism should give way to cultural particularism (Bell, 2008). In response, we propose that the arguments of Asian values advocates do not necessarily demonstrate any inherent flaws with liberal ideas and that the emphasis on cultural particularism suggests the necessity of a classically liberal order as being best positioned to deal with this challenge.

Specifically, we make the following claims:

1. Western countries have indeed been poor exemplars of the values they preach, but this is insufficient to conclude that liberal values themselves are undesirable.
2. Western countries indeed suffer from serious problems of their own. Much of these problems in the West, as this chapter will highlight, stem not from any inherent defect of liberalism, but a failure to preserve their liberal heritage.
3. Theorists and advocates of the Singapore school that defend East Asian cultural particularism and political meritocracy do not take into account the serious problem of cultural diversity and its accompanying moral disagreements. Institutional plurality is thus needed to cope with this problem, revealing the value of epistemic liberalism.

We make these arguments from the unique perspective of classical liberalism. By doing so, we provide new insights into the discourse on Asian values, which had begun in the 1990s. We agree with much of the criticisms made by the Singapore school thesis, but conclude that liberalism remains an attractive model that is worthy of emulation by others. We acknowledge that Western countries have indeed used highly illiberal means in their quest to promote human rights and democracy around the world, often with negative results. That concession, however, should also be balanced with the fact that numerous developing countries remain trapped in under-development due to the absence of inclusive, market-based institutions, which are the basis of prosperity and progress. We reinforce the concerns of the West's critics that liberal reforms cannot be imposed exogenously, but insist that they should be grown organically.

We also acknowledge that there have been serious socio-economic problems in Western societies, namely in the United States, the chief promoter of democracy and human rights globally. While these problems are real, we insist that they do not necessarily lead us to the conclusion that *liberalism has failed*, or that it is inherently defective. The "visible social consequences" in the West, which we acknowledge, do not stem inexorably from "unfettered individual freedom" (Mahbubani, 2018a, p. 112). Instead, these concerns provide liberals and non-liberals alike an opportune moment to reflect on how the West has gone astray from its classical liberal heritage, and the enduring value of classical liberalism in the world today.

Crucial to our argument is the acknowledgment that Asian societies have very legitimate concerns and values of their own, which may diverge from their Western counterparts. We are by no means saying that individualism, freedom, and autonomy should trump all other indigenous, local values of non-Asian peoples. Classical liberalism does not assume that we know best about what is right for others. The classical liberalism we outline is instead based on the conviction that we do not know, or more precisely, *cannot* know what's best for the multitude of individuals that make up the complex society in which we live today. This epistemic humility also entails policymaking humility. It is precisely because no central agent can accumulate all knowledge about what's best that a decentralised system of governance is preferred, and non-interventionism, a guiding principle for policymakers.

On the Dogmatic Insistence of Democracy and Human Rights for Developing Nations

Asian values advocates have criticised the West for dogmatically pushing an agenda of liberal democracy and human rights in developing countries. The argument is that this is inappropriate because many countries, including Western developed countries themselves, had traditionally achieved development first before attaining democracy. Therefore, the insistence of "democracy now" is akin to putting the cart before the horse (Mahbubani, 2018a, pp. 97–106).

On a deeper level, the argument is that there are multiple pathways to development, and it would be incorrect to insist on "one standard path" as dictated by the Western agenda. What developing countries need, the argument continues, is not necessarily a democratic government that protects human rights, but rather a "strong and firm government, one that is committed to radical reform" to "break out of the vicious cycle of poverty" (Mahbubani, 2018a, pp. 98–99).

We agree with the above argument, to a limited extent. It is indeed true that there is no one single path to development, and the road to prosperity must necessarily be organic, drawing from the cultural resources of each community (as will be explained in the following section). Economic reforms will not be successful if they are imposed exogenously from far-flung Western development offices.

It is also true that liberal democracy is not a fundamental requirement for successful economic growth. The story of East Asia, and Singapore for that matter, clearly illustrates that authoritarian governments can coexist with high rates of economic growth. However, what classical liberals insist is not that democracy is the precondition for growth, but that sustained development requires a set of inclusive, market-based institutions, both in politics and economics (Acemoglu & Robinson, 2012; Easterly, 2014). While this does not require a Western-style government that prizes human rights above all else, state constraints are still necessary for the private, entrepreneurial sector to flourish.

Prosperity necessarily results from individuals being able to experience the gains from trade, specialisation, exchange, and innovation. Such productive economic activity, in turn, requires a conducive political

infrastructure that gives economic agents the confidence, clarity, and simplicity to conduct their affairs. Just as a state needs to be strong enough to raise revenue, provide public goods, and make necessary investments into society — in other words, possess sufficient state capacity — it has to at the same time be constrained by a set of rules, lest it degenerates into a predatory regime. In other words, development success requires what Daron Acemoglu and James Robinson (2019) have aptly described in their latest book as a "shackled Leviathan". The state capacity necessary for providing essential public goods, building infrastructure, and making much-needed investments has to be coupled with state constraints if they are to be sustainable and not descend into a regime of predation (Johnson & Koyama, 2017).

Many scholars, including the pantheon of classical liberals, have clarified that this simply means that political, democratic freedom is not necessary for growth, as long as economic freedom exists. Simply put, even an authoritarian government that maintains a free market will still be able to achieve economic growth. On the surface, that is empirically true. However, we argue that such a dichotomy between economic and political freedom is misleading and, frankly, unhelpful. For economic freedom to take place, i.e., the freedom to trade, exchange, and contract, we do not necessarily require the freedom to criticise Lee Hsien Loong on national television and conduct regular protests on the streets. Still, we do need a state that is somewhat constrained. In other words, *some limits on political power* characterises every prosperous developed society.

The case of Singapore is not at odds with the argument we make, but very much coheres with it. While the Singapore political system may rightly be described as authoritarian, given its restrictions on civil liberties and past clampdowns on civil society and opposition politics, it nonetheless is not a predatory government that regularises extraction of private wealth. Individuals and firms in the non-state sector do enjoy a degree, albeit restricted, sphere of action in which to pursue their plans. The high degree of confidence that investors, multi-national corporations, and expatriates have in Singapore is sufficient proof of that.[2]

---

[2] Property Rights Alliance. (n.d.). *2019 International Property Rights Index Singapore*. Retrieved from https://internationalpropertyrightsindex.org/country/singapore.

Therefore, we argue that Asian values advocates are right that liberal democracy and human rights are not preconditions for successful development and that Western leaders have been short-sighted to the extent they force this on developing countries. These concerns are consistent with the insights made by classical liberals. We emphasise the additional point however: constraints on political power are still necessary if society is to be characterised by peaceful social cooperation.

On Western Hypocrisy and Policy Failures

Foreign Policy

Another related problem identified by Asian values advocates is that *even if* liberal democracy and human rights are desirable, the West have themselves not practiced what they preach. The hypocrisy they demonstrate on the world stage not only undermines their moral authority to preach the virtues of freedom to others but have also caused harm to developing countries they profess to help (Koh, 2000; Walker, 2008; Cromwell, 2012; Baraka, 2013). While all governments, including those in the non-West, have double standards, what is especially striking is that "none of the governments outside the West pretend to be as virtuous as Western ones do" (Mahbubani, 2008, p. 166). This makes Western advocacy for human rights especially infuriating.

Professor of International Law, Onuma Yasuaki (1999), has made a similar argument, which is that Western governments and non-governmental organisations (NGOs) have not considered the historically subordinate role that non-Western societies have experienced in the international order, such as that arising due to the colonial experience. Once this is considered, it is only understandable when non-Western societies dismiss human rights advocacy as "nothing more than another beautiful slogan by which great powers rationalise their interventionist policies" (Yasuaki, 1999). Yasuaki also calls out the self-righteousness Western liberals demonstrate when they criticise other countries for human rights violations while ignoring similar problems at home, and also questions the supposed universality of human rights claims (Yasuaki, 1999).

It is indeed true that the United States has committed gross violations of human rights in various developing countries. American foreign policy

has rested on the neoconservative belief that Western liberal democracy can and should be exported to the rest of the world, by force if necessary (Preble, 2019). These nation-building exercises have involved the deliberate practice of Central Intelligence Agency (CIA) covert operations, political assassinations, and the fomenting of unrest. American activities in the Middle East, in particular, have seen them support dictatorial regimes when it suits them and abandon those same regimes when political winds shift (Bacevich, 2017; Carpenter, 2019). The recent American opposition to Qaddafi and al-Assad, for instance, speaks to the hypocrisy that Asian values advocates decry, since these were rulers who were first supported by the West in the past.

Does this put liberalism on trial? The West's illiberal tactics on the world stage should be rightly condemned. But in no way should these foreign policy failures be seen as an inherent defect of liberalism. There is a rich tradition within American constitutional history of emphasising humility and non-intervention in global relations. The Jeffersonian insistence of "peace, commerce, and honest friendship with all nations & entangling alliances with none" succinctly captures this non-interventionist tradition in American foreign policy thinking (Paul, 2007).

That many American administrations in recent history have deviated from this sound principle is highly regrettable, of course. The American empire around the world has also imperilled America's national security, considering the staggering costs of foreign intervention and nation-building (Coyne, 2013; Bacevich, 2017). This self-inflicted wound of America's own making points to the warnings of numerous classical liberal scholars that true liberalism requires a small government, and that war is often a source, if not the main source, of tyranny.

Economic Practices

On the economic front, the United States, and Western-dominated global institutions, have also done harm through their advocacy of neoliberal policies. The Washington Consensus was foisted upon many developing countries after the Cold War, with an insistence on the virtues of privatisation, liberalisation, and deregulation. However, these virtues have been counter-productive, breeding corruption and forming new political elites in countries where they have been applied. This has stymied the genuine transition to a better economy. The case of Russia is instructive. Rather than experiencing a genuine transition to a market economy, it has degenerated into a rule by oligarchs who control the levers of power till the present day (Guriev & Rachinsky, 2005). The prominent economist Joseph Stiglitz (2003) has written emphatically that "neoliberal reform produced undiluted economic decline" in Russia.

These neoliberal political reforms have also been tied to the practice of 'conditionality', whereby monetary aid is given upon the fulfilment of some conditions. It has been largely acknowledged that foreign aid has had mixed results at best, and adverse consequences at worst. Indeed, numerous American aid programmes have benefitted authoritarian rulers with poor human rights records. It was shown by Christopher Coyne and Matt Ryan (2009) that the United States, up until 2009, had provided nearly "(US)$36 billion in net disbursements and almost (US)$53 billion in total commitments" and "more than (US)$46 billion in military aid" to the world's worst dictators, including Robert Mugabe, Bashar al-Assad, Hosni Mubarak, and Muammar al-Qaddafi.

Therefore, Asian values advocates are spot on in their denunciations of the Western development establishment. In the same token, Kishore Mahbubani (2008, p. 262) has pointed out that "if the true story of Western aid the developing world is told, however, it may well emerge the story of the Big Lie". He elaborated that such aid programmes were not done out of altruism, but that "interest has almost always trumped altruism", serving special interests at the expense of the actual intended beneficiaries (Mahbubani, 2008).

Interestingly, these policy failures provide us good reasons to learn the insights made by classical liberal political economists. First, aid programmes have never been a policy prescription of classical liberals, largely because it involves a top-down approach driven by imperfect bureaucracies. That aid money has ended up in the hands of consultants, bureaucrats, and special interests is unsurprising, given the ever-present possibility of rent-seeking (Easterly, 2006). Additionally, another important insight made is that market-liberal economies cannot be established through illiberal means. Transitions to functioning market economies require an economic and political culture that supports market institutions. The absence of such a supportive culture will mean that institutional reform stalls, which in turn would imperil whatever neoliberal policies being tried, however desirable they may be. Indeed, the neoliberal reforms forced on Eastern Europe failed not because there was something inherently defective about free markets, but due to the failure to acknowledge the importance of supporting market institutions (Nicoara & Boettke, 2015).

Thus, the failure of Washington Consensus policies by global organizations points to the critical political economy insights that classical liberal scholars have written about: how the most lasting and sustainable reforms must be homegrown, and pay respect to indigenous customs, values, and concerns. When such cultural sensitivity is present, institutions are more "sticky", and will spur progress (Boettke, Coyne, & Leeson, 2008).

The unique contribution of this classical liberal perspective being offered here is that, on the one hand, it acknowledges the practical failures, whether deliberate or unintended, of Western liberals in development circles, but at the same time defends the continued value of market freedoms as a pathway to prosperity. Our argument may thus be contrasted by the one made by legal scholar Yash Ghai in an edited volume on the East Asian challenge for human rights (see Bauer & Bell, 1999). Ghai (1999) had pointed out how the contemporary international human rights regime fails to protect economic and social rights, on top of civil liberties. This argument was based on a sceptical attitude towards the market economy, which he says has led to an erosion of social and economic rights in an era of rapid globalisation (Ghai, 1999). Our classical liberal perspective supports the underlying spirit of criticism against the Western development establishment but rejects this conclusion in the need for greater controls on corporations and its scepticism towards economic globalisation.

We reiterate that Asian values advocates have made a valuable contribution in the way they puncture the myth of Western superiority. We, however, further the conversation by pointing out how these very failures of the West provide an opportunity for another important lesson: that the West has abandoned its classical liberal heritage.

On Socio-economic Problems in Western Society

Asian values advocates have identified socio-economic problems in Western society so as to charge liberalism as being defective. The Great Financial Crisis of 2008, which originated in Western countries, has been portrayed as evidence of the weakness of Western liberal economics. The economic malaise Western economies suffered since then, coupled with the rapid rise of non-Western economies, yields a forecast that the future is Asian. This seems to be further reason to doubt the inherent superiority of the Western economic model, let alone the minimal state classical liberalism explored in this book.

The Asian values advocate Kishore Mahbubani has written extensively about the 2008 financial crisis and what this means in the *Financial Times*, which, in 2009, named him one of the Top 50 individuals who would shape the debate on the future of capitalism.[3] In a *Financial Times* article titled "Western capitalism has much to learn from Asia", he characterised the 2008 episode not as a fundamental problem with "capitalism itself", but rather, a peculiar form of *Western capitalism*.[4] He outlined the numerous strategic errors that the West committed in the way it has practiced capitalism. One of the problems that he charged the West was failing to realise that "for capitalism to work well, governments have to play an essential regulatory and supervisory role", which is a lesson he points out "was forgotten by many western governments". He also added that:

> "For all its flaws and defects, capitalism remains the best system to improve human welfare. This is why the whole world (barring North Korea) has accepted it, in one form or another. But it is also an inherently imperfect system, as Adam Smith warned us from day one. It requires careful government regulation and supervision. Asians never forgot this".

This argument is part of a general argument suggesting that Western capitalism is not the only good economic model to follow and that there are other paths to capitalist development. This argument is valuable. Political economists have indeed clarified that there are varieties of capitalism,

---

[3] Financial Times. (2009, March 10). Future of Capitalism: Fifty People Who Will Frame the Debate. *Financial Times*. Retrieved from http://ig-legacy.ft.com/content/7f6f08da-0d7d-11de-8914-0000779fd2ac#axzz2yHlqre00.

[4] Mahbubani, K. (2011, January 25). Asia has had enough of excusing the west. *Financial Times*. Retrieved from http://mahbubani.net/articles%20by%20dean/Asia%20has%20had%20enough%20of%20excusing%20the%20west.pdf; Mahbubani, Kishore. (2012, February 7). Western Capitalism Has Much to Learn from Asia. *Financial Times*. Retrieved from http://www.mahbubani.net/articles%20by%20dean/Western%20capitalism%20has%20much%20to%20learn%20from%20Asia.pdf.

rather than one single blueprint to be emulated (Hall & Soskice, 2001). Asian societies have indeed used the developmental state model to much success. Even Asian capitalism exhibits much internal diversity, from the city-state model of Hong Kong and Singapore to their larger counterparts (Hundt & Uttam, 2017).

What we take issue with is the omission of a very important classical liberal perspective in this account of the global financial crisis, one which obscures its important contributions to policy discourse. Numerous economists have analysed the 2008 financial crisis and found that it had stemmed from the failed monetary policy by the Federal Reserve, specifically, its maintenance of artificially low interest rates and the government sponsorship of affordable housing (Horwitz, 2010). Both of these policies had led to capital malinvestments and an associated housing bubble, which inevitably burst.

This is not to say that regulation did not play any role in the crisis. We also do not argue that capitalism must be completely unfettered, which is what Mahbubani presents as a "strategic flaw" of Western capitalism. Rather, the point is that regulation has to be simple, predictable, and conducive to market exchange. The economist Jeffrey Friedman had shown that the financial crisis was very much triggered by "the complex, constantly growing web of regulations designed to constrain and redirect modern capitalism" (Friedman, 2009, p. 127). This web had interacted with one another and eventually leading to the securitisation of subprime mortgages and their wrongful rating as AAA, which was nothing more than the proximate, rather than the fundamental cause of the crisis (Friedman, 2009).

This account of the 2008 financial crisis is, in turn, part of a more extensive classical liberal explanation for the perils of government intrusion in the financial and monetary system. It has been explained that much of the economic instability in the 20th century has not been a result of any inherent flaw in capitalism, or "Western capitalism" for that matter, but the state-created distortions in the realm of money and banking (Rothbard, 2008; Veryser, 2013; Schlichter, 2014).

Of course, the financial crisis of 2008 is not the only problem that Western economies have faced. Indeed, many Asian values advocates, and general commentators, have pointed to a general sense of malaise in

Western societies. For Mahbubani, the West has suffered the "dangers of decadence", providing important lessons for the rest of the non-Western world (Mahbubani, 1993). To give a complete diagnosis of the West's decline on the world stage would be beyond the scope of this book. But there are several points worth examining.

What we take issue with is the notion that these social problems are a result of "unfettered liberty", or what has been called a "hero-worship" of "individual freedom" (Mahbubani, 1993). Kishore Mahbubani's denunciation here is curious:

> "The same hero-worship is given to the idea of individual freedom. Much good has come from this idea. Slavery ended. Universal franchise followed. But freedom does not only solve problems; it can also cause them. The United States has undertaken a massive social experiment, tearing down social institution after social institution that restrained the individual. The results have been disastrous. Since 1960 the U.S. population has increased 41 percent while violent crime has risen by 560 percent, single-mother births by 419 percent, divorce rates by 300 percent and the percentage of children living in single-parent homes by 300 percent. This is massive social decay. Many a society shudders at the prospects of this happening on its shores. But instead of traveling overseas with humility, Americans confidently preach the virtues of unfettered individual freedom, blithely ignoring its social consequences" (1993, p. 14).

This is not an esoteric academic quote. It is generally believed that liberalism cannot work in a primarily conservative Asian society since it would sweep away all kinds of social-moral restraints. What if liberalism means the freedom to shoot others indiscriminately in the streets? To do as one pleases without a modicum of moral inhibition?

To blame violent crime, divorce rates, broken families, and such social decay on individual freedom is a strange point to make. What we maintain is that while many of these problems exist in American society, they are contingent problems stemming from policymaking failures, rather than "structural weaknesses in its core values and institutions" as Mahbubani (2018, p. 111) believes. In fact, many of these social problems that this passage highlights explicitly, single-parent families, divorce, and violent

crimes, were the product of failed interventionist social policies (Sowell, 1996; Rector, 2014; Murray, 2015). Today, two serious socio-economic problems, opioid abuse, and drug-related violence, stem from the failure of the war on drugs and its overly punitive orientation (Mirron *et al.*, 2019; Redford, 2019).

Also, it is doubtful that any self-respecting liberal political philosopher would advocate unbridled libertarianism, or for that matter, "hero-worship" of individual freedom. Certainly, the classical liberalism highlighted in this account believes that much of our prevailing institutions are a result of cultural evolution over time, and one would be guilty of a fatal conceit if social engineering is practised. The best form of change is gradual, involving the spontaneous actions of individuals. Granted, such evolution might lead to results that some may not anticipate or even endorse, such as changes in the family structure and marriage relations (Horwitz, 2015).

But the key point to note here is that there is a clear, fundamental, and qualitative difference between changes in the social fabric, which are products of gradual evolution, and top-down impositions of government policies that tear away social institutions. As such, one is spot on to criticise the disastrous results of the United States' "massive social experiment" (Mahbubani, 2018a, p. 111). But it would be wrong to associate such dangers with suspicion of liberalism and individual liberty more generally.

Asian Culture and Classical Liberalism

A much deeper criticism has been made against Western liberal democracy, in that it wrongly claims to be universally applicable, even while many non-Western societies have their distinct set of values and cultural beliefs. This criticism is most trenchant in its East Asian form, which asserts that in place of the emphasis on individualism and autonomy in Western societies, Confucian values such as community, family life, and tradition feature more strongly in East Asian cultures.

This argument is best articulated in the writings of the political philosopher Daniel Bell, who has presented arguments criticising the liberal claim to universal applicability, and that liberal democracy and universal human rights may not be desirable. At the same time, these Asian values advocates have also presented another alternative that is seen as more desirable in the East Asian context: that of political meritocracy, a Confucian system that emphasises rulers who are selected based on their superior ability to make informed political judgements (Bell & Li, 2013; Bell, 2018). Theorists have developed variants of these arguments, some insisting that political meritocracy can deliver better outcomes than democraciers, with others considering the possibility of building political meritocracy based on Western liberal democratic institutions and values (see Bell & Li, 2013, ch. 1).

In response to this ongoing debate between political theorists, we contribute the perspective of classical liberalism, which has been absent thus far.

We do so by clarifying here at the outset that classical liberalism is not synonymous with liberal democracy. Classical liberalism is not primarily a defence of the political system of democracy, and has in fact, been quite critical of its illiberal effects (see Caplan, 2011; Somin, 2013; Brennan, 2017). Conversely, a democratic society need not be liberal, let alone classically liberal. Many liberal democracies today are characterised by high levels of state intervention into the economy and society.[5] This clarification is important because it highlights the unique contribution of this chapter to the literature. Much of the scholarly literature in the Asian values debate criticising Western advocacy of liberal democracy deals with how Western liberal democracy is unsuitable for Asian societies, which has invited others to respond by showing their mutual compatibility.

We instead advocate classical liberalism, not liberal democracy. The key distinction is that classical liberalism emphasises the importance of circumscribing the extent of political authority in society, which is separate and distinct from the other issue of how political leaders are to be selected and the basis for their legitimacy.

We make two arguments in this section. First, we take the lead from other scholars in the Asian values debate and show that East Asian cultural traditions provide the resources for local commitment to values and practices similar to Western countries (Bell & Li, 2013). Such work

---

[5] In Europe, there are many countries that can be described as liberal democracies. However, they are clearly not libertarian because they are social democratic, welfare states, where redistribution and equalisation attempts are heavy. Liberal democracies today mostly align with modern liberalism rather than classical liberalism.

has already been done from the perspectives of Confucianism, Islam, and Buddhism (Othman, 1999; Satha-Anand, 1999; Chan, 2013). These scholars show that one need not jettison the pursuit of liberal democracy and human rights, and may indeed justify these principles on the basis of Asian values itself.

In this spirit, we contribute a new classical liberal perspective, which has not been attempted before. We look specifically at Confucianism, a key plank in ancient Chinese political theory. We briefly show how some Confucian ideas lend some credence to classical liberalism, which has not previously been considered. We also introduce another school of thought from within ancient Chinese political theory, that of Daoism, which makes warnings against political authority that are strikingly similar to many classical liberals.

We acknowledge, and indeed anticipate, that many will not find this argument convincing. After all, seeking to defend classical liberalism from the basis of Confucianism or Daoism seems to be forcing a square peg into a round hole. It would be a stretch of the imagination to imply that believers in ancient Chinese values must be classical liberal. At worst, such an exercise falls foul of the same ethnocentric bias that Asian values advocates accuse Western liberals of.

This is why we present classical liberalism as ultimately resting not on any particular, narrow set of cultural values, but rather, on an epistemic basis. Classical liberalism is justified because it rests on a practical realisation that no one is in the position to gather the necessary knowledge to determine what is "right" or "best" in the realm of morality, social practices, or economic resource allocation. State planning of society should be avoided not because everyone is, or must be American individualists, but that it would be incompatible with a complex society characterised by diverse standards of moral evaluation and deeply held moral commitments.

Three Schools of Political Thought in Ancient China

Much of the debate concerning Asian values and its compatibility with Western liberal democracy and human rights centres around Confucian political philosophy, which is said to be the dominant tradition in East Asian history. Not only have Asian political figures cited Confucianism as the basis to reject Western liberal democracy, academic scholars have also written on how, or indeed whether, Confucianism is compatible with it.

However, Confucianism is only one of many schools of political thought which emerged in the late Chou period of Chinese history.[6] According to the influential text *A History of Chinese Political Thought* by Kung-Chuan Hsiao, Confucianism existed alongside Legalism and Daoism, representing three ideal types with different visions of the ideal society. Briefly, they are Confucianism, Legalism, and Daoism, which respectively translate into three models of government: "government of men", "government of laws", and "non-governing" (Hsiao, 1979).

The Confucian school envisions a "government of men". The Confucians had expressed a conservative nostalgia for the fading old order and endeavoured to reconstitute it. The ideal Confucian society is a well-ordered hierarchy with virtuous rulers at the apex, exercising benevolence and wisdom on behalf of the masses. The ideal gentleman-ruler is a type of "superior man", who "combined in one person both the perfection of his ethical nature and the possession of office, and who in consequence could bring about beneficial results by cultivating his person, regulating his family, righting governing his state, and making the world tranquil and happy" (Legge, 1960). In short, the Confucian world is an elitist meritocracy that prizes virtuous rulership, with good character defined in terms of a code of conduct that prizes benevolence and righteousness as two key values.

Legalists envision a "government of laws". Directly opposed to the Confucians, they sought to justify and strengthen the new authoritarian order. They believed that good government cannot depend on the availability of virtuous men and must rely on harsh punishments and laws, essential elements of sound governance. Clearly articulated laws, rigid regulations, severe punishments, and heavy fines are the ideal methods of government. Importantly, in the world of Legalism, governance is divorced from moralistic considerations — like those emphasised by the Confucians — which allows the exaltation of the ruler and the aggrandisement of the state

---

[6] The old feudal order fell apart and was replaced by increasing political centralisation during the Warring States Period. The first Chin Emperor operated within this context and established himself as an all-encompassing authoritarian ruler.

(Hsiao, 1979). Legalist government entails an authoritarian state with the ruler having wide discretionary powers.

Daoists envision a "non-governing" model. Rejecting all institutions, the Daoists, most famously represented by Lao Tzu and Chuang Tzu, favoured simple living and small communities with little central control. With the central principle of "*wu-wei*", or non-action, they held as their ideal a polity that was run spontaneously (*tzu-jan*), with minimal direction from centralised political entities; this explains why the Daoists rejected the new authoritarian order and the former feudal system with a specific aim of the "liberation of the individual" (Hsiao, 1979). In modern parlance, the Daoists advocated a semblance of libertarian individualism.

Singapore's System

This tri-fold classification is useful for situating Singapore's style of governance, which may be seen as a blend of the Confucian and Legalist types. Clearly, Singapore adopts a meritocratic system. There is a strong rejection of affirmative action and welfarist policies, with a corresponding belief in "work for reward, and reward for work". This is applied in the education system, the civil service, armed forces, and even in government-linked corporations. The meritocratic principle is championed because it allows individuals to be judged based on merit alone and not on ascriptive factors like race, or ethnic background; this allows social mobility and equality of opportunity for all.

On deeper analysis, Singapore is not just any meritocracy; it possesses a specifically elitist form of meritocracy that resembles Confucian elitism. This is seen in different public policies. Most obviously, the Singaporean polity is fundamentally structured in such a way as to promote the selection of highly capable, educated leaders with good character into top civil-service positions, and even into party positions. The use of government scholarships, high salaries, and promotion of scholars within the system is used to identify and retain the top talents. These elites are deemed as the top five percent society who are "more than ordinarily endowed physically and mentally and in whom we must expend our limited and slender resources in order that they will provide that yeast, that ferment, that catalyst in our society which alone will ensure that Singapore shall maintain its pre-eminent place in South and Southeast Asia" (George, 1973, p. 186). The PAP consciously portrays itself as having an important obligation of serving the nation virtuously and 'leading by example': for instance, the PAP does not tolerate corruption or ostentatious lifestyles, believing they must be seen as living up to their high standards. This reflects a form of "noblesse oblige" that brings to mind the moral and dutiful obligations of the Confucian-gentlemen ruler (Mauzy & Milne, 2002, p. 54). The world of Confucianism is hierarchically structured with rulers at the apex ruling with virtue and leading by example, and this to a large extent is reflected in Singapore's elitist meritocracy, with the PAP "men in white" resembling the class of virtuous Confucian gentlemen.

Not only is Singapore an elitist meritocracy, authoritarianism is a core part of the political system. Civil liberties of liberal democracies are eschewed in favour of the values of stability, efficiency, and honest government. Political reform that entails an embrace of human and civil rights has been repeatedly resisted (Freedom House, 2019). A strong reflection of their political conservatism, the PAP ideology has put in place harsh punishments for certain vices, like drug consumption and trafficking. Besides harsh punishments, the state has a heavy hand in socio-economic engineering to bring about certain national outcomes. The strong presence of the state in Singaporean society is a clear reflection of the Legalist political frame mentioned above.

It is clear then that the Singaporean polity rests on a peculiar combination of both the Confucian and Legalist frames. Both frames are combined because meritocracy in Singapore is managed and heavily shaped by state elites. The next chapter of this book demonstrates this. Other Singapore scholars have also shown how meritocracy has been utilised as a strategic tool by the state to maintain political hegemony: it has been argued that through the use of "competitive scholarships, stringent selection criteria for party candidacy, and high ministerial salaries, the PAP has been able to co-opt talent to form a technocratic government for an administrative state", such that meritocracy ultimately becomes the key "ideological resource for justifying authoritarian government" (Tan, 2008). In the same vein of thought, this explains why even the policy of multiculturalism has been utilised as a political tool for social control (Chua, 2003).

Confucianism and Market Liberalism

What we contribute to the discourse on Confucianism, Asian values, and governance is a classical liberal perspective. Just as some scholars have shown the compatibility of that Confucianism with Western liberal democracy, we show how Confucianism may also be compatible with classical liberalism. It bears repeating that we do not claim that Confucianism must imply a classical liberal political order. What we aim to do, rather, is to identify classical liberal themes for the first time in the social philosophy of Confucianism, something that has not been done in the debate on Asian values.

According to the philosopher Roderick Long (2003), Confucianism is not simply an authoritarian worldview but has numerous classical liberal themes in its early variant.[7] Significantly, Confucians have advised restraint on the part of state officials, cautioning them from acting coercively.[8] Specifically, rulers should lead by moral example, rather than by coercion: "if you try to guide the common people with coercive regulations and keep them in line with punishments, the common people will become evasive and will have no sense of shame" (Confucius, 2003, p. 8). Confucius adds that people only become genuinely virtuous when "the heavy burden of oppression has been lifted from their shoulders" (Schwartz, 2009, p. 107). Confucius observes that the "natural universe" maintains order without giving commands, and the ruler should therefore do likewise, "remaining motionless like the north star and letting the people revolve spontaneously around him"[9] (Confucius, 2001).

The Confucian emphasis on virtue brings to mind the contributions of virtue ethics as a philosophical school of thought. Yet, it is not correct

---

[7] Roderick Long demonstrates that even in early Confucianism, there were many thinkers that exhibited pro-capitalist and pro-market understanding, like the Confucian historian Sima Qian (Long, 2003).

[8] This sense of non-coercion, although not as consistent as the Daoist "*wu-wei*", nonetheless contributed to their lack of enthusiasm for strong laws and punishments: "when punishments and penalties accumulate, the people turn away in resentment...when they are bludgeoned with laws and commands...the prevailing mood among the people is one of sadness". (Hsiao, 1979, p. 78) This quotation comes from the 2nd century Confucian, Jia Yi.

[9] This is echoed by Confucius' disciple, Mencius, who emphasised the value of spontaneous order over imposed order (Mencius, 1970, p. 78).

to portray Confucian politics ethics as a form of state paternalism where officials dictate virtuous behaviour from on high. It is emphasised by Confucius that righteous behaviour should be exemplified by rulers themselves, who are models to emulate. Mencius specifically contributed to our understanding of how virtue is developed: he explained that virtue is formed when ordinary people will behave virtuously given the right environment. He does so through his parable of a farmer inspecting his crops. Mencius noted the error of the farmer when, in his haste to get his crops harvest-ready, he began to pull on the sprouts to expedite their growth, which inadvertently caused the plant to shrivel (Mencius, 2009, p. 17). Mencius pointed out the lesson to be learnt was that one cannot artificially force a result, but must allow virtue to be grown organically; chiding the impatient farmer, he said: "not only does this not help, but it even harms it" (Mencius, 2009, p. 17). Beyond echoing the classical liberal warnings about unintended consequences that occur through state interventionism, the parable also points to the arguments of classical liberal philosophers who have used virtue-ethics approaches to show how minimal states best facilitate the cultivation of virtues (see Lebar, 2016 for a useful review of such approaches).

Confucianism also emphasises the important role of rituals in society, which also highlights its aversion to coercion. One specific ritual, *shu*, is heavily shaped by the ethic of reciprocity, which is, by definition, non-coercive, since coercion implies unequal domination of one over another. This is important because the ethic of reciprocity has recently been used to ground the classical liberal non-aggression axiom, that "no man may initiate the use of force against other except in self-defense"[10] (Huemer, 2013). With this in mind, it is instructive that certain Confucian scholars have studied the implications of *shu* and its norm of reciprocity, and insist that a consistent Confucian must be "a kind of anarchist in the respect that he is radically opposed to the use of force, compulsion, coercion, or punishments in government or in human affairs generally" (Fingarette, 1978, pp. 513–514).

---

[10] The ethic of reciprocity is linked to libertarianism's non-aggression axiom. It is the idea that I should refrain from using force against you just as you do the same; non-aggression flows out of this reciprocal recognition.

In the same vein of thought, Confucians have warned that state authority is never unlimited, and its legitimacy depends on whether it rules justly and righteously. If a ruler demonstrates virtue, then "people from other states will flock to him with their children swaddled on their backs" (Confucius, 2001, p. 133). However "if a ruler ill-uses his people to an extreme degree, he will be murdered and his state annexed; if he does it to a lesser degree, his person will (rightly), be in danger and his territory reduced" (Mencius, 1970, pp. 118–119). The key point is that an unjust king has no legitimate claim over his subjects' allegiance, according to a conversation between Master Kong and Duke Ding in *Analects*.[11] Mencius drew on Confucius' "rectification of names", and affirmed the idea that a ruler deserves the title of "king" to the extent he behaves as such, failing which, defying him involves no disloyalty; political legitimacy accrues to the one who outdoes others in ruling rightly over the people (Mencius, 1970, p. 143).

What about Confucianism's relationship with market exchange, a key tenet of classical liberalism? While it would be wrong to infer from Confucian writings a fully developed theory of economic exchange, there are nonetheless junctures where Confucian writers reveal their appreciation for important concepts such as the division of labour, exchange, and the market's ability to coordinate action. Mencius had specifically warned against the recommendation by Hsu Hsing that everyone should take up agriculture as a vocation, by explaining how such a view does not consider the benefits of the division of labour. He responded that "to trade grain for implements is not to inflict hardship on the potter and the blacksmith. The potter and the blacksmith, for their part, also trade their wares for grain" (Lau, 2003, p. 113), and further clarified a few passages down that "if everyone must make everything he uses, the Empire will be led along the path of incessant toil" (Lau, 2003, p. 115).

---

[11] Duke Ding said: "One remark that can lose a state — is there such a thing?" Master Kong replied: "One remark cannot do something like that. However, there is one close to it. One man's saying goes: 'I find no joy in being sovereign except that, whatever I say, no one disobeys me.' If what he says is good and no one disobeys him, is it not good? If it is not good and no one disobeys him, is it not almost true that one remark can lose a state?" A similar example is offered by Mencius, in Ivanhoe and Van Norden, *Readings in Classical Chinese Philosophy*, pp. 120–21.

In addition to the writings of Mencius, Confucians have also made contributions to our understanding of the market as a system of spontaneous economic coordination. Leslie Young (1996) had argued that Adam Smith's concept of the "invisible hand" was not only anticipated by the Confucian-inspired historian Sima Qian from the Han dynasty, but done so in a way that was deeper than Smith's own insight (Young, 1996). Sima Qian's passage here is significant:

> "There must be farmers to produce food, men to extract the wealth of mountains and marshes, artisans to process these things and merchants to circulate them. There is no need to wait for government orders: each man will play his part, doing his best to get what he desires. So cheap goods will go where they fetch more, while expensive goods will make men search for cheap ones. When all work willingly at their trades, just as water flows ceaselessly downhill day and night, things will appear unsought and people will produce them without being asked. For clearly, this accords with the Way and is in keeping with nature" (Young, 1996, p. 138).

It is worth reflecting on the relationship between Confucianism and market exchange. The leading advocate of East Asian political meritocracy Daniel Bell has insisted that Confucianism would imply a very different form of capitalism as opposed to an "unfettered property rights regime" that is supposedly unique only to Western history (Bell, 2006, chs. 9–11). In response, we acknowledge the truism that the dynamics of market exchange are always filtered through a cultural lens, an insight that numerous classical liberal scholars have emphasised in their criticisms of mainstream neoclassical economics (see Laroie & Chamlee-Wright, 2001, ch. 4). This insight, at the same time, is also entirely consistent with the separate point we emphasise: that complex markets have existed throughout history in various cultures, and are not a uniquely Western imposition (Baechler, 1975; Anderson & Latham, 1986; Berger, 1987). A defense of a private-property, market-based economy need not be charged with Western ethnocentrism.

In the end, we concede that Confucianism is mostly committed to communitarian values, and eschews the self-interested actions of rulers. For example, Confucians may allow rebellion against authority, but this is always done for the common good, and never for self-gain. This absence of a commitment to individualism means that Confucianism's affinity with classical liberalism is imperfect. Yet, the point of this section is to emphasise that Confucianism has many ideas friendly to classical liberalism and cannot be narrowly interpreted to justify a strong authoritarian state.

Daoist Classical Liberalism

Although the link between Confucianism and classical liberalism is imperfect and often tenuous due to the former's inherent commitment to communitarianism, Daoism, the third school of thought, is *consistently and explicitly individualist.*[12] It contains consistent denunciations of political power and calls for minimalist government, for the sake of the "liberation of the individual"[13] (Hsiao, 1979). The commitment to individual freedom of the Daoists has been to such a degree that Lao Tzu, the chief pioneer of this school, has been considered as the world's first libertarian (Boaz, 1997, p. 27). Subsequent Daoists like Chuang Tzu and Pao Ching Yen carried the classical liberal inclination even further in its anti-statism.[14]

Classical liberals are generally united in their sceptical view of the state, greatly resonating with Daoist political thought. While there are many reasons for why this is so, state action is generally viewed by classical liberals as being rife with numerous unintended consequences and thus ineffective in achieving stated intentions. This counterproductive nature of state intervention was emphasised by Lao Tzu, who wrote that "the more artificial taboos and restrictions there are in the world, the more people are impoverished. The more that laws and regulations are given prominence, the more thieves and robbers there will be".[15]

This scepticism of government intervention leads both classical liberals and Lao Tzu to call for the state to be limited. Classical liberals believe

---

[12] We should point out the curious omission of Daoism as a major school of thought in Daniel Bell's (2006) investigation of how East Asian ideas transcend liberal democracy.

[13] This consistency is significant, since this paper is not seeking to square a circle by forcing Daoism into a libertarian framework.

[14] The link between anarchism and Chuang Tzu for instance, is well documented in Elbert D. Thomas's *Chinese Political Thought* (1927), E. R. Hughes's *Chinese Philosophy in Classical Times* (1942), and Sebastian de Grazia's *Masters of Chinese Political Thought* (1973).

[15] Tao Te Ching 57.

in minimalist political institutions, allowing individuals to act according to their conception of the good. Similarly, Lao-Tzu, animated by his core principle of "*wu-wei*" (translated as inaction), believes that the state must be kept limited as possible, because when government is kept simple and inactive, then the world may "stabilize itself"[16] (Rothbard, 1995). This stems from his belief that an application of "*wu-wei*" would allow the individual to flourish and achieve *his own* happiness (in other words, his own conception of the good life): "therefore, the sage says: I take no action yet the people transform themselves, I favour quiescence and the people right themselves, I take no action and the people enrich themselves".[17]

This desire for the circumscribing of political authority is also related to a fear of tyranny. Indeed, tyranny has been a common theme running through world history, with the 20th century alone witnessing brutal murders by states enjoying unlimited powers (Rummel, 1997). This historical evidence of state tyranny led the classical liberal philosopher Chandran Kukathas (2006) to conclude that "the state is a difficult institution to defend even with mild enthusiasm". It is with this in mind that the following writings are apt. Lao Tzu pointed out that the state, with its "laws and regulations more numerous than the hairs of an ox", was a "vicious oppressor of the individual" and "more to be feared than fierce tigers"[18] (Marina, 1998). This belief is not unique to Lao Tzu alone. In a striking resemblance, Chuang Tzu does not believe that concentrated power will amount to any good: "there has been such a thing as letting mankind alone; there has never been such a thing as governing mankind [with success]" (Giles, 2013, p. 106). It is, therefore, no surprise that Daoism has been co-opted by many political movements throughout history opposing state authoritarianism.

---

[16] In Tao Te Ching 60, Lao Tzu argues, "governing a great state is like cooking a small fish". He means that the government should adopt a light touch, and not be intrusive and constantly interfering. In fact, the government that "which is meddling, touching everything", is the "most unwise" and will bring "disappointment" (Lao-tzu, 1891). Tao Te Ching 58. Retrieved from: http://www.sacred-texts.com/tao/taote.htm.

[17] Tao Te Ching 57.

[18] These ideas have also revealed many pro-capitalist and free market leanings. Reynolds, Neil. (2018, May 8). China's greatest adversary: Mickey Mouse. *The Global and Mail.* Retrieved from: http://www.theglobeandmail.com/report-on-business/rob-commentary/chinas-greatest-adversary-mickey-mouse/article4187281/.

Daoism is a radical political doctrine, with some anarchistic leanings. The anarchistic leanings of Chuang Tzu and Pao Ching Yen are evident. Chuang Tzu believes that individuals can live in a state of "natural freedom", such that the world "does simply not need governing; in fact it should not be governed"; he has therefore been considered as the first-ever libertarian anarchist (Rothbard, 1995). Pao Ching Yen was even more anarchistic since he believed that in a stateless age, before governments wreaked havoc, there was no warfare and no disorder, and where "people munched their food and disported themselves; they were carefree and contented" (Rothbard, 1995). Though many classical liberals are, rightly, sceptical about radical political claims to abolish the state, some have emphasised the importance of private governance, specifically, how much of the rules, institutions, and norms that govern social life are a product of bottom-up evolution over time, rather than creations of the state.

Another significant similarity between Daoism and the classical liberalism espoused in this book is a sceptical attitude towards the faculty of reason. Daoism is a highly anti-rationalistic philosophy, emphasising the subjectivity and relativity of knowledge claims (Kjellberg & Ivanhoe, 1996). Daoists believe that, in relation to reason and language, "all abstract categories and linguistic distinctions falsify our lived experience", hence the opening of Tao Te Ching: "the way that can be spoken is not the constant way", and "the name that can be named is not the constant name" (Long, 2003, p. 37). This is in concordance with the classical liberal emphasis on epistemic humility, which is why many classical liberal political philosophers have been influenced by notions of scepticism (see Kukathas, 2003).

Asian Values, Culture, and Epistemic Liberalism

The section above attempted to provide some interpretations of Confucian and Daoist thought — two important planks of ancient Chinese philosophy — friendly to classical liberalism. We point out that this exercise is necessarily imperfect because it is easy for one to read into any philosophy, let alone Asian philosophy, principles that one favours. We also take seriously the charge of ethnocentrism (or perhaps, Western cultural superiority) that Asian values scholars have levelled against

Western liberals, a charge that we wish to avoid. Hence, we make the case for classical liberalism not based on Confucianism, Daoism, or any transcendental, universal moral principle of freedom and autonomy, but rather, on a very different, epistemic foundation.

Asian values scholars have made an important contribution by challenging Western liberalism's claim to moral universalism. Human rights may not be as universal as one thinks, they insist. Liberal values of individualism, freedom, and autonomy are not ubiquitous or even commonplace in many societies, and in the end stem from a narrow Western historical experience, they insist. One has to realise that millions of people live in societies very culturally distinct from the West. In other words, Asian values advocates provide us with an important reason to treat cultural particularities very seriously. The leading academic scholar on Asian values, Daniel Bell (2008), has thus written that East Asian political theory's valuable contribution to Anglo-American political theory is its emphasis on cultural particularism over liberal universalism.

Due to the existence of these distinct sets of values, it would not be practically feasible, or normatively desirable, they claim, for East Asian societies to implement the institutions of liberal democracy based on universal human rights. There is, in addition, a legitimacy component. Government institutions need not be legitimated based on democratic consent, but may be so through other criteria, for example, performance legitimacy, an important legitimating principle in political meritocracy.

Response

We argue two inter-related points. First, it is important to take seriously the problem of cultural diversity and not just cultural particularism. In a world of cultural diversity and different standards of moral evaluation, it is disingenuous to posit an ideal blueprint of East Asian political meritocracy [i.e. "China Model" (Bell, 2018)] as more suitable for any society, let alone an East Asian society. Second, and on a deeper level, cultural identity is not an unchanging, static whole, but rather something subject to constant evolution, re-evaluation, and change. It is only in the course of cultural evolution on a micro-level do individuals "discover" their true selves, including their cultural identity. For these reasons, a classical liberal regime that emphasises decentralisation, bottom-up evolutionary processes best allow individuals and communities to live out their cultural commitments.

The first problem is that many Asian values advocates fail to seriously take cultural diversity into account, a concern that is resolved through the unique classical liberal perspective offered in this book. They are right to consider how cultural factors in East Asian societies may affect the prioritisation of rights and the justification of rights, and provide moral foundations for distinctive political practices (Bell, 2008). However, there is much more cultural diversity that has been suggested, and certainly so within East Asian societies themselves.

East Asia is a highly heterogenous, diverse region, both historically and present-day. There is a myriad of communities, with thousands of languages and ethnicities, some of which have intermingled for many years. It is not a leap of imagination to argue that there is no singular culture or set of values — whether this is "Confucianism", or some other variant — that adequately capture and transcend this diversity. What this diversity results in is the inevitable problem of moral disagreement, which numerous political theorists today have increasingly been discussing. How does one adjudicate between different moral claims by cultural groups? Why should particular East Asian values of family, community, and the nation be normatively more desirable than Western values of individualism? Why should Confucianism be the leading representative of East Asian values? How do we decide between different interpretations of Confucian philosophy? This does not even touch the difficult question of applying different political rules and institutions in the real world that would best comport with abstract Confucian principles. These questions provoke a variety of answers, and predictably, deep disagreement.

In a world with diverse standards of evaluation, it would be far better — if the peaceful resolution of moral conflict is to be achieved — to favour a regime that allows for different conceptions of the good to coexist peaceably, rather than insist on a singular theory of justice (Gaus, 2015). This is best explained by what the epistemic liberal Adam Tebble (2016) has called the "cultural knowledge problem", where "the ethical knowledge relevant to arbitrating between differing and sometimes conflicting identities and conceptions of the good, as well as the specific rules, conventions, and practices that constitute them, is never given in its totality in a directly accessible form". In the face of such moral diversity, and most likely disagreement, Tebble (2016) articulates a more sensible task for political theory, which is "not to justify terms of political association that presuppose or promote a particular identity or conceptions of the good, as if the cultural knowledge problem had already been solved", but rather to "justify...a procedure that facilitates arbitration between differing and sometimes conflicting conceptions and their constitutive rules and conventions".

Consequently, it is classical liberalism, which favours decentralisation, that allows different groups, communities, and individuals to freely associate or disassociate. It should be clear that such a society would best accommodate the cultural diversity that is to be found in any human society today. If Asian values advocates emphasise the importance of allowing communities to live out their particular values, rather than have a universal hegemonic narrative imposed on them, classical liberalism's attractiveness should be obvious.

There is a deeper and related problem. Not only is there a diversity of cultures and moral values, the very notion of "culture" is itself highly "mutable", even "unstable", as the philosopher Chandran Kukathas (2003, p. 80) pointed out in his influential account of minority rights. He points out that "all human associations, including cultural groups, are not fixed but highly mutable things which change with economic, legal and political circumstances" (Kukathas, 2003, p. 78). It is with this fluid conception of social identities that he advocates a model of a free society as an archipelago of competing and overlapping jurisdictions.[19]

Considering the mutability, variability, and fluidity of culture, one may question the usefulness of the very concept of "Asian values". This term obscures more than it reveals. There is no singular set of *Asian* values. The Asian region has historically comprised a mind-boggling variety of

---

[19] Chandran Kukathas has made a similar argument to this chapter, in response to the Asian values debate. The key difference however, is that he (2000, p. 428) believes that "what passes for Asian values is little more than a set of assertions tied to a manufactured national sentiment, an armoury of weapons of social control wielded by elites seeking to silence dissenters and critics". We acknowledge that while this may be true in some cases, there nonetheless exists a credible body of theoretical contributions made by academic scholars worth taking seriously, see Bell (2008) for a useful summary.

ethnicities, racial groups, and cultures, let alone Confucian values, which typically informs much of the Asian values debate. Not only is there a plurality of cultural values in Asia itself, every particular cultural group, to the extent they can be identified, is subject to constant renegotiation as distinct individuals interact and transmit their values. The cultural character of East Asia may be very different in the years to come, and this process of cultural evolution is one that knows no particular trajectory and cannot necessarily be predicted in advance.

Aside from the diversity of cultural values and the problem of moral adjudication, one should also peer deeper into the very concept of "cultural identity" in the first place. One's "identity" does not exist as an unchanging, fully-formed entity, but is rather negotiated continuously through a myriad of social interactions. What we understand today to be a society's dominant culture is itself a product of cultural evolution over generations, as values, norms, and practices are tried out by various groups, with some being transmitted over time to the present day (Boettke, 1990b; Horwitz, 2015). This process of cultural evolution is the product of "human action, but not human design", and is not one that can be predicted in advance, with no particular endpoint.

This realisation leads us to argue that the very concept of "Asian values" is one that is similarly subject to a process of constant renegotiation daily. "East Asian culture", to the extent that it exists, *emerges* from the spontaneous interactions of individuals who themselves have their own particular — and possibly conflicting — understanding of what it means to be an Asian, an East Asian, a Confucian, etc. One would thus be guilty of "constructivist rationalism", in the words of Friedrich Hayek, to posit a full-blown theory of East Asian political theory and the resulting institutions that supposedly flow from such a conception.

Aspects of Asian cultural identity have undergone much evolution over time, rather than being a static entity. Food is an important aspect of social life in Singapore. The sociologist Lily Kong (2015) has provided a useful investigation of the 'kopitiam', a key cultural institution in Singapore. She specifically showed how its story is "deeply embedded within a larger historical and social narrative of migration and cultural diversity", in terms of its origins as an ethnic venture in colonial Singapore and how it has evolved to become today a focal point of everyday social life (Kong & Sinha,

2015, p. 127). The numerous, far-flung cuisines available at *kopitiams* reflect the cross-pollination of diverse influences in multicultural Singapore. Even on the global stage, culture is ever-contested and evolving. Contrary to the expectations of some, globalisation has not created a homogenous Western culture but facilitated cultural creative destruction that has enhanced cultural diversity (Cowen, 2002).

Thus, it is through a daily process of social interaction — which on a larger level leads to cultural evolution — that one *discovers* what it means be "Confucian", or to be "living according to the precepts of East Asian culture". Just as the knowledge necessary for rational economic coordination is not given in totality to a single mind, the required knowledge for society to align itself to a set of cultural values is itself not centralisable but has to be discovered through a process of trial-and-error learning. Think, for example, about the very concept of national identity, in the Singapore context. What is the Singapore identity? What does it mean to be a Singaporean? This is itself subject to debate, disagreement, and negotiation.[20]

Therefore, we urge the discourse on Asian values to answer a deeper question: in the face of a diversity of cultures and identities people subscribe to, many of which are themselves constantly in flux, how do we adjudicate between different moral claims offered by various cultural groups? Asian values scholars criticise one comprehensive doctrine of governance (Western liberalism). Yet, they offer another ethical ideal that's supposedly more appropriate for East Asian societies: that of political meritocracy (see Bell, 2018). They therefore beg the question that is worth answering: what institutions are necessary to cope with a plurality of cultural claims? What institutions allow for the discovery of one's cultural convictions?

Epistemic liberalism is normatively desirable and practically feasible, *precisely* because there exists a diversity of cultures, each of which may have their own very deeply held preferences for how they wish to be governed. It is not enough just to point out that the world does not share narrow

---

[20] Han, F. K. (2017, July 23). Is Singapore's identity less clear today? *The Straits Times.* Retrieved from: https://www.straitstimes.com/opinion/is-singapores-identity-less-clear-today.

Western values, and that Asian values are equally legitimate. Western liberal democracy may not be suited to East Asian societies, but does this mean that political meritocracy is the final answer? On what basis do we decide which is the better option? There is a multiplicity of values in the world, beyond a simple dichotomy of Western liberal democracy against East Asian political meritocracy. Epistemic liberalism's emphasis on a polycentric institutional order is precisely attractive because it can accommodate cultural diversity, i.e., enabling different social groups to live in ways that align with their deeply held values (Kukathas, 2003; Pennington, 2011; Tebble, 2016; Gaus, 2017).

Not only that, epistemic liberalism envisions a society where different communities try out different conceptions of the good, and compete in an "evolutionary process". This process of trial-and-error learning allows people to live out their cultural commitments, but at times also "break away" from the norm as they advocate their particular conception of the good. A polycentric institutional order, rather than a monocentric one, is best placed to facilitate this process. The legitimate concerns of Asian values advocates, which find the hegemonic claims of Western moral liberal universalism to be suspect, are not only heard but resolved within epistemic liberalism. Epistemic liberalism supports the desire of any indigenous, local community to act on their own particular knowledge and subscribe to their own cultural values and political institutions but does not assume that there is any one ideal end state to be pursued.

The leading academic proponent of East Asian particularism and advocate of political meritocracy, Daniel Bell (2008), argues that with greater cross-cultural understanding between East and West, one may achieve a "genuine, unforced consensus" on human rights, borrowing the idea from the communitarian theorist Charles Taylor. In response, we argue that we should face the real likelihood that such consensus may not be possible, or if it is to be realised, may come at a frightful cost. Rather than looking to a consensus, we should allow for a plurality of commitments to be simultaneously realised, and this is why a free society based on private property, with limited political interventionism, is morally attractive.

Conclusion

Advocates of Asian values have made a valuable contribution to policy discourse by criticising the hubris many Western liberals demonstrate when imposing their liberal agenda on others, and the hypocrisy of not living up to their own ideals. They have also rightly taken cultural diversity seriously and rightly insisted that Western democracies do not offer a yellow brick road to success. It is in this spirit that liberalism may be considered in its classical sense, with its unique emphasis on epistemic humility. Given its non-interventionist thrust in public policy emphasis, Asian values advocates would have much to favour in classical liberalism.

3

Meritocracy and Elitism in Singapore: What Both Sides Get Wrong About the Debate on Meritocracy

This chapter will present a classical liberal perspective on meritocracy, a key pillar of governance in Singapore, which has come under increasing criticism in recent years, particularly with regards to how it entrenches socio-economic inequality and elitism. We argue that both the perspectives of conservative supporters of meritocracy and the new progressive-leftist criticism of it are incomplete. While critics of the People's Action Party's (PAP) meritocracy offer a positive argument that is true, it unfortunately reaches misguided normative conclusions.

In this chapter, we argue that meritocracy[1] is fundamentally at odds with market economies, which allow people a degree of economic freedom. Second, even if meritocracy was normatively desirable, there would be simply no way for governments to enact it in the face of immense epistemic and logistical problems. Finally, we conclude by arguing that the insights of

---

[1] In the present chapter, we understand meritocracy simply as a system that determines leadership positions by merit, as opposed to wealth, race, age, gender, or other variables of socio-economic status. What constitutes "merit", however, can be highly subjective and contingent on background circumstances that are out of control. We elaborate on this in the third section. For the purpose of the following discussion however, meritocracy can be broadly thought of as the values of hard work that populates rags-to-riches stories, and self-determination and reliance on one's own effort to pull yourself up by the bootstraps.

classical liberal philosophy would provide the foundation for an improved and more pluralistic meritocracy that better serves the welfare of society.

Meritocracy in Singapore

The PAP's Rhetoric of Meritocracy

When one speaks of meritocracy in relation to Singaporean politics, it brings to mind a specific discussion that is rooted in a unique context. Since the country's independence in 1965, Singapore's politics has historically been monopolised by one political party, with virtually no formal parliamentary competition. Since its beginnings, the PAP government has propagated meritocracy as the heart of its political philosophy and championed it as an ideal form of political governance. Unlike most liberal democracies where interparty competition is visible, the ideological rhetoric that dominates Singapore's political landscape is relatively homogeneous. By exerting tight control over the media, the PAP government has stifled competing narratives out of the public eye (George, 2012).[2] Consistent with its approach, communication channels in the Internet era have also been subjected to harsh licensing regulations.[3]

Mainstream political discourse in Singapore is not conducted along a traditional left to right-wing spectrum. Instead, the spectrum is typically represented along a pro-PAP versus anti-PAP dichotomy, often debating the veracity of "pragmatism" and "meritocracy" — both distinctive styles of PAP's governing philosophy. Indeed, Singapore's founding father Lee Kuan Yew often highlighted the importance of a non-ideological government, a philosophy that has reverberated through to the current generation of political leadership (Lee H. L., 2018).

A distinct rhetorical thrust of the PAP has been an emphasis on the value of a strong work ethic. From a young age, children are taught in public schools the moral virtue of hard work and that the rewards of Singaporean society are availed to anyone as long as one is committed to

---

[2] To a significant extent, this can be explained by the government's control over the education system as well.
[3] See the Broadcasting Act and more recently, the Protection from Online Falsehoods and Manipulation Act.

diligence. Equal opportunity and non-discrimination, it is said, forms the foundation of Singaporean society that allows anyone to reap the fruits of success. Weaved into the National Pledge which students recite daily through elementary to middle school, Singaporeans are reminded of its country's multiculturalist values: "We, the citizens of Singapore, pledge ourselves as one united people, regardless of race, language or religion…".

That merit plays a pervasive role in Singaporean culture is telling when one examines the style of rhetoric that political leaders employ in speaking to the general public. From its earliest beginnings, Lee Kuan Yew, along with his political party, firmly believed in a political system governed by meritocracy. As early as just six years after independence in 1971, Lee made a now-infamous remark:

> "The main burden of present planning and implementation rests on the shoulders of some 300 key persons. They include key men in the PAP, MPs, and cadres who mobilise mass support and explain the need for policies even when they are temporarily inconvenient or against sectional interests. Outstanding men in civil service, the police, the armed forces, chairmen of statutory boards and their top administrators — they have worked the details of policies set by the government and seen to its implementation. These people come from poor and middle-class homes. They come from different language schools. Singapore is a meritocracy. And these men have risen to the top by their own merit, hard work and high performance. Together they are a closely-knit and co-ordinated hard core. If all the 300 were to crash in one jumbo jet, then Singapore will disintegrate" (National Archives of Singapore, 1971).

He frequently cited Singapore for being a non-discriminatory nation that rewarded people for their hard work and talent, aspects of which he credited for being critical reasons for its successful economic development. Even in remarking on the uncertainties of globalisation trends and a burgeoning knowledge-based economy three decades later, Lee continued to adhere to tenets of a meritocratic society:

> "That we have succeeded in the last three decades does not ensure our doing so in the future. However, we stand a better chance of not failing if we abide by the basic principles that have helped us progress: social

cohesion through sharing the benefits of progress, equal opportunities for all, and meritocracy, with the best man or woman for the job, especially as leaders in government" (Lee, 2000, p. 691).

The promise that "anyone can be successful if you work hard" is a highly visible incentive for Singaporeans to persevere and excel. Material possessions, a comfortable life, or social esteem are all visible signs of meritocratic success that encourages Singaporean to be ambitious about their lot in life. More importantly, it told Singaporeans that their success was not held back by factors out of one's control, such as race and socioeconomic status, but only by one's personal disposition to excel. This is telling in the way Lee dignified a merit-based business culture and the role of the entrepreneur:

> "… we must adopt … a national emphasis on personal independence and self-reliance … respect for those starting new businesses … acceptance of failure in entrepreneurial and innovation efforts … tolerance for a high degree of income disparity. For over 30 years, we in Singapore have aimed for an egalitarian society. If we want to have more successful entrepreneurs, Singaporeans must accept a greater income disparity between the successful and the not so successful" (Lee, 2002).

Similarly, the second Prime Minister Goh Chok Tong called on Singaporeans to "encourage enterprise and reward success, not envy and tax them" (Goh, 1988, p. 5).

Politicians over the years frequently credit meritocratic values as the bedrock of Singapore's developmental success. Founding PAP leader S. Rajaratnam put it blatantly: "I believe in a hierarchy of merit simply because I cannot think of any other way of running a modern society — for that matter even a primitive tribal society" (Chan & Haq, 1987, p. 539). Former top diplomat Kishore Mahbubani reflects on how he owes his life's success to Singapore's meritocratic system:

> "In my life, I have lived the meritocratic dream … Through unusual good fortune, Singapore had remarkably wise leadership upon independence in 1965. These leaders decided that Singapore's only resources were human resources. None should be wasted. Any talent anywhere in society would

have an opportunity to grow and flourish. Hence, with financial aid and scholarships, and through a merit-based promotion system, I escaped the clutches of poverty" (Mahbubani, 2005, p. 5).

The third and current Prime Minister Lee Hsien Loong echoes this repetition of reference to hard work determining success: "I ask myself if we're not going on merit, what are you going to look at?" (Choo, 2012). Just before the 2015 General Elections, he continued to uphold the ideals of meritocracy:

"One of our most remarkable achievements over these last 50 years, has been our racial and religious harmony. It stems from a strong belief in the ideal of a multiracial society where everybody is equal, regardless of race, language or religion... we have held firmly to the belief that before race, language and religion, first and foremost, we should all be Singaporeans together and so, we have built a fair and just society, based on meritocracy, where ability and not your background or the colour of your skin, determines how well you do, determines what contributions you make, and what rewards you get" (Prime Minister's Office Singapore, 2015).

Wherever one looks in Singapore's post-independence political radar, talk of meritocracy in Singapore's political discourse is prevalent. The rhetoric of a merit-based society is prominently featured in popular discourse and continues to permeate the social fabric of Singapore.

A Meritocratic Public Policy

The PAP's public policy has, to a great extent, created equality of opportunity, and strongly emphasises the value of self-reliance. This reminds Singaporeans to forge one's success by individual merit — the state acts only as an extreme safety net. As Neo & Chen (2007) puts it,

"Singapore's governance philosophy — the stress on the link between work and rewards, encouraging self-reliance and the application of rationality and logic to problem-solving — and the resulting emphasis on economic principles in policymaking, is reflected in the key features of public policy: no inter-generational transfers; no subsidies to consumption, and wherever possible, using the market and pricing mechanism to allocate resources" (p. 171).

The prominence of the meritocratic foundation of Singapore society is most clearly visible in the education sector and upper echelons of its political class. Lower levels of education are subsidised to ensure universal access to education for every Singaporean child. The Compulsory Education Act makes it mandatory by law for all citizens to attend education, reflecting the meritocratic ethos that every Singaporean citizen is guaranteed a start in the race of life regardless of socio-economic status (Ministry of Education, 2019).

Politicians and public figures who fill top political appointments or key positions in government-linked companies (GLCs) typically display an exemplary academic background, having studied in top universities on prestigious government scholarships, availed only to the cream of the crop. That the best-performing of Singaporean society populate key leadership positions is no coincidence. The PAP has long pursued a policy of recruiting the brightest and most talented into the public sector to cultivate an elite technocratic class that can run the machinations of the state. The defining characteristics of the government's selection criteria have been academic achievement and professional expertise, as we elaborate in the next section. The meritocratic ideology of the PAP has been said to parallel a market allocation mechanism for mobilising the "best" labour into the state bureaucracy (Sai & Huang, 1999).

Consistent with the meritocratic narrative, the early leaders of the PAP sought to ensure a non-discriminatory society where "no race would have an advantage" (The Straits Times, 2011, p. 219) in multiracial Singapore. As seen by a slew of PAP policies that aimed at creating a level playing field for all races and general racial cohesion, this bold vision of equality of opportunity that is blind to race would be pursued uncompromisingly. Racial quotas for the public housing system, which houses more than 80% of Singaporeans, were implemented in 1989 to thwart existing racial enclaves. Such a policy served to deter racial clustering, ensuring that children from all walks of life, no matter their economic background, grow up in a similar sociocultural environment as the rest of society. English, instead of Chinese, Malay, or Tamil, was established as a neutral lingua franca and the main language of instruction in the professional workplace. The British-inherited electoral system was changed to reflect the meritocratic narrative; the Group Representation Constituency (GRC) scheme was introduced, requiring parties to field a team of candidates (as opposed to the traditional single-member scheme) that mandated a minimum of one minority candidate, typically a Malay or Indian. As Article 39A of the Singapore Constitution states, the purpose of the GRC scheme was to ensure that minority communities were sufficiently represented in Parliament. Most recently in the 2017 presidential election, the seat was reserved for candidates of only the Malay minority race under the reasoning that all races had served as a presidency since 1970 except for a Malay.

The PAP's social welfare policy arguably best embodies its meritocratic philosophy of self-reliance and individual responsibility. Where welfare assistance is offered, it is structured in a way that discourages welfare dependency and does not disincentivise personal hard work. Indeed, it is not easy to qualify for welfare in Singapore. The government's stance is that families and communities should provide the first line of welfare before turning to the government as a last resort (Fund, 2015). The state, in other words, should not act as a guarantor of means, but merely a guardian of final recourse. Even society's most vulnerable demographics, such as the disabled or elderly, must prove that they do not have a family member they can depend on financially before being able to qualify for public welfare.

One substantial form of welfare is the government-supported self-help community groups. These self-help groups advocated the "Many Helping Hands" welfare approach of the Singapore government, where welfare is not exclusively provided by the state, but also by private and grassroots organisations (Moore, 2000). The communities exist to date and are structured along racial lines. Its objective is to tackle poverty alleviation through various schemes of cultural lessons and general education for the poor to improve their economic opportunities. The programme started within the Malay community in 1981. It was deemed so successful by the end of the decade that the government gradually expanded it to form similar self-help organisations for the "under-performing" groups of the Chinese, Indian, and Eurasian communities too. In an eye-opening revelation, Lee Kuan Yew spoke about the early PAP leaders' reluctance to organising the welfare groups along racial lines as this went against the meritocratic ideals that the PAP leaders advocated. PAP pioneer and Singapore's first Minister for Foreign Affairs S. Rajaratnam saw it as "backsliding" from Singapore's multiculturalist "ideal[s] of a colour-blind policy" (Lee, 2000, p. 211).

The same approach of instilling self-reliance can be seen in "Workfare" programmes, where government welfare is contingent on the worker's ability to upgrade their productivity output (Teo, 2018). Workfare programmes encourage low-wage workers to upgrade their skills or re-join the workforce, as opposed to simple handouts that disincentivise them from working altogether. Singapore's alternative to a minimum wage — the Progressive Wage Model — provides low-wage workers with the opportunity to acquire new skills by subsidising training costs. Reflected again in this policy is the lesson of self-sufficiency and an anti-entitlement mindset.

This philosophy of self-reliance and responsibility is replicated in the Singapore government's approach to retirement savings, healthcare, and housing. For instance, the state's preferred policy of ensuring individuals have adequate financial means for essential expenses is via the Central Provident Fund (CPF), a government-mandated savings account where a portion of one's monthly salaries is deducted and deposited into. These funds can be withdrawn incrementally at the age of retirement for critical healthcare expenses or the purchase of an apartment flat. The overriding philosophy undergirding CPF is to instil self-reliance in Singaporeans where you should "help yourself first before asking others for help".

The CPF savings system is at the crux of Singapore's successful healthcare system. Research by William Haseltine (2013) has shown how Singapore manages to spend exponentially lower on healthcare in comparison to other first-world economies while achieving comparatively on par or superior health outcomes of low infant mortality rates and higher life expectancies. Because CPF savings can only be used for critical health issues, Singaporeans are forced to pay out-of-pocket for minor health expenses. This helps to control government healthcare costs while instilling in Singaporeans a crucial sense of self-responsibility for their savings and healthcare expenses/expenditure.

In sum, the concept of meritocracy goes beyond superficial political rhetoric. The PAP does not pay mere lip service to lofty notions of meritocratic virtue; it is put into serious policy practice, consistently affirming the official rhetoric. However, the PAP's policy is not without its criticisms, as we elaborate in the next section.

Is Singapore a True Meritocracy?

Any country that tries to govern whole societies on one encompassing philosophical principle inevitably runs into its inconsistencies and flaws. The PAP's style of meritocratic governance is not an exception. Since the 21st century, its meritocratic philosophy, for all its usefulness, has come under increasing scrutiny and criticism.

Perhaps the most authoritative analysis of the PAP's meritocratic philosophy is offered by Kenneth Paul Tan. Tan (2011b) argues that meritocracy, as practiced, strives to fulfil four main criteria. First, it aims to provide equality of opportunity for all citizens by ensuring universal access to education, housing, and healthcare. Second, meritocracy is a public policy tool of resource allocation for revealing the best and brightest talent. Such leaders are groomed from young for top civil service roles through Singapore's highly competitive education system and the offer of prestigious government scholarships. Upon entry to the civil service, public servants are continuously subject to a stringent evaluation system (Quah, 2010). Third, the meritocratic ideal that "anyone can succeed if they work hard" serves an economic incentive for individuals to compete with their peers and strive for excellence. Fourth, it promises rewards in the form of better-paying jobs, material comforts, and general social prestige for its winners.

These factors form the benchmark of Tan's criticism of PAP's meritocratic system, which he argues is riddled with contradictions and inconsistencies in actual policy implementation. The PAP's implementation of a meritocracy, according to Tan, has been unfaithful to its principles, allowing the breeding of an elitist minority of upper echelon political leaders.

What this critique of meritocracy brings to the forefront is the way by which the Singapore system neglects and underplays the fundamental economic inequalities at starting points. While the rules of the game might select the best performers, the players (Singaporeans) do not begin at the same socio-economic line. This manifests most ostensibly by the way wealth and social advantages of privileged families enable them to step up and ahead of others in the education system. Critics hold that the rules of PAP's meritocratic society have historically advantaged a higher social stratum of Singaporeans, mainly families who can indirectly "buy their way up" in the form of extensive supplementary classes. This is a common criticism of Singapore's highly competitive education system, where well-meaning parents participate in a competitive race to the bottom, sending their children for intensive enrichment classes at an increasingly young age (Gee, 2012). An article from *The Straits Times* in 2015 reported that an overwhelming 7 in 10 parents sign up their children for enrichment lessons in a booming billion-dollar tuition industry, despite acknowledging that it might not significantly impact their children's grades (Davie, 2015). Because one of the criteria for admission is geographic proximity, some Singaporean parents even go as far as to relocate near the best school to improve the chances of enrolment.

As a result, Singapore's meritocracy has been polluted by advantageous wealth and social capital. While merit has been professed in lip service as an objective indicator of the most well-deserving individuals, in practice, factors of various socio-economic circumstances are used for assessment such as, "inheritance, marriage ties, social connections, cultural capital, opportunities arising from developments in the economy, and plain luck" (Tan, 2008, p. 10). In a closely related line of argument, Barr (2006) argues that the PAP's brand of meritocracy is systemically biased against a non-Chinese minority. His criticism fixates on the fact that a Chinese majority predominantly occupies much of the government's most prestigious scholarships and top leadership positions in the civil service, damning evidence of what he believes reveals "a charade of meritocracy" in the PAP regime.

A second prominent challenge to the PAP's brand of meritocracy is the charge that it has been manipulated for political and policymaking goals. Critics contend that the system of meritocracy has been increasingly co-opted and manipulated by its early beneficiaries. This has allowed the early winners of PAP's meritocratic society to gradually tilt the political scales to favour their own normative vision of what good governance should constitute. This has manifested in mainly two ways. First, merit has been exclusively delineated to the narrow definition of academic expertise or professional business acumen. This is most prominently witnessed in political recruitment where "… the PAP recruits top achievers directly from the civil service, military sector, legal and medical professions, academia, and business community" (Tan, 2008, p. 14).[4] In addition, winners of prestigious government scholarships tend to be disproportionately individuals who have displayed an exemplary academic record (Barr, 2006). Second, the machinations of politics are increasingly "professionalized" to limit national decision-making to an elite administrative state of technocrats, under the reasoning that "modern governance [is] too complex for mass participation" (Tan, 2008, p. 16). In sum, while the PAP's rhetoric of meritocracy promises the highfalutin ideals of equal competition and rewards for the most well-deserving, the reality is that the boundaries of what determines leadership are increasingly defined by the incumbent elite class of leaders to exclude a majority of the Singaporean population.

The typical running theme in these critiques points to crucially fundamental tensions in the PAP's narrative of meritocracy. What critics maintain is that existing rules systematically benefit an increasingly narrow class of elite citizens who has the resources to ensure staying a step ahead in this race. In light of these contradictions, Singapore's political society cannot be said to be genuinely meritocratic. "Meritocracy," as espoused by the government, serves as a useful ideological tool to defend an elitist mode of governance and for "justifying authoritarian government and its pro-capitalist orientations" (Tan, 2008, p. 11). Although Tan acknowledges that meritocracy has served the country in the past, he ultimately concludes that the advent of 21st-century globalisation, its accompanying new information communication technologies, and rising income inequality will lead to increasing exposure to alternative worldviews, resulting in the deepening of these tensions and contradictions if left unresolved.

What Both Sides Get Wrong

In this section, we elaborate on what critics get right and wrong about Singapore's meritocracy. We offer two broad objections: one positive and

---

[4] After years of similar criticism, the government has in recent years responded by shifting the focus of its education policy away from academic excellence in science, technology, engineering, and mathematics (STEM) fields, but also to encourage a "broad meritocracy of skills", such as the creative pursuit in the arts (Ong, 2018).

one normative. Finally, we offer some policy solutions from the perspective of classical liberal philosophy.

Response to Starting Line Argument: Why Meritocracies are Incompatible with a Market Economy

Kenneth Paul Tan argues that meritocracy in Singapore is perverse because individuals do not begin at the same starting line. We agree. This is a trivially obvious point: no two individuals enjoy the same advantages in life, be it in the form of financial wealth, talent, intelligence, or luck. Yet, it carries significant implications. Meritocracy is fundamentally a desert-based theory of justice. Its key tenet says that justice is served when people get the rewards they deserve. Therefore, determining merit requires knowing a person's actions, behaviours, and their advantages or disadvantages. For example, we disqualify Olympic gold medallists if they were found to be abusing performance-enhancing drugs. The underlying reason points to the idea that the winner was not *deserving* of the medal since he had an advantage over his competitors, i.e., the starting line was unequal.

Similarly, meritocracies require the same starting line. For a meritocrat, the child of a millionaire who has enjoyed economic and social advantages to get to his position of success cannot be said to be as meritorious as the child who grew up in conditions of hardship and poverty and arrived at the same end state. Such a statement can only be true if we could hypothetically go back in time to remove the advantages of the privileged child, to equalise the starting points.

Yet it is hard to conceive of a world where such starting points could be made equal. If we are to live in a society that allows individuals the free decision-making power to spend their time and resources, income inequalities will arise as a natural state of affairs. A hardworking person will amass more income than a sloth, as will the wise investor over the mistaken investor, and a thrifty spender over the reckless gambler. The libertarian philosopher Robert Nozick illustrated this in his famous Wilt Chamberlain thought experiment. He showed how a society that began from a state of pure equality would result very quickly in drastically unequal outcomes so long as people have basic economic freedoms. A famous athlete, thanks to his fame and talent, would be infinitely wealthier than the average person if millions were willing to pay just another cent to watch him play.

Nozick's broader point was that under a regime that respects economic liberties, "… no end-state principle or distributional patterned principle of justice can be continuously realized without continuous interference with people's lives" (Nozick, 1974, p. 163). The pursuit of any form of end-state theory of justice, including meritocracy, would provide a never-ending justification for governments to tax, restrict, and disrupt personal liberties.

It is easy to see then that a meritocracy, at a fundamental philosophical level, is incompatible with a market economy (Mulligan, 2018). The meritocrat is faced with a tricky task — how far should the state go to ensure an equitable starting line? To what extent might a government persecute the wealthy for their above-average incomes and owned properties to prevent these privileges being given unto their children? Would the Singaporean policymaker ban supplementary tuition or regulate the use of social capital to ensure admission? If he is willing to take that step, how might he control for sociocultural circumstances that inhibit a child's educational environment? Once we realise the potential extent of government overreach that the consistent pursuit of meritocratic principles might entail, we see that it comes at a high cost.

One might even push the envelope further to try and account for genetic differences that individuals have no personal control over, what the philosopher Ronald Dworkin (2000) refers to as outcomes of "brute luck". Individuals who are more talented, better-looking, more charming, or intelligent are sure to enjoy superior social advantages. How might a meritocratic regime account for these differences in genetic make-up?

The simple truth is that people with liberties pursue different things with their freedom. The problem with trying to equalise the starting line is that people are radically different in their capacities, talents, interests, and personalities. Any attempt to do so only proceeds in a purely philosophical game to flatten social differences, curbed only by the boundaries of a wild imagination.

What this analysis suggests is that if the Singapore state wishes to maintain a genuine market economy where citizens are allowed to keep their incomes and inheritances, then the principle tenets of meritocracy will have to come at its expense, since both are fundamentally at odds with one another. It also means that critics of Singapore's meritocracy, many of whom advocate the equalisation of incomes and wealth (we explore this in other chapters of this book), run into problems as well, since even the equalisation of "starting points" will license and require a level of economic authoritarianism that most democrats in Singapore will be averse to.

Response to "Politically Defined" Argument: There is No "Fix" to Meritocracy

The second criticism that meritocracy is politically and narrowly defined mounts a serious challenge to the PAP's meritocratic rule. We agree that the PAP's conception of meritocracy is biased in that it uses an overly narrow meaning of "merit". Political leaders might make grandiose promises of how the fruits of success are attainable by any hardworking Singaporean. In practice, however, the institutional implementation through the education sector and government scholarships has favoured Singaporeans who excel in academic study or the business sector. Such a narrow conception of merit has until now excluded a more pluralistic account of meritorious ability. For example, talent in the arts has traditionally been neglected as STEM fields were emphasised for its "practical" purposes of economic growth (Stead & Hoo, 2014). "Meritocracy," as practiced until now, has lacked an appreciation for a wide account of meritorious talents that might include creative talents in music, film, and sports.[5] As much as the system purports to be neutrally selecting the most meritorious leaders, it has until now marginalised many.

In response to a flawed meritocracy, the prevalent criticism in Singapore's political discourse believes the solution is for the state to expand the definition of merit by accounting for a more diverse set of talents.[6] These critiques ultimately see the problem as one rectifiable by policy changes, rather than an inherent problem within meritocracy itself. We argue that this is ultimately a misdiagnosis of the real problem. There are three reasons why this argument fails.

State-defined meritocracy leads to rent-seeking

The first reason is political. Critics condemn the PAP for increasingly co-opting the rules of politics to their political purposes under the guise of a meritocracy (Tan, 2008, pg. 9–10). Kenneth Paul Tan recognises that

---

[5] The government has since reversed its policy to capture the cultural potential of economic growth (Kong, 2000).

[6] See popular commentaries by the Lee Kuan Yew School of Public Policy (2018) and Yip (2019).

a meritocratic system has an internal bias toward existing rules of the status quo:

"The winners, though initially convinced of their deservingness to win, may grow secretly diffident and begin to misdirect their energies on preserving their position by eliminating competitors and augmenting their own material rewards. A lack of focus and self-cultivation will lead to a depreciation of talent, and eventually the initial winners will become the wrong people for the job, as they spend most of their creative energies trying to convince the system that they are the right people for the job" (Tan, 2008, p. 10).

This can be seen as a form of rent-seeking, an important contribution from the field of public-choice economics (Tullock, 1993). Rent-seeking is the phenomenon by which political actors are able to influence and capture legislative rules for self-benefit. This preferential treatment can come in the form of a special regulation, tax, or tariff that serves to block potential competitors from entry or deter the activities of existing competitors.

Assuming that political actors act in their self-interest, it is hardly surprising then that the winners of meritocracy would be in favour of the incumbent system. After all, the biggest beneficiaries of a system are unlikely to be critical of the rules that have served them well. This might best explain why the rules of Singapore's meritocracy have remained entrenched for decades until now, with marginal changes. From a public choice perspective, there is very little reason to believe that the rules of meritocracy would be considerably modified to ensure an equal playing field. What is more likely to happen is what we see taking place — a co-optation of the rules to favour the motives of the existing winners. This may manifest in political corruption, nepotism, and other kinds of state-granted privileges. In Singapore, what we specifically see is the way meritocracy, as practiced in Singapore's public institutions, has been calibrated to serve the PAP's public policy goals of economic growth by attracting the brightest and most talented into the civil service through its competitive education system. It is plausible to see how meritocracy is subject to a high likelihood of political capture, to be warped to serve the most pressing electoral purposes of the day.

People cannot pursue what meritocracy means to them

Second, "merit" is notoriously subjective and means something different for each person. While most people think of merit as synonymous with hard work and effort, it is a fiendishly complex affair to pin down what exactly would be *most* meritorious when making public policy considerations. We intuitively see famous entrepreneurs, athletes, and celebrities as having won the meritorious game, but it is not necessarily true that the unsuccessful would be deemed unmeritorious. After all, recall that a meritocracy is not concerned with outcomes, but with the process. An unsuccessful songwriter or a physically-handicapped athlete may not be selling out packed stadiums, yet can be seen as highly meritorious for their unwavering determination and persistent grit to their craft.

Depending on a person's values and worldview, diametrically different meanings could be extracted from the term "merit". A child whose parents are scientists might see a career in the life sciences as a socially meritorious goal. At the same time, one with a creative arts background would likely place a higher premium on a career that demands creativity. Chinese cultures that dignify and celebrate a life of wealth and prosperity would consider a financially lucrative corporate career to be meritorious, but a Muslim who believes in the immorality of profit-making would differ sharply on the virtue of a good life. As the familiar adage goes, one man's meat is another man's poison.

As we document in Chapter 6, we show that many Singaporeans have the opportunity for social mobility, but are nonetheless somewhat disadvantaged by an education system that predominantly defines merit in a narrow academic manner. Many of the interview subjects expressed that they were "fortunate" to have had some academic talent, allowing them to do well in the meritocratic race of Singapore. When government policies and institutions are structured according to the state's vision of meritocracy, a diversity of ends is necessarily stifled.

It is hard to see how the institutions of meritocracy might be arranged. In light of how different people's value systems are, any form of top-down government-imposed determination of merit would simply reflect one account of meritorious ability, while marginalising alternative visions of merit.

Knowledge problem relating to meritocracy

Third, the discussion of merit in Singapore has until now underestimated how difficult it is to assess it. The meritocratic notion that a person should be rewarded according to their merit carries huge presumptions that we can judge how well people use their abilities within the context of all the circumstances that made possible using these abilities.

Take two billionaires: famed author J. K. Rowling and Donald Trump. Rowling was a single mother on public welfare who overcame her hardships to produce the wildly successful Harry Potter novels, whereas Trump's business empire was built on inherited wealth. Most people would intuitively agree that Rowling was a far more meritorious person than Trump. We can say this reliably because of knowledge of Rowling and Trump's background circumstances are public. But from the perspective of a policymaker who crafts the rules of a meritocratic society, this is an insurmountable task. How will public policymakers acquire the necessary knowledge of an individual's historical life trajectory to determine whether one person has adequately played to his strengths, grasped their life's opportunities, and is more meritorious than another?

The Nobel Laureate F. A. Hayek pointed out poignantly in his magnum opus *The Constitution of Liberty* the many problems with trying to arrange a society based on merit. The judge of merit is possible only:

> "… where we possess all the knowledge which was at the disposal of the acting person, including a knowledge of his skill and confidence, his state of mind and his feelings, his capacity for attention, his energy and persistence, etc. The possibility of a true judgment of merit thus depends on the presence of precisely those conditions whose general absence is the main argument for liberty…" (Hayek, 1960, p. 95).

For Hayek, merit-based accounts of justice demand an overwhelming epistemic weight that would cripple attempts to judge what might be "meritorious":

> "… we are not in a position to judge the merit of their achievements. To decide on merit presupposes that we can judge whether people have made such use of their opportunities as they ought to have made and how

much effort of will or self- denial this has cost them; it presupposes also that we can distinguish between that part of their achievement which is due to circumstances within their control and that part which is not" (Hayek, 1960, p. 95).

Policymakers cannot possibly afford the necessary resources to study how millions of its citizens navigate the courses of their lives (putting aside the Orwellian nightmares that might accompany such a venture). Yet in a meritocracy where governments must determine the rules of what constitutes merit, these would be the onerous requirements necessary to meet. Even if citizens can philosophically agree that meritocracy is most desirable, there is no reason to assume that governments would have access to the private knowledge needed to assess individuals by merit.

In summary, we argue that the popular belief to "fix" meritocracy by simply expanding its scope is unlikely to be successful. First, this is because meritocracy is fundamentally at odds with a regime that respects private property rights and economic freedoms. Insofar as we want to allow people to freely trade and associate, the rules of meritocracy will be continually put at tension, giving a meritocratic government an increasing onus to equalise socio-economic starting lines via drastic measures. Second, state governments are bound by the rules of politics and electoral trends, making it unlikely that they will effectively enforce a meritocratic regime when it comes at the expense of their own interests. Third, in the unlikely event that states will act in the interest of the public, what counts as merit is highly subjective and notoriously difficult to assess. In this context, a meritocracy is both epistemologically and logistically impossible to implement.

Classical Liberalism as a Solution to Resolve Tensions in Singapore's Meritocracy

It is for all these reasons that one should be sceptical of a meritocracy when its institutional rules are being designed and imposed top-down by a state government. As a purely philosophical exercise, we are convinced that meritocracies are incompatible with capitalist economies and are tempted to discard meritocracy as an ideal. As a matter of public policy however, we argue that this does not necessarily have to be the solution. Meritocracy, imperfect as it is, has served Singapore well. The classical liberal approach can offer insight into bridging these existing tensions in the status quo. Therefore, assuming that Singapore policy wants to continue adhering to meritocratic principles, we argue that market forces and competition should be harnessed in the education sector to allow a diverse account of "merit" to exist.

Assuming that a meritocracy (in the broadest sense) is collectively desirable, public policy is best oriented towards a decentralised approach that allows for a competing set of education choices. Such decentralisation of rules would first and foremost enable existing public schools in Singapore more freedom to create its own education syllabus and grading criteria. If a school believes academic excellence to best reflect merit, they are free to provide an intensive educational syllabus with stringent grading criteria. However, if another school thinks that inculcating creativity and innovation in children is a better reflection of merit, they will be free to provide an alternative mode of assessment. Within such a regime, the administrative decisions that schools make will be subjected to the commercial pressure of market competition. If parents realise that their child is incompatible with an overly "grade-obsessed" syllabus, they are free to uproot and relocate their children to a different education programme.

Unlike a state meritocracy, the classical liberal approach is one that allows room for diversity. It makes a case for enabling a market-oriented education system, where a multiplicity of merit-based conceptions can coexist simultaneously. It allows multiple authorities and jurisdictions to cohabit at the same time, without any one single institutional authority being able to exert a set of homogeneous rules across the board. Therefore, the classical liberal approach is particularly liberating because it allows parents a scope of exit from the status quo in Singapore, which at present amounts to a grade-obsessed race that is not necessarily equivalent to learning.

Rather than being locked into the PAP's narrowly-defined version of "merit", it gives families the freedom to define merit within the scope of their own households and sociocultural rules, and pick and choose from a variety of education options that are best compatible with their normative vision of a meritorious life. Parents would have the freedom of association and disassociation to pursue their subjective versions of merit by enlisting their children in the schools that best meets their choices.

Most fundamentally, the classical liberal acknowledges the radical difference in individual potentials, capacities, and diverse human values.

Therefore, it is critical of the notion that only one set of institutional rules should be governing a merit-based education system, where a central authority is able to impose a rigid conception of "merit" on others. In a classical liberal regime, individuals, households, and groups can customise their lifestyles according to what is best for them. In the area of education policy, for instance, it would preclude the state's careful selection of certain subjects and skills worth funding in favour of a neutral alternative, driven by private actors and civil society groups.

As it is, parents do not have any choice but to enlist their child into a state-defined version of "merit". The existing government-oriented education system, by its very structure, disallows a plurality of different merit-based views to coexist. Students are introduced to a fixed set of test subjects and grading criteria at the primary, secondary, and tertiary school levels. Parents enlist their children in identical enrichment classes that help them "game" the state examinations, all in a bid to secure a university course of their choice. Because the route to the top is designed the same way, students cannot help but participate in the same grade-oriented educational arms race. This is shown in our interviews with local Singaporeans, some of whom have complained about the narrow, state-defined understanding of "merit".

The unique contribution of classical liberalism is that on the one hand, it endorses the meritocrat's desire for excellence to be rewarded, yet minimises the problems of the existing meritocracy. Classical liberalism advocates an institutional framework of choice, competition, and evolutionary discovery. It is when firms, individuals, and various communities compete with each other that positive outcomes emerge from this trial and error process. This is achieved in a bottom-up manner, precluding any attempt by the state to define the scope of merit or to engineer a meritorious endpoint. Consequently, critics of Singapore's system of meritocracy, who condemn its narrow scope and favouring of elites, would find much to praise in our alternative.

Conclusion

The main purpose of this chapter has not been to defend the government's conception of meritocracy or argue for its abandonment, but rather to diagnose why is it these tensions exist. An imperfect meritocratic regime

is still an admirable form of governance. It provides incentives to cultivate a strong cultural work ethic. Even in its flawed form, it is hard to deny that this work ethic has been an effective guiding principle for Singapore's public policy and economic development.

However, so long as conventional thinking is restricted to the premise that "merit" is up to the definition by Singaporean policymakers, a system that suffers from prejudice and bias is unavoidable. The problem is not with meritocracy per se, but with the notion that only one version of state-defined meritocracy can exist. Critics believe that the solution to the status quo is to simply widen the scope of merit, but we argue that this mode of thinking continues to underestimate the congenital differences among people and the radically different institutional environments they come from. A "meritocracy" that is imposed top-down by the state will inevitably discriminate against certain groups of individuals over others in an inconsistent fashion because it cannot possibly accommodate a pluralist account of merit. Therefore, we conclude that a classical liberal regime that allows for individuals to pursue their individual conceptions of "merit" is a morally attractive alternative, and this starts with a decentralised, market-based education system that allows parents to pick from different education programmes.

4

Singapore's Technocratic Paternalism and How Behavioural Economics Justifies More of the Same

Singapore's reputation of a nanny state in popular culture stems from its highly technocratic and paternalistic approach. One of the principles that guide the Singapore government is that of pragmatism, where policies are justified based on whether they produce concrete and tangible results, rather than being subject to consistent rule-based ideals. This has been consistently demonstrated by the People's Action Party's (PAP) willingness to make intrusive interventions into the personal lives of its citizens from religion, public housing racial segregation, abortion, or something as trivial as a ban on chewing gum. Indeed, Lee Kuan Yew once famously praised the merits of this approach:

> "I am often accused of interfering in the private lives of citizens. Yes, if I did not, had I not done that, we wouldn't be here today. And I say without the slightest remorse, that we wouldn't be here, we would not have made economic progress, if we had not intervened on very personal matters — who your neighbour is, how you live, the noise you make, how you spit, or what language you use. We decide what is right" (BBC, 2015).

Not only is the state paternalistic, such practices are conducted by an elite group of officials and scholar-bureaucrats who believe they possess the superior wisdom needed to steer the ship of the state. That Singapore governance is *paternalistic and technocratic* is an open secret. What we add to the discussion, in this chapter, is the insight that in recent years, this form of technocratic paternalism has been *further entrenched* due to two new and related developments. First, and most significant, is the "behavioural" revolution in academia. Second, the rise of new technologies has further given the technocratic state tools to harness in their central planning of society.

The first development is the rise of the popular paradigm of behavioural economics. Today, it is pervasive in mainstream economics and has permeated the world of public policy. So widespread is the use of behavioural nudging that to date, more than 150 countries are said to have resorted to it in their policymaking.[1] It is no surprise then to find that behavioural economics too has gained significant attention and traction in Singapore policy discussions. Advocacy of behavioural-style policy is highly visible in the Civil Service College, a government-funded educational institution that grooms young high-potential Singaporeans for a policymaking career. Published under the same institution is *Behavioural Design and Policy Design* (Low, 2012), an extensive collection of essays that studies and advances the application of behavioural economic insights to Singaporean policy. The book provides a comprehensive survey of how behavioural insights have been historically utilised in Singapore's policy, with case study examples of road traffic congestion management, retirement savings, organ donations, and more.

The second trend is the rise of new information technologies, including the use of "Big Data" and artificial intelligence-related technologies, which strengthens the government's long-running practice of central, national planning. In Singapore, through the use of its elaborate Risk Assessment and Horizon Scanning (RAHS) digital tools, policymakers have deployed these new technologies toward a wide variety of ends from national security to strategic policy planning. While this practice recognises the behavioural shortcomings of policymakers due to the increasing complexity of the

---

[1] OECD. (2017). *Use of behavioural insights in consumer policy.* Retrieved from: http://www.oecd.org/officialdocuments/publicdisplaydocumentpdf/?cote=DSTI/CP(2016)3/FINAL&docLanguage=En.

globalised world, it nonetheless believes that these limitations may be overcome. While the new agenda of behavioural economics seeks to improve and modify individual behaviour at the micro-level, this second trajectory is a macroeconomic approach that makes use of gaming simulations and scenario planning in order to achieve normatively superior outcomes of public governance.

Both trajectories are, however, united in its acknowledgement of modern social complexity, as well as its rejection of neoclassical economic rationality. In the globalised market societies of today, it is argued that because both consumers and policymakers deviate from standard models of economic rationality, policies must develop a more nuanced approach that accounts for the fundamental nature of human irrationality.

This chapter takes issue with the practice of technocratic paternalism today through a classical liberal lens, especially in light of the increasing application of behavioural insights into local policymaking. We question the methodological foundations that the behavioural paradigm rests on, as well as its practical applicability in public policy. Although proponents of the behavioural approach painstakingly emphasise its distinctiveness from traditional hard-handed governance, we argue that what the so-called behavioural revolution ends up enabling is more of the same old technocratic paternalism, and is therefore very much wanting from a classical liberal perspective.

Behavioural Economics in Public Policy

The key defining feature of the school of behavioural economics is its methodological positioning away from neoclassical economic forms of rationality. It begins by questioning the traditional construct of *homo economicus*, where individuals and firms are modelled as being strict utility or profit maximisers, operating on rational preferences and on the basis of full information, a common analytical construct used in Econ 101. The implicit assumption of neoclassical modelling assumes actors are faced with all relevant costs, benefits, and probabilities to conduct a flawless cost-benefit analysis to always make the right choice.

Behavioural economists reject the methodological device of *homo economicus*. The basic argument is that consumers do not behave as rationally as traditional economic models suggest (Tversky & Kahneman, 1974; Camerer & Lowenstein, 2004; Ariely, 2008). Instead, the decision-making processes of individuals operating in markets are heavily flawed. We are riddled with a slew of cognitive biases that prevent us from making optimal outcomes. Consumers mistakenly save too little for their retirement, smoke too much when they know it's terrible for them, and fall prey to unhealthy food when they would rather be fit and healthy.

The biases that behavioural economists have mapped out are extensive. One prominent bias is known as hyperbolic discounting, which describes a person's lack of foresight to commit to long-term goals.[2] People give in to instant gratification for a smaller payoff, whereas if they had exercised patience, they would have reaped a superior reward in the future. Where traditional neoclassical economics would assume a decision-maker to possess a consistent discounting rate, behavioural economics argues that people more often than not have *inconsistent* discounting rates, causing them to underestimate the costs of current trade-offs. In other words, a person may plan to commit ex-ante a portion of their income to savings, yet succumb to the temptation of splurging it when they receive their paycheck, only to suffer in ex-post regret. Hyperbolic discounting is popularly drawn upon to explain a wide range of "self-control" problems in the behavioural economics literature in regards to retirement savings and consumption of unhealthy food or drugs.

Other popular biases in the behavioural economics literature include the availability heuristic, where people overestimate the importance or probability of events due to accessibility or overexposure to information; the bandwagon effect, where people attribute truth and falsehoods to popular belief, i.e. groupthink; the anchoring effect, where we mistakenly base our decisions on the first piece of information that comes their way and subsequently disregard others; or the endowment effect which describes the tendency to place a higher value on objects already in possession.

The policy implications that follow from the behavioural economics diagnosis is manifold. The less coercive policy involves "nudging", where policymakers have sought to frame the consumer decision-making process in a way that induces more optimal selection for the decision-maker.

---

[2] Behaviour Lab. (n.d). *Hyperbolic Discounting*. Retrieved from: http://www.behaviorlab.org/Papers/Hyperbolic.pdf.

For example, Thaler and Sunstein (2008, p. 104) have advocated the practice of automatically enrolling employees in savings plans, with the voluntary option for the employee to opt-out. The underlying rationale is that present-biased employees may suffer from inertia to adopt a savings scheme. Therefore, automatic enrolment serves to make for consumers a choice they would already prefer and as judged by themselves.

Behavioural economists make a central normative argument. Because people do not make sound decisions within the scope of their private lives, policymakers need to ensure that these mistakes are corrected. By nudging people toward optimal decision-making, governments help save people from their own suboptimal decisions. Advocates of behavioural economics, however, have been explicit about nudging people in a way that preserves the liberty of choice (Thaler & Sunstein, 2003b, p. 1185). The claim is that nudging should help people make choices that already align with their own self-interests, rather than that of the policymaker.

Therefore, it can be said that this form of paternalism departs from traditionally hard-handed forms of paternalism where so-called sin goods are outright banned or regulated. This economic philosophy has been referred to by behavioural economists themselves as "libertarian paternalism" (Thaler & Sunstein, 2003a), a middle-way between the absolute freedom of choice that free-market libertarians champion, and an overbearing paternalistic oversight of a nanny-state government.

That being said, behavioural economists do not necessarily restrict themselves to such less coercive nudges and have kept the door open for more aggressive regulation — a slippery slope that we discuss in the third section of this chapter. Behavioural economists have also advocated sin taxes that raise consumption costs in the present, so as to offset hyperbolic discounting biases and push the consumer towards making more "rational" decisions (O'Donoghue & Rabin, 2006). In the context of Singapore policy, much of the discussion surrounding the application of behavioural insights have to do with introducing or improving already existing and coercive government laws where an opt-out option is not availed. For example, it is suggested in the book *Behavioural Design and Policy Design* that consumer myopia in the energy market means it "makes sense for governments to introduce mandatory energy performance standards to remove the most inefficient appliances" (Ong, 2012, p. 82). In Chapter 8, which discusses social welfare policy, the analysis is wholly dedicated to refining the existing mandatory Central Provident Fund (CPF) welfare programme through the use of behavioural framing in public consultation, without considerations for an exit option. As such, the rhetoric of "libertarian paternalism" at times diverges from its actual policy application, raising scepticism about the real intent of behavioural proponents.

Behavioural Paternalism in Singapore

Governance in Singapore has always exhibited a clear paternalist tendency, which may have preceded the rise of behavioural economics as a discipline but is now subtly accelerated because of it. Technocratic paternalism in Singapore is evident in the type of policies being passed, the rationale articulated behind those policies, and in the very structure of the public sector.

Technocratic paternalism in Singapore can be traced to the very identity of the People's Action Party's conception of itself and its legitimacy to govern. One of the foundational elements of the PAP's ideology is that of elitism, which has been explained by the Singapore scholars Diane Mauzy and R.S. Milne as "the belief that there is always a small group of people at the top who make the important decisions influencing society, whatever the political system" (Mauzy & Milne, 2002, p. 53). Elite governance has always existed in history. Thomas Jefferson, the father of American democracy, himself acknowledged that "there is a natural aristocracy among men".

However, what we point out is that in the unique context of Singapore, what legitimates this elite group is not socio-economic status or superior moral virtue, but rather, the possession of *superior intellect*. In other words, the PAP elites believe that there exists a natural aristocracy of more knowledgeable individuals within society who are more fit to govern and that they themselves constitute this elite. Governance in Singapore is based on an elitist foundation defined in terms of the superior knowledge of political elites. State paternalism in Singapore is thus a by-product of technocratic elitism.

This is evident, first of all, by the rhetoric of the PAP state elites over the years. By now, most Singaporeans would be aware of the (in)famous quote by Lee Kuan Yew that in every society, there is about five percent "who are more than ordinarily endowed physically and mentally and in whom we must expend our limited and slender resources in order that they will provide that yeast, that ferment, that catalyst in our society...".[3] This belief in the necessity of elite leadership in society is also associated with Lee's distrust of the collective wisdom of the democratic masses, when expressed: "So when people say, 'Oh, ask the people!' it's childish rubbish. We are leaders. We know the consequences. You mean the ice-water man knows the consequences of his vote? Don't tell me that." (Lee & Han, 2011, p. 135).

It is also evident through the very structure of the public service. While recruitment into politics and the civil service is based on the principle of meritocracy, in reality, this has been based on a deeper, elitist foundation. Generous government scholarships are provided to the best and brightest in Singapore society on the basis that they would form the next generation of leaders who will steer the ship of the state. Scholars and commentators have previously shown how students from top schools are overwhelmingly selected in these programmes, sent to top universities, and promoted rapidly within the ranks of government. The representation of highly educated elites in government jobs forms the basis of the "government-knows-best" mentality that is pervasive in Singapore society.

The technocratic elite in the Singapore state has passed numerous paternalistic policies. Singapore has been described as a nanny state where personal consumption choices, lifestyle choices, and public behaviours are subject to social engineering, prohibitions and regulations. Besides the common point made by foreigners of how chewing gum is banned in Singapore, what Singaporeans put into their mouths is subject to active public health campaigns.[4] The use of moral suasion by the government to shape Singaporeans' lifestyle choices is conducted through numerous media: on television, radio, public transportation stations, and printed media. The very structure of CPF, the social security system, is itself based on a paternalist premise, which is that some Singaporeans may not take responsibility for their own health, retirement, and lifestyle and thus

---

[3] Lee, K. Y. (1967). *Transcript of Speech by the Prime Minister Lee Kuan Yew on 19 June 1967.* Retrieved from: https://www.nas.gov.sg/archivesonline/data/pdfdoc/lky19670619.pdf.
[4] Singapore Infopedia. (2005). *National healthy lifestyle program.* Retrieved from: https://eresources.nlb.gov.sg/infopedia/articles/SIP_339_2005-01-06.html.

may become a social burden. This in turn necessitates the practice of forced savings *for the own good* of Singaporeans.

The economic historian Deirdre McCloskey has called behavioural economics the "applied theory of bossing people around".[5] This is because it provides a theoretical justification for an elite to socially engineer the choices of a supposedly irrational public. It is thus unsurprising that the technocratic and elitist PAP government has embraced behavioural economics, both as a means of descriptive analysis and a policy tool to shape social behaviour.

Behavioural economics has been used in various levels of policymaking in Singapore. Its applications are extensive, and in fact, pervade the everyday life of Singaporeans. Reports have documented how rubbish bins are strategically placed to separate smokers from other bus users, gyms are located in heartland areas to remind passers-by of the need to exercise, and how train stations have coloured signs to guide and hasten the movements of commuters.[6] On a larger level, behavioural insights are also harnessed to tackle what are deemed as national challenges, such as healthcare, water shortage, and environmental conservation. Nudging is extensively used to steer Singaporeans to have healthier diets and reduce the incidences of diseases such as diabetes, which has recently emerged as a public health concern. Behavioural insights were also used to curb water consumption during showers by providing real-time information on water usage and goal setting.[7] Nudging is also practiced in the environmental arena in Singapore, such as through the presentation of energy labels encouraging the use of energy-efficient technologies and posters, campaigns, and messages to socially sanction environmentally unfriendly behaviour (Boh, 2017, p. 25).

The commitment of Singapore to the use of behavioural insights and its applications is also seen through the establishment of the National University of Singapore (NUS) Centre for Behavioural Economics, the

---

[5] McCloskey, De. (2018, Febr). *The applied theory of bossing people around.* Retrieved from: https://reason.com/2018/02/11/the-applied-theory-of-bossing/.
[6] Keating, S. (2018, February 20). The nation that thrived by nudging its population. *BBC.* Retrieved from: https://www.bbc.com/future/article/20180220-the-nation-that-thrived-by-nudging-its-population.
[7] Public Utilities Board, Singapore. (n.d.). *Smart Shower Programme.* Retrieved from: https://www.pub.gov.sg/savewater/athome/smartshowerprogramme.

first research centre that is exclusively devoted to behavioural economics research in Singapore; the Behavioural Sciences Institute at the Singapore Management University (SMU); and the grafting of behavioural insights into the work of the Public Service Division.[8] The Civil Service College has also made available course offerings to Senior Officers and above on the use of behavioural insights to craft policy interventions and also organised events to discuss its usefulness.[9] Behavioural economics is not merely a passing fad, but increasingly forms an integral component of Singapore policymaking (see Low, 2012 for more).

Big Data and Public Governance

That the Singapore government engages in technocratic national planning is, of course, no secret. Scenario planning is an integral component of the government's policymaking toolkit, both for macroeconomic planning and the crafting of social policies. However, in recent times, and due to the rise of new information technologies, the Singapore government has been more confident in its long-standing practice of technocratic paternalism. Today, Singapore's technocracy is augmented by the deployment of Big Data scanning tools and "scenario planning" methods under the Risk Assessment and Horizon Scanning (RAHS) Centre.

The origins of RAHS go as far back as 2004 when the 2001 Jemaah Islamiyah terrorist attacks and the 2003 SARS disease outbreak jumpstarted its usage and provided the Singapore government with a justification to use it. Inspired by the US Defense Department's "Total Information Awareness" (TIA) system, the system deploys "Big Data" technologies that allow users to screen through vast amounts of data from varied sources to pick up on signals in the economy that might indicate an impending shock or systemic disruption.[10]

---

[8] Chang, C., & Mohamed, J. (2018, November 22). How to make government more agile. *GovInsider*. Retrieved from: https://govinsider.asia/innovation/how-to-make-government-more-agile/.

[9] Civil Service College. *Introduction to Behavioral Insights*. Retrieved from: https://www.cscollege.gov.sg/programmes/pages/display%20programme.aspx?epid=a7jes1t1d7864srt9pcnlj3nqe; Civil Service College. (2017, June 14). *Behavioral Insights: Fact or Fad?*. Retrieved from: https://www.csc.gov.sg/articles/behavioural-insights-fact-or-fad.

[10] For a more detailed and technical explanation of how the Singapore government utilises RAHS, see Habegger (2010).

Perhaps the biggest proponent of this policy approach is Peter Ho, ex-head of Singapore's civil service. The policy justification for RAHS is derived from the central belief that nations and cities in the globalised world of today are characterised by high levels of complexity. Due to rapid technological improvements in communications and transport that have greatly increased the complexity of goods and labour flows, the causes and effects of socio-economic phenomena are no longer easily discernible (Ho, 2015). Therefore, biased policymakers are prone to underestimating the nuanced complexities of modern economies, and are potentially blindsided by their conceit in policymaking. In particular, these complexities are wrought with unpredictable events (what the popular intellectual Nassim Taleb refers to as "black swans") and unclear solutions, such as terrorist attacks, epidemic outbreaks, natural disasters, and economic recessions.

The dominant policy approach that the Singapore government has taken in tackling these problems is steeped in what is often termed a "whole-of-government" approach that emphasises inter-agency collaboration between government organisations. Because such complex problems often lack clear stakeholder ownerships, it is best tackled by a diverse team of government actors that collectively pool their knowledge and experiences. As such, it is imperative that the government overcomes institutional tendencies in the public sector to operate within siloed units and aim toward horizontal integration and cooperation.[11]

This preference for a "whole-of-government" approach is related to some key insights from the field of behavioural economics. Peter Ho, for instance, has drawn from the insights of behavioural economics when he acknowledges that even the smartest statemen are not flawless, as "the most forward-looking government, leaders and officials will have their own mental models and cognitive biases, and seek confirmation for them" (Ho, 2010; see also Ho, 2012). Second, he recognises that the knowledge required of policymakers to plan around such complex and unpredictable events lie out of reach in the dimension of "tacit" knowledge. Tacit knowledge is difficult to transfer and convey, and only acquirable through actual learned experiences, distinct from explicit and theoretical knowledge that can be acquired through reading a book.

---

[11] The construction of the Marina Barrage water reservoir in central Singapore is cited as an achievement via the "whole-of-government" approach (Ho, 2015, p. 6).

Based on this behavioural insight of the knowledge limitations of policymakers, Ho advocates for governments to conduct simulator exercises and games that parallels real-world experiences for would-be policymakers. It is argued that these simulations would help thwart the many biases that individuals suffer from, and "mitigate issues of cognitive dissonance and consistency biases" (Ho, 2010). Further to that, it would arm policymakers with valuable forms of tacit knowledge that will help combat these unforeseeable shocks, by "embedding patterns in the memory of participants, which can be recalled later for making decisions in real-life situations" (Ho, 2016a; Ho, 2016b). While he acknowledges that the exercises are imperfect, these training simulations nonetheless serve as a crucial way to increase the readiness of a civil service by allowing policymakers to immerse themselves in similar environments so as to reduce the element of surprise when the actual crisis hits.

The overarching objective of scenario planning is to enable better governance through its attempt to predict and pick up on exogenous shocks to the economy beforehand and soften its damage. RAHS was initially utilised mainly for Singapore's national security. However, its use-cases in recent years have been extended to a wide range of purposes in economic policy such as informing economic forecasts, planning national budgets, and guiding housing, education, and immigration policies (Harris, 2014). In summary:

> "Scenarios make people aware of problems, uncertainties, challenges and opportunities that such an environment would present, and opening up their imagination and initiating learning processes. For the past two decades, the Singapore government has been using scenario planning. National scenarios are developed at the Whole-of-Government level every few years. These then help the ministries and agencies in anticipating in their policies, plans and even budgets of the challenges and opportunities that could arise in the future" (Ho, 2015, pg. 9).

Where Technocratic Paternalism Goes Wrong

We offer three broad objections to the technocratic paternalism characteristic of Singapore's governance under the PAP. First, we present objections highlighting the theoretical problems at the root of the new behavioural economics. The second objection takes issue with epistemological problems that technocratic paternalists face. The third and final objection raises public choice problems that plague the policy suggestions technocratic paternalists recommend.

The Theoretical Problems of Behavioural Economics

As we pointed out in the previous section, the defining feature of behavioural economics is its methodological departure from the standard norms of neoclassical economic rationality. As the argument goes, people are deeply irrational creatures who operate at a suboptimal level than they would in an ideal world. This suboptimality then is best corrected by the deployment of governmental policies.

It is at this methodological starting point that the behavioural economics project is theoretically problematic. Although neoclassical rationality is claimed to be an impossibility, *homo economicus* is nonetheless upheld as a normative standard of human rationality. This is explicit in the writings of Thaler and Sunstein themselves:

> "We intend 'better off' to be measured as objectively as possible, and we clearly do not always equate revealed preference with welfare. That is, we emphasise the possibility that in some cases people make inferior choices, choices that they would change *if they had complete information, unlimited cognitive abilities and no lack of willpower*" [emphasis added] (Thaler and Sunstein, 2003a, p. 175).

Camerer and Loewenstein state it more explicitly:

> "At the core of behavioral economics is the conviction that increasing the realism of the psychological underpinnings of economic analysis will improve the field of economics on its own terms — generating theoretical insights, making better predictions of field phenomena, and suggesting better policy. This conviction does not imply a wholesale rejection of the neoclassical approach to economics based on utility maximisation, equilibrium, and efficiency. The neoclassical approach is useful because it provides economists with a theoretical framework that can be applied to almost any form of economic (and even noneconomic) behavior, and it makes refutable predictions" (2004, p. 3).

Therefore, while behavioural economists tell us that individuals cannot possibly behave like the fully-informed and lightning-fast calculators that populate neoclassical economic models,[12] they simultaneously argue that people *should* act that way in an ideal world. But this line of logic is severely puzzling. If the all-rational man is a myth, then what sense does it make to judge real people by such impossible standards? By doing so, the behavioural economics project has already ex-ante framed the inevitable discussion of how people are wholly biased and flawed in a multitude of ways, thereby requiring correction. If *homo economicus* is an unrealistic description of the individual, then adherence to it as a normative standard is highly questionable. In other words, Superman is not real, yet you shall be evaluated according to the standards of Superman.

As Boettke *et al.* (2013) point out, there is a stark similarity in the behavioural economics project today to the dominant "market failure" welfare economics paradigm of the 20th century. In its simplest form, the neoclassical welfare economics paradigm is oriented around two main theorems.[13] The first theorem starts with a set of assumptions about what an ideal market would look like when it is fully competitive and perfectly efficient. The second theorem states that when there is a deviation from the first theorem, i.e., market failures, governments can theoretically make lump-sum transfers to achieve efficiency. Therefore, by claiming that real-world markets are always imperfect, the two theorems together provide an ideological justification that is ever-present for governments to intervene and reach full efficiency in the economy (Wagner, 2017, p. 139). Similar to market failures in the welfare economics paradigm, individuals in behavioural economics suffer from a type of "decision-making failure" where their actions fail to match the supposedly rational standards, providing a paternalistic onus for correction.

Indeed, we agree with behavioural economists that the narrow treatment of economic man is analytically problematic. However, because the behavioural economics project is ultimately wedded to neoclassical rationality assumptions, it continues to operate within the parameters

---

[12] Rizzo (2017a) has pointed out the strawman in this argument; *homo economicus* is meant to serve as a methodological tool for performing analysis, not a positive description of human nature.

[13] For more on the welfare economics paradigm, see Munger (2018).

of neoclassical economics that fundamentally underestimates the truly radical and complex nature of human action. This line of argument has been notably developed by scholars associated with the "Austrian school", who have long pointed out the errors of neoclassical economics.[14] In a seminal essay, Israel Kirzner writes:

> "At the individual level, Austrians have taken sharp exception to the manner in which neoclassical theory has portrayed the individual decision as a mechanical exercise in constrained maximisation. Such a portrayal robs human choice of its essentially open-ended character, in which imagination and boldness must inevitably play central roles... such decision making is seen as being made in the context of known probability functions. In the neoclassical world, decision-makers know what they are ignorant about. One is never surprised. For Austrians, however, to abstract from these qualities of imagination, boldness, and surprise is to denature human choice entirely" (Kirzner, 1997, p. 62).

The key difference between Austrian methodological individualism and the new behavioural economics paradigm, however, is that the former goes one step further in disengaging from such a normative standard of neoclassical rationality. Indeed, the "open-ended" character that Kirzner speaks of is at the heart of Austrian methodological individualism. From an Austrian perspective, individual action is always purposeful and operates under ever-present conditions of uncertainty and doubt. Man is not assumed to be an all-rational utility-maximiser but a flawed decision-maker operating under cognitive limitations. He pursues a diverse range of values, of which every decision involves tradeoffs. The judge of whether an action is "rational" depends on the context in which the choice is taken and the agent's internal preferences. But most crucially for the discussion

---

[14] Austrians have also been long sceptical of the pervasive use of *homo economicus* constructs in the neoclassical economic paradigm. As Ludwig von Mises writes, *homo economicus* "... does not deal with the behavior of man as he really is and acts, but with a fictitious or hypothetical image. It pictures a being driven exclusively by "economic" motives, i.e., solely by the intention of making the greatest possible material or monetary profit. Such a being does not have and never did a counterpart in reality; it is a phantom of a spurious armchair philosophy. No man is exclusively motivated by the desire to become as rich as possible; many are not at all influenced by this mean craving. It is vain to refer to such an illusory homunculus in dealing with life and history" (Mises, 1998, p. 62).

at hand, individual rationality is not measured against a theoretically ideal standard of rationality,[15] where deviations from such a standard would prompt correction by the behavioural paternalist with a sin tax or a nudge.

Similar criticisms have been levelled against the new behavioural economics paradigm by the prominent behavioural psychologist Gerd Gigerenzer (Gigerenzer & Todd, 1999). Like Austrian economists, Gigerenzer takes issue with the way that the new behavioural economics paradigm omits the institutional context by which decision-making takes place. By doing so, the analysis of the behavioural paternalist is blinded to the way by which individual decisions are shaped by the various factors in that particular environmental circumstance, such as time constraints, limited information, and tacit knowledge acquired from historical experience.

When the environmental context is introduced back into the analysis, decisions previously seen as "biased" are in fact highly rational and optimising. Rather than being seen as unreliable coping mechanisms,[16] heuristics serve as exceptionally useful guides of human action according to the standards of *ecological rationality*, which "involves analysing the structure of environments, the structure of heuristics, and the match between them" (Gigerenzer & Todd, 1999, p. 18). Such heuristics are based on simple, sequential rules of guidance that allow the user to navigate a world of high uncertainty and time constraints.

The famed psychologist Herbert Simon, most famously known for his models of bounded rationality, could not have been more explicit about the analytical importance of the institutional context in economics:

"[The] study of bounded rationality is not the study of optimisation in relation to task environments. It is the study of how people acquire strategies for coping with those environments; how those strategies emerge out of problem space definitions; and how built-in physiological

---

[15] In the same vein, Herbert Simon was explicit that bounded rationality is a model "… of human judgment and decision making [that] should be built on what we actually know about the mind's capacities rather than on fictitious competencies" (Gigerenzer & Todd, 1999, p. 12).

[16] The term "heuristic" has dual meanings; while it used to mean a cognitive tool that individuals use to discover new forms of knowledge, today it is more commonly associated with cognitive impairments (Gigerenzer & Todd, 1999, p. 26–28).

limits shape and constrain the acquisition of problem spaces and strategies. At each of these steps there is room for alternative processes, any of which would meet satisfactorily (not optimally) the requirements of the task environment. The environment cannot predict which of these alternatives will govern the adaptive behavior" (Simon, 1989, p.16).

It is particularly strange then that advocates of nudge policy in Singapore often cite Simon favourably for their purposes (see Low, 2012, p. 22) when the methodology of the nudge paradigm is guilty of committing this blundering error.

In other words, the context matters when judging human rationality. The behavioural economist omits the ecological context by which action takes place, and his judgment of "irrationality" is blindsided because he cannot truly understand why the subject is behaving a certain way. Furthermore, when the subject's actions are evaluated against the very same neoclassical standards of rationality that behavioural paternalists find fault with, it amounts up to a fruitless exercise that produces the obvious conclusions that individuals do not operate like flawless robots. Mario Rizzo summarises it well:

> "Both behavioral and neoclassical economists maintain a concept of strict rationality that is exceptionally narrow. Neoclassicists use it as a tool both to explain what agents actually do and as a prescriptive framework. Behavioralists do not believe it adequately explains actual behavior but that it is still a good prescriptive framework... The appropriate concept of rationality for evaluation purposes must be 'liberal' or broad reflecting the complexities of human decision-making. Behavioral economists are blind to much of this at a normative-prescriptive level. So their critique of [the] market or other outcomes is impoverished" (2017b, p. 3).

This theoretical confusion at the heart of behavioural economics provides reason to be sceptical of its larger enterprise. Behavioural economics has been too quick to point out the errors in human decision-making, yet jumping to the conclusion that said errors are to be corrected to match the standards of perfect rationality. It has, importantly, also lacked an institutional analysis, which if included reveals that many seemingly "irrational" actions were simply context-contingent circumstances, and not a fatal problem of human behaviour needing governmental correction.

Knowledge Problem Objections

The second major objection to the technocratic paternalism project can be categorised under the broad umbrella of what we refer to here as "knowledge problem" objections. At the core of the nudge project is its attempt to use government policy to correct for cognitive biases that individuals lack on their own willpower and self-discipline to do so. Rizzo & Whitman (2009b) have argued comprehensively that behavioural paternalists underestimate the epistemic weight required to employ nudge policies. Left unaddressed, nudges may crowd out desirable forms of self-regulation and even do more harm than good.

We make two objections here. Firstly, individuals in the real world are inflicted with multiple biases at any given time. These biases can interact in different ways that will exacerbate the adverse effects, improve the positive effects, or invalidate the other biases for a person.

Consider a hypothetical individual Moses, who struggles with obesity because he lacks the discipline to (1) commit to a fitness regime and (2) abstain from unhealthy foods. Suppose the behavioural paternalist subsidised gym memberships in order to nudge people like Moses toward healthy exercise. A free membership will increase the likelihood of Moses exercising. But suppose now that the newfound confidence in committing to a gym routine might greatly worsen his bias to indulge in unhealthy junk food (if I'm working out, I can eat whatever I like), thereby offsetting the healthy benefits of his exercises. In this scenario then, nudging runs the risk of leaving individuals worse-off than before from the way it creates interaction between both his biases.

Granted, in our hypothetical scenario, there is no reason to assume that Moses' secondary biases will inevitably be aggravated in a welfare-reducing direction. It is entirely plausible that Moses' nudge-induced workouts might inspire him to forgo unhealthy foods altogether. But this is an empirical question that cannot be settled by economic theory. The point of significance here is that for nudge policies to be successful, policymakers must be able to successfully account for how an agent will resist, accept, or counteract the forces of a policy nudge in various ways.

Yet, it is highly unlikely that technocrats would have access to these forms of knowledge in order to design the optimal nudge policy not just for Moses, but for an entire population. How might the technocrat possibly know the almost infinite possibilities by which individuals' biases would interact? Given that people have different inclinations towards "sinful" activities and exhibit varying extents of different biases, the epistemological burden that is placed on the technocrat denotes a fiendishly impossible task.

Secondly, individuals employ their own self-debiasing measures to counteract biases they are aware of (Rizzo & Whitman, 2009b, p. 943). It is naive to assume that individuals are helpless sheep who are wholly incapable of defending themselves. In reality, we willingly adopt credit card limits to curb our spending, commit to year-long fitness gym memberships to prevent slacking off, and deliberately avoid social situations where we might be tempted to consume alcohol or other unhealthy foods.

Therefore, nudge policies need to account for these various coping mechanisms that individuals self-adopt. By ignoring the fact that people do already employ forms of self-regulation, the behavioural paternalist's attempt to alleviate biases may go too far and result in welfare-reducing outcomes. It might even crowd out self-regulation to the extent that individuals believe they no longer have to worry since the government is looking out for them.

The need to account for such nuances is unlikely from the fact that all policies (including nudging) construed at a top-down manner will come in a "one-size-fits-all" character that cannot account for such radical heterogeneous differences between people. Because people are drastically different, assessing the policy effectiveness will require extensive knowledge of the distribution and extent of the bias, and the elasticity rate of how agents will respond (Rizzo & Whitman, 2009b, p. 905). As such, the behavioural paternalist is ill-equipped on his mission to nudge people towards healthier states. Nudge policies are more likely than not to benefit some at the expense of others. Whether or not the eventual outcome is a welfare-improving situation then is by no means certain and highly questionable.

The knowledge problem, on a final note, also means that policymakers are prone to cognitive, mental, and intellectual biases too. Regulators that fill the nudge units are not perfect robots. They are humans, just as flawed and endowed with inherent biases and psychological heuristics as the very consumers they have set out to nudge. These biases include:

"... (1) action bias, which is defined as a tendency to overact in the face of risk and uncertainty. (2) Motivated reasoning, which is a tendency to reach the conclusions we prefer for other reasons. (3) Focusing illusion, which is a bias that appears when experts consider the impact of one particular factor and overestimate its significance. (4) Affect heuristics, which suggest that our reasoning is to a great extent the product of our emotions, and (5) illusions of competence, which is overconfidence with respect to one's own knowledge" (Thomas, 2018, p. 20).

It is important to clarify that the knowledge problem we have outlined is not a problem that can simply be overcome through the recruitment, selection, and development of intelligent individuals within the government. We acknowledge that civil servants are better equipped to tackle the task of governing a country than the average citizen. The complex system of public administration — with its scholarship policies, performance based tools, and attraction of private sector professionals (Quah, 2010) — is said to be why this is so.

Yet, to believe that the knowledge problem can be overcome simply by recruiting the smartest civil servants to steer the state is a profound misunderstanding of what it is. Cognitive limitations are present in all individuals, including the highly educated. Elites may themselves have additional biases that afflict them uniquely, giving rise to the possibility of expert failure (Tetlock 2017; Koppl 2018). The knowledge problem transcends the individual's cognitive make-up, and also stems from the complexity of the wider economy and social world that people inhabit, and from the fact that central authorities are not situated in a context where relevant knowledge in society is discovered and transmitted (Kiesling, 2014). It is this multidimensional nature of the knowledge problem that must be taken seriously in policymaking.

The knowledge problem indeed has serious implications for Singapore policymakers, who have already adopted behavioural insights in their work. This is especially so considering the greater socio-economic diversity of Singaporeans, their needs, unique circumstances, and the challenges they face. Additionally, Singapore is a highly open society and is thus vulnerable to new disruptions that originate elsewhere. Complexity is thus especially pronounced in the context of Singapore as an open global city. Given this, the choice of behavioural nudge interventions confronts a serious knowledge problem that should give any policymaker reason for caution, regardless of how educated, qualified, and experienced they are.

Public Choice Objections

Finally, we turn to the third set of objections from the tradition of public choice economics. Public choice arguments highlight the many problems of liberal democratic politics that technocratic paternalists are subject to. Even if we grant the assumption that regulators can overcome the knowledge problems raised in the previous section, the effectiveness of nudge policies is bogged by various problems that underlie the process of politics in democracy.

The problem is that most of the research in the field of behavioural economics simply assumes that the political process is smooth sailing. In a literature review of the field, Berggren (2012) finds that a startling 95.5% of behavioural economic research that advocates for paternalist policy action fail to conduct any analysis whatsoever on whether policymakers are likely to succeed in implementing their policy suggestions. In other words, much of behavioural economics commits what the economist Harold Demsetz (1969) referred to as the "nirvana fallacy", where idealised alternatives (in this case a perfect government) are held up against the imperfect status quo — invariably the *modus operandi* for justifying statist intervention. There is an over-eagerness to point out how actors in the market economy are prone to decision-making-failure while failing to consider whether actors (and institutions) in the political arena are subject to the same types of failures and breakdowns. Instead, a fair political economy analysis requires analytical balance by conducting a comparative institutional analysis. Public choice objections ask the questions of *how* exactly they will be implemented, by *whom*, and the likelihood of implementing a well-calibrated nudge policy given the chaotic process of democratic politics. In the following section, we raise three broad objections from a public choice perspective.

The first objection is concerned with the types of slippery slopes that nudging might open the door to. As Rizzo & Whitman (2009a, p. 705) argues, there is a multitude of unforeseen factors that might lead even relatively well-implemented nudge policies to provide ever-increasing justification for more paternalism. People might react to nudging by adapting their behaviour in a way that invalidates the nudge, providing further incentive for the policymaker to double down on its policy goal.

Increasing intervention is also more likely when the particular policy area has a multifaceted nature which makes it hard to predict complex interactions. For example, the behavioural paternalist might enact an auto-enrolment savings program aimed at increasing retirement savings, justified on the grounds of the status quo bias (Thaler & Benartzi, 2004). Yet, the success of the policy might inadvertently trigger separate biases of hyperbolic discounting (preferring a smaller, sooner payoff versus a larger, future reward) and spur workers to splurge their increased savings on "sinful" consumption, negating the original policy goal of increasing retirement savings.

It is highly unlikely at this point that the policymakers involved will sit back and reluctantly accept the failure. What is more likely to happen is that policymakers will look for alternative methods to tinker around the edges of the existing policy in a bid to set out and achieve the original public policy goals. Yet what would be the institutional checks that restrain policymakers from escalating the initial policy? Behavioural economists do not seem to pay much attention to these slippery slope problems. To the extent that there is such a bias, it is not hard to see how the policymaker will soon find more coercive methods attractive (such as by simply restricting workers from spending a certain percentage of their salaries) and thereby abandoning the initial promise of non-coercion altogether.

Secondly, nudge regulatory units are subject to risks of private sector rent-seeking. Producers of artificial sweeteners will lobby for a sugar tax while financial service firms will throw support behind savings schemes. Conversely, incumbent players will resist these legislative efforts. When soda taxes were implemented in Philadelphia, Big Soda corporations, whose bottom line were hurt by the tax, poured millions of dollars into deterring the legislation (White, 2019). Rent-seeking efforts increase the likelihood of inducing "political capitalism", where political elites and economic elites enjoy a reciprocal relationship that helps entrench their top statuses at the expense of the ordinary voter (Holcombe, 2018). Indeed, a key insight of public choice theory is that we should not assume political actors behave as benevolent angels with their electorate's best interests at heart (Buchanan, 1999). Policymakers and public servants face an array of perverse political incentives to engage in predatory political behaviour such as electoral bribery on the eve of election terms and a bias toward maximising budgets to produce politically-pleasing outcomes to win voters.

It is widely believed that Singaporean civil servants and political office-holders are immune to the various incentive problems just explored. After all, stringent checks and balances are put in place to sanction corrupt activities. The PAP-constructed political system is also based on the selection of morally virtuous men who fulfil strict standards of the public interest. Given this, we acknowledge that outright and systemic political corruption is unlikely in the current Singapore context. However, it is reasonable to suggest that all political agents, even those in Singapore, are also motivated, to some extent, by political self-interest. In fact, there have been numerous actions taken by government elites in Singapore which have been criticised as being motivated by narrow electoral interests, such as the selective upgrading of public housing areas during elections. The PAP state elites have also constructed new political innovations which have raised the barrier for electoral competition (Tan, 2011a). Although this has been commonly justified as being in the interest of the public, it is not inconceivable that some electoral advantage is being sought through such schemes. What this means is that incentive problems, however curtailed in Singapore, is always a real concern to be wary of.

Due to the knowledge and incentive problems just highlighted, the behavioural paternalist is then faced with a conundrum: who will watch the Watchmen? If regulators are just as subject to narrow self-interest and knowledge limitations as the subjects they seek to regulate, we should be sceptical of putting them in charge of producing nudge policy. While Low at least acknowledges that the behavioural economics project is vulnerable to public choice problems, he nonetheless maintains that the government should simply be "cognizant of its vulnerability to biases and to take active steps to correct for them" (Low, 2012, p. 11). Yet this is neither an analytical nor scientific statement; it is to simply brush aside the problem of asymmetric analysis that behavioural economics suffers from. After all, saying the government should be aware of its own biases in order to correct for them is no different from saying irrational consumers in the market economy should do the same. If that is so, then the paternalistic onus to nudge people is utterly irrelevant.

How Far can Big Data Tools Take us?

The elite technocratic governance in Singapore has recently been enhanced through the use of Big Data tools and the latest technologies. Arguably, this system has reached its zenith in the complex Risk Assessment and Horizon Scanning system (RAHs), which has traditionally been used for national security purposes but have gone to even socio-economic planning.

In this section, we take issue only with its evolving usage for economic planning. We argue that Big Data systems such as RAHs, just like behavioural economics, lacks a comparative institutional analysis between state policy and markets. As a result, its analysis does not take into account how market institutions of property rights, price systems and profiteering facilitate the adaptation to and mitigating of economic complexity in societies. We argue in this section that the Singapore government's Big Data assessments fail in this regard when put up against classical liberal arguments.

Big Data is not Big Knowledge

The notion of incorporating Big Data technologies into economic policy is not new. The much improved storage capacities, data processing speeds, and analytical abilities that the technological revolution of the 21st century has given us have prompted much speculation by intellectuals and journalists into whether Big Data would be the missing key to solving the perennial socialist quest of central planning (Thornhill, 2017; Wang & Li, 2017).[17] Chinese billionaire entrepreneur Jack Ma too famously extolled the virtues of Big Data in reviving the ideals of centrally planned economies (Global Times, 2017).

As the argument goes, the gargantuan amounts of data that are managed daily by tech corporations such as Facebook and Amazon today could, in theory, be similarly organised by government planners to modulate the economy carefully. If private corporations can do it, so can states. According to this line of argument, the economic failures of the old socialism were due to a lack of informational inputs that, if available, could

---

[17] Elsewhere, Sunstein (2014, p. 11) has contemplated the value of Big Data toward fine-tuning cost-benefit analysis for regulatory purposes.

better inform managerial processes and solve inefficient organisational processes, thereby enabling efficient central planning.

RAHS does not aspire to the ambitions of central planning. Indeed, Peter Ho fully acknowledges that the RAHS system is not intended to be able to make pinpoint predictions of how the future will develop. Having said that, the economic philosophy of "scenario planning" has much in common with the popular talk around using Big Data to plan economies. It is ultimately a tool that nonetheless aims at making *some* predictions. In a 2018 interview, Ho stylised this as "futures thinking":

> "Some of us call this [RAHS] foresight, or futures thinking. It helps policymakers in government devise strategies and formulate policies to maintain positive trajectories and shift negative ones into a more positive direction. The goal is to make better decisions today that can help shape the future, rather than to predict the future, which would be a futile exercise anyway" (2018, p. 14).

Big Data indeed enables government planners to obtain and much better analyse high volumes of data for valuable historical patterns. These arguments, however, do not succeed in undermining the classical liberal case against central planning. At the root of these arguments is a severe epistemological misunderstanding of the type of knowledge required for economic planning. There is a conflation of two seemingly similar but crucially different concepts: data and knowledge. "Data" is what proponents of this argument seek to mobilise with new age computers; it represents an empirical datapoint of the past. Purchase data, for instance, tells us about the time, place, price, and quantity of a transaction. However, it is silent on the context by which it happened and fundamentally an incomplete representation. "Knowledge", on the other hand, exists within a unique context of time and place. Knowledge is specific and personal thoughts, subjective beliefs, values, and preferences in the minds of individuals are contained in scattered forms across millions of people in society.

In the socialist calculation debates of the early 20th century, F. A. Hayek (1945) pointed out in his seminal article *The Use of Knowledge in Society* the crucial distinction between data (what he refers to as "scientific knowledge") and knowledge that exists in the present time and place.

The latter is precisely the type of knowledge that is required of the central planner. Economic planning at the state government level is impractical for the reason that such knowledge is never available in its entirety to the central planner. The epistemological burden required of the planner would amount to an impossible task because all the knowledge required would be isolated far out of reach in dispersed forms. In *The Sensory Order* (1952), Hayek further develops his argument to show how subjective forms of knowledge are also grounded in the local institutional rules that govern social exchange in society (culture, social norms, legal rules, etc).

It is on this note that the RAHS-like policy makes its first misstep. The notion that governments can amass large datasets to steer the economy is to make the mistake of treating "data" as "knowledge". A dataset might indicate a decline in imported steel last year, but it does not shed any insight into the value-laden decision-making processes by thousands of entrepreneurs pursuing different business plans. Big Data, with all its processing power, cannot offer such a reason. Technological improvements do not assist the central planner in his quest because the knowledge needed to plan the economy is, as Hayek argued:

> "... knowledge of the kind which by its nature cannot enter into statistics and therefore cannot be conveyed to any central authority in statistical form. The statistics which such a central authority would have to use would have to be arrived at precisely by abstracting from minor differences between the things, by lumping together, as resources of one kind, items which differ as regards location, quality, and other particulars, in a way which may be very significant for the specific decision. It follows from this that central planning based on statistical information by its nature cannot take direct account of these circumstances of time and place..." (1945, p. 524).

In a 1968 lecture, Hayek similarly contended that:

> "... all the collective supply and demand curves that we use so happily are not really data, but rather outcomes of the constantly ongoing process of competition. Thus, statistical information can never disclose to us what price or income changes will be needed to bring about the necessary adjustment to an unavoidable change of the data" (2002, p. 18).

Thus, no matter how advanced artificial intelligence (AI) tools become and how much citizenry data governments might collect, such data tells the planner nothing about consumer preferences and the circumstances by which these preferences are formed. Human choice is a procedural action that exists within a unique time, place, and mode of exchange. My purchase of a particular car might be induced by the seasonal forecast, my projected household income levels, and sociocultural norms that dictate what would be "normal" (a Prius) or "too obnoxious" (a Hummer) or "prestigious" (a Mercedes) to drive, but all that is not visible to the analyst with a spreadsheet.

Making sense of the data requires the analyst to impute his own normative judgments about what the reason might be. An economy's decrease in imported steel might be due to an international trade war, emerging markets/technologies that would reduce steel dependence, economic forecasts of recession, etc. Policymakers would have to try and control for such exogenous effects in the Big Dataset, but this task would prove bewilderingly complex considering the infinite number of possible reasons that could be present in the context of the globalised world.

Moreover, by trying to marshal historical data to steer the economic future, RAHS commits the folly of assuming that consumer values and preferences are static across time when they are not. By making this implicit assumption, the government planner proceeds on the task as a mere problem of computation. After all, if we could already *know* ahead of time what consumers would prefer, the remaining task would simply be one of mathematical distribution.

When these assumptions are abandoned, however, the problem we face becomes not one of mathematical computation but what Hayek refers to as an "economic problem", where the conditions of economic planning are now highly complex; individuals have differing preferences, risk attitudes, and conflicting values that are dynamically changing in accordance to their institutional environments. How then can opposing goals among millions in a free economy be *coordinated* in a way that avoids disagreement? From the perspective of a socialist central planner, this is the same as asking: "How might a planner privilege certain production methods or the manufacturing of some goods over another?" The reality of economic scarcity entails that every goal cannot be simultaneously achieved at the same time. The planner must choose where to commit limited resources. It is to this question that Hayek and other scholars have explained how the market institutions of private property rights, the free market price system, and the profit-loss calculus enables such coordination of conflicting goals. We elaborate on this in the next section.

Adaptation in a Complex World

The central motivation for RAHS stems from the recognition that policymakers are epistemologically ill-equipped to cope with the radical complexities of modern societies. This premise is, in fact, very much within common ground with classical liberalism, as we shall see. Harnessing the insights of behavioural economics, it is argued that RAHS and scenario planning would help mitigate the institutional biases of policymakers and help "search and discover" new solutions in order to be "adaptive" in complex environments (Ho, 2012, p. 8). We contend that RAHS-like policies severely underestimate the problem of complexity and falls short of their goal to facilitate adaptiveness under such complex circumstances.

As highlighted in the previous section, the nature of knowledge needed to plan the economy cannot be encapsulated in datasets, but exists as dispersed forms in a specific context. Therefore, Big Data offers a superficial form of economic "adaptation" at best. Planning an economy based on historical datasets is not only based on a muddled understanding of "data" as "knowledge", but also depends on unrealistic assumptions such as non-changing preferences that bear no reality in the real world. Even if the Big Data planner recognised this shortcoming, the rapidly changing circumstances of any complex modern economy would subject such a proposal to the endless problem of trying to play "catch-up" by mining new empirical data.

In light of these limitations, it is unpersuasive how Big Data could facilitate economic adaptation in the highly complex and globalised economy of today. Unlike RAHS, the classical liberal case for free markets is grounded in an institutional framework that is highly sensitive for adaptation to rapidly changing circumstances. It does not assume that the required knowledge for economic planning can logistically be centralised in the institutions of the state. Instead, it is a process that allows decentralised actors to pursue their subjective economic plans within the scope of their own private spheres, giving birth to a competitive order that generates the very knowledge needed to adapt to complex and changing circumstances.

It is within the context of the Hayekian knowledge problem that classical liberals have long emphasised how free-market economies enable coordinative adaptation. Such market regimes are characterised by three key market institutional mechanisms: private property rights, an unhampered free market price system, and the profit-loss calculus.

1. Firstly, decentralised private property ownership permits capital-holders to practice discretion in pursuing their own visions of entrepreneurship that is in line with their subjective forms of knowledge, as opposed to a policymaker that monopolises these production decisions.
2. Second, the market price system plays the role of informing business owners on the most economising methods to undertake in their decisions of capital investment and production. In a now-classic example, Hayek illustrated how the price system induces tin users to reduce their consumption by observing rising prices, without having to expend high costs of time and research to understand why exactly tin supply is increasingly expensive (1945, p. 526).
3. Third, the profit-loss calculus provides an ex-post evaluation that reveals wisdom and error in business decisions. Profits are a sign that businesses are correctly providing value to consumer demand, while losses indicate a lack of value provision or simply that current production methods are not economically sustainable. From a perspective of economic efficiency, the profit mechanism is useful because it helps guide entrepreneurs to make the necessary adjustments or go bust.

Against the classical socialists that sought to abolish prices, property rights, and profiteering, Ludwig von Mises (1990) famously argued that without these market institutions, rational allocation of scarce resources in an economy would be impossible. It is precisely because the economy is too complex for a single central bureau to manage that market mechanisms are instrumentally valuable in coordinating economic activity. Private property incentivises entrepreneurs to invest capital in accordance with their future projections of supply and demand shifts. The price system acts as informational signals that guide entrepreneurs toward undertaking economically sensible production processes. Business ventures would be continuously subject to the test of profits under market competition, discouraging misled entrepreneurial decisions and halting inefficient production methods. Above all, the free market system permits the Schumpeterian (2006) gale of creative destruction that weeds out bad existing economic projects and permits new experiments.

These coordinative mechanisms would be absent in Big Data central planning. The viability of the RAHS project is only further complicated by a separate Hayekian argument of "tacit knowledge" that would be necessary for economic planning. By tacit knowledge, we refer to inarticulate forms of knowledge that are difficult to convey, such as the way we ride a bicycle without being able to explain the underlying physics and science (Lavoie, 1986). The problem for the central planner is that tacit knowledge is endogenous to the market process and does not exist outside of it. It is only when entrepreneurs *act* on these inarticulate intuitions (for example, the alert awareness of profit opportunities) that it might generate economic value and become observable to an outsider, making it inaccessible to central planners and market competitors alike. As such, the process of market competition is an ongoing discovery procedure that divulges relevant economic knowledge, without which it will be unavailable (Hayek, 2002).

Ho (2016b) seems to be cognisant of the concept of tacit knowledge. To mitigate problems of tacit knowledge for policymakers, he has explicitly proposed for incorporating simulations and games into public policy. But this argument is predicated on a misunderstanding of tacit knowledge. As said, the relevant tacit knowledge pertaining to economic planning is generated only within the context of rivalrous market competition. Such knowledge, as we have argued, is not the same as statistical data, much less attainable through gaming simulations where the rules of the game are a shallow representation of real-world market economies in the absence of market incentives, private stakeholdership, and rivalrous competition. Boettke, Coyne, & Leeson (2007) have argued that the types of knowledge generated out of market competition are fundamentally different than knowledge generated out of political competition. Feedback mechanisms in markets allow the identification of error and continuous alteration.

In democratic politics, however, feedback mechanisms such as the ballot box and elections encourage political efficiency that is wholly different from economic efficiency.

Even if simulations could help policymakers overcome *some* problems of tacit knowledge, such across-the-board simulations will be, in all likelihood, privileging certain forms of "trained" tacit knowledge and pattern recognitions over an infinite amount of variations. Yet if the priority is macroeconomic adaptation to the complex "unknowable unknown black swans" that Ho constantly warns us about, it is unconvincing how simulation games would be a realistically credible solution.

From a classical liberal perspective, it is precisely because the economy is complex and that tacit knowledge is hard to grasp that we desire a polycentric context where a plurality of actors can exercise their own tacit intuitions in the competitive market arena. Knowing "what works" requires a trial and error process where competing methods can be put into practice simultaneously. It is the knowledge generated from such a competitive process that allows society to adapt to the complex environment.

Why Should We Care?

The weaknesses of behavioural economics, Big Data, and its applications matter much for policymaking in Singapore. To the extent that policymakers rely now on such theories and instruments to analyse social behaviour and judging to craft policies,[18] the risk of policy failures is heightened, especially when elite policymakers are subject to knowledge limitations themselves. This potentiality is real, though deceptively subtle: behavioural economics imbues policymakers with excessive confidence in their superior wisdom in the face of a supposedly irrational public.

The limitations of Big Data specifically affect economic policy. The Singapore state has, since its independence, engaged in careful economic planning for industrial restructuring, skill-upgrading, and moving the economy to ever-higher levels of value-added (Chia, 2005). This has most recently culminated in the comprehensive national plan in the Committee

---

[18] There is strong evidence to suggest this is now the case, considering that the Civil Service College has sought to embed behavioural economics training to civil servants and their work in government agencies.

for Future Economy in 2017, which in turn entailed the creation of detailed Industry Transformation Maps for 23 different industries, amongst other industrial policy initiatives.[19]

Given the severity of the knowledge problem just described, we have reason to be sceptical of the effectiveness of such central economic planning for the purpose of future economic competitiveness. The problem may, in fact, be more pronounced in the Singapore case, considering the small and open nature of our economy, which results in the fact that the latest technologies and industry trends typically emerge offshore before being adopted domestically. Singapore's exposure to the vicissitudes of global competition, and disruption inherent in the global economy makes accurate future-oriented economic planning much more difficult.

When it relates to nudging policy, we acknowledge that evidence-based policies that *attempt* to account for the psychological makeup of its target agents are a step up from traditional policy that does not. However, these methods do not go far enough in recognising radical complexity and are merely reinforcing the Singaporean style of technocratic government and paternalism where "government knows best". The right answer to complexity, we argue, would entail embracing the classical liberal case for a polycentric order of competition in markets and civil society where competing solutions can coexist.

Granted, we do not intend for the criticisms in this chapter to be taken as a wholesale rejection of behavioural economics or Big Data analytical tools. Much of our objection here takes issue with its application in public policy as opposed to private sector use cases. This distinction should be strongly emphasised. It is precisely because these methods are implemented under the monopoly of the government that its effectiveness should be held to a much higher standard. Private corporations that make use of behavioural insights and Big Data may err in so doing, yet the repercussions would be internalised by shareholders.

There are larger ramifications of our argument. The legitimacy of the PAP state has always been derived not from the democratic principle of

---

[19] Ministry of Trade and Industry, Singapore. (2017). *Report of the Committee on the Future Economy*. Retrieved from https://www.mti.gov.sg/-/media/MTI/Resources/Publications/Report-of-the-Committee-on-the-Future-Economy/CFE_Full-Report.pdf.

the consent of the governed, even though Singapore is an electoral, though authoritarian democracy, but rather from performance legitimacy that is characteristic of developmental states (Wong & Huang, 2010). Behavioural economics provides further fuel to the PAP state's attempt to shore up this performance legitimacy. Behavioural nudging adds one more arrow to the large quiver of policy tools the Singapore state utilises to maintain social harmony, economic progress, and social order, the very basis for this legitimacy. The actual, or even perceived, success of nudging policy in Singapore allows the state to strengthen their message that "we indeed know best". Indeed, a BBC article has already written that Singapore is a nation that "thrived" by nudging its population.[20] Those concerned with the cause of democratisation in Singapore should turn their critical gaze at the paradigm of behavioural economics, its use of nudging, and the way it entrenches the norms of paternalist government.

---

[20] BBC. (2018). *The nation that thrived by nudging its population.* Retrieved from https://www. bbc.com/future/article/20180220-the-nation-that-thrived-by-nudging-its-population

5

Appreciating Digital Media and How It Empowers Civil Society

The Nobel Laureate free-market economist Milton Friedman had a famous thesis: For any society to enjoy political freedoms, it must achieve basic economic freedoms (Friedman, 1962). This thesis has proven mostly true. In the 21st century, countries that score high in economic freedom indexes are strongly correlated with high ranking scores in the Economist Intelligence Unit's (EIU) Democracy Index. The case study of Singapore stands out, however, as an anomaly. Singapore has consistently ranked at the top of every economic freedom index (The Heritage Foundation, 2019), yet remains a country that lacks fundamental civil rights like freedom of speech, the right to protest, and press freedoms (Vasquez & Porcnik, 2019). Against the standard of Western politics, Singapore's style of governance is judged as illiberal and non-democratic.

Although political restrictions continue to be enforced by formal legislation, politics in Singapore has undergone a subtle democratic upheaval in the 21st century. In this chapter, we look at how the Internet, digital networks, and social media play a fruitful role in strengthening one core pillar of democracy: civil society. Our attention to civil society is natural given classical liberalism's strong emphasis on decentralised organisation, making civil society groups a prominent fixture.

The first section establishes the importance of civil society in classical liberal philosophy, with reference to classical liberal thinkers. The second

section considers how the Internet has empowered civil societies in the 21st century. We provide an economic explanation for how this widening scope of democratic participation is in part largely enabled by the Internet. In the third section, we extend this analysis to Singapore's context and look at how it has enabled a plurality of voices in the public sphere, and its impact on local politics, the media, and civil society. Finally, we conclude.

Classical Liberalism and Civil Society

Classical liberals have long emphasised the importance of civil society (Palmer, 2002; Scalet & Schmidtz, 2002). Civil societies are valuable because its decentralised mode of organisation makes them well-positioned to address a broad spectrum of social, political, and economic problems on the ground that are out-of-reach to a centralised nation-state. By civil societies, we mean all forms of associations that are organised voluntarily: businesses, families, religious institutions, the media, labour unions, humanitarian and philanthropic groups, and various forms of non-governmental organisations and non-profit grassroots communities and clubs that organise around similar hobbies and professional pursuits.

The French classical liberal political scientist Alexis de Tocqueville studied civil societies extensively. When we think of democracy today, we often think of it in its formal institutions, that is, how "freely contested" elections are, the spectrum of political parties, the separation of powers and checks and balances, and the relationships between state representatives and the voting electorate. Tocqueville, however, understood "democracy" in a broader sense. His analysis extended beyond democracy's formal institutions into the informal sphere of civil societies and associations.

In exploring the vulnerabilities of democracies, Tocqueville argued that civil society was one pillar in a robust democracy that guarded against a tyrannical government. He warned that the durability of a democratic republic depended on a citizenry that was willing to remain vigilant. As one writer describes the Tocquevillian conception of civil society, "... civil society never stands still. It is a sphere of restlessness, civic agitation, refusals to cooperate, struggles for improved conditions, the incubator of visions of a more equal society" (Keane, 2015).

Tocqueville's study of democracy was driven by his interest in the maintenance of this unprecedented and newfound equality from monarchy. He feared that just as easily were democratic freedoms achieved, it would also just as quickly wither away. For that reason, he paid great attention to the relationship between democratic citizens and the state. Governments tended to overreach their duties and circumscribe an incrementally larger scope for public policy, indirectly seeking to relieve citizens of their democratic duties. Tocqueville feared that citizens would abandon their self-responsibilities to the government, growing increasingly complacent and indolent, indirectly encouraging the growth of a nanny state and failings of democracy:

> "The more it puts itself in the place of associations, the more individuals, losing the idea of associating, will need it to come to their aid. These are causes and effects that engender each other without stopping. Will the public administration end up directing all the industries for which an isolated citizen cannot suffice? … The morals and intelligence of a democratic people would run no lesser dangers than their trade and industry, if the government came to take the place of associations everywhere" ([1835] 2010, p. 900).

The more a person is regulated according to a formal set of rules, the larger the incentive to abide only by these specific prescriptions while looking around the edges of the rules for loopholes. Heavy regulation disciplines us into a mode of thinking where our actions are shaped by explicit reward and punishment, rather than an internal evaluation of such explicit costs *and how they weighed against our values and morality.*

Over time, our senses of self-regulation are slowly eroded, thereby justifying the government's role to further intervene in the lives of a helpless citizenry. In other words, regulations beget more regulations, simply because the citizenry, conditioned to being pampered, has grown incapable of self-governance. As the familiar adage goes, you feed a man for a day if you supply him with a fish. But you feed him for a lifetime if you equip him with the skill to fish. Tocqueville enquired the appropriate role of the state in "teaching" its citizens, and warned the potential harms from such an overextension:

> "The will of man is not shattered, but softened, bent, and guided: men are seldom forced by it to act, but they are constantly restrained from acting: such a power does not destroy, but it prevents existence; it does

not tyrannise, but it compresses, enervates, extinguishes, and stupefies a people, till each nation is reduced to nothing better than a flock of timid and industrious animals, of which the government is the shepherd" ([1835] 2010, p. 1252).

Building on Tocqueville's insights, Vincent Ostrom argued that sustaining a "culture of inquiry" was one crucial factor in the viability of a democracy (Ostrom, 1997, p. 15). Given the short lifespans of humans, a robust democratic polity must be able to successfully transfer the teachings of eternal vigilance and "appropriate habits of the heart and mind" to its younger generations. These lessons are the "skills of association" that people use to pursue their individual private goals and objectives in life through a complex web of relationships with their friends, family, and broader civil society. Such lessons cannot be formally taught in a classroom but must be self-learnt in an unending process of navigating the communities in which they live in. It is cultivated through a lifetime of succeeding, failing, compromise, and healthy scepticism.

A public that is used to being mollycoddled by its paternalistic masters would suffer from a lack of understanding as to how communities function and soon lose this democratic spirit of inquiry. Lacking these essential lessons, the fabric of democracy would grow increasingly vulnerable to exploitation from "strongman" figureheads and market power.

Further to losing this culture of inquiry, a nascent and weak civil society loses its ability of self-governance. David Beito's research finds that in 20th century America, poverty alleviation and healthcare were governed by private mutual aid societies that comprised of voluntary charity efforts, religious associations, and self-help communities (Beito, 2000; Beito, Gordon, & Tabarrok, 2002). Approximately 18 million Americans were registered in such societies in 1920. These private and decentralised solutions of poverty relief were eventually eroded and crowded out by the modern welfare state, as governments took over the role of welfare provision.

The Internet and Civil Society

We turn now to the Internet's unprecedented impact on democratic civil society, particularly in the way it has changed how information is produced and distributed, thereby changing *who* is allowed to participate and increasing the plurality of voices in the public sphere. This fact has transformed the trajectories of modern politics to a large extent. In some cases, it has given rise to many democratic revolutions in authoritarian regimes, such as the Arab Spring. Elsewhere in the developed world, protests also erupted in Spain (Indignados Movement), Israel (2011 housing protests), and the American Occupy Wall Street protests.

Seen through a Tocquevillian lens, a far-reaching impact of new media technologies has been its strengthening of civil society. The digital public space of the 21st century has radically energised "civic agitation" in the political arena, of which we bear witness to today in the form of a series of uprisings and protests across the geopolitical landscape. Digital networks reduce the costs of political organisation, thwarting Mancur Olson's (2009) perennial collective action problem. With the Internet, it is easy to circulate protest calls to activists and citizens who share similar social concerns and grievances. The low costs of self-assembly sowed the seeds for democratic uprisings, enabling an activist public to raise awareness on social issues, and more crucially to *act* on it by organising and coordinating action against political elites. As seen in Egypt, the Mubarak dictatorship fell because it acted too late to curtail the social media platform YouTube, home to vast swathes of anti-Mubarak content (Gurri, 2018, p. 54).

The common underlying denominator in many recent political uprisings was how online tech platforms provided a space for a variety of voices across the political spectrum. It enabled the average citizen to voice their grievances and collectively organise in a way where an elite class of political leaders, scientists, academics, and journalists could not afford to ignore them. Perhaps the most prominent and latest example of such a circumstance is the 2019 pro-democracy Hong Kong protests, ongoing as this is written. Hong Kong protestors leverage on a wide variety of social media platforms and tools to sustain a year-long demonstration against the perceived encroaching reach of authoritarian China, changing and synchronising their protest strategies as authorities begin to censor the Internet (Shao, 2019).

The geopolitical analyst Martin Gurri (2018) offers a persuasive explanation for this phenomenon. The Internet has created a revolution in society's main modes of communication, destabilising the system by which elites could exert top-down control on the public throughout the 20th century. Where the people were previously ignorant, digital access to information has now equipped them with an informational advantage that only the elite class previously enjoyed. The lens by which the average citizen interpreted modern politics used to be confined to the news agendas that the mainstream mass media prescribed. With the public's wider exposure to alternative news agendas and viewpoints, the "realities" portrayed on state-controlled or state-influenced media are quickly contradicted by a different set of realities circulating on social media in the form of trending Twitter tweets, popular YouTube commentary, and viral Facebook posts. This expansion of how the public cognitively interprets politics gives birth to internal contradictions that eventually stirs a "revolt of the public" against age-old elitist and hierarchical institutions.

In this section, we provide an economic analysis of the media to explain *how* a plurality of voices emerged.

The Economics of the Media

The Internet is commonplace today, and many of us take it for granted. For that reason, we often underappreciate how the Internet has been the greatest advancer of individual freedoms in the 21st century for the way it has changed the functioning of politics (Benkler, 2006).

Consider that in the pre-Internet era, topical issues in politics were largely determined and shaped by the mainstream corporate media. The dominant communication model of old media can be typified as a unidirectional "one-to-many" information flow. This hierarchical institutional structure is well explained by the underlying economics of the media industry. Since the mid-19th century onwards, to be in the business of information production, i.e. a news organisation required sizeable up-front capital investment costs for setting up a broadcast station, printing presses, and mainframe servers. The huge budgets essential for starting a media enterprise meant that it was limited to a wealthy class of professional businesspersons. Therefore, investors sought a return on their investments through a mass-production business model, paid for by advertising revenue and print subscriptions.

The one-to-many communication model of 20th-century mass media was not one that allowed variety. Because the mode of communication resembled that of a "megaphone", old media necessarily discriminates against coverage of topics outside the median appeal of news consumers. News production was bound by a for-profit business model that needed to provide a commercially viable readership to attract advertisers. Accordingly, this meant a business model that prioritised "newsworthy" topics because it took place on a national or global scale, or simply stories of a sensationalist nature. It was economically sensible for news corporations to dedicate limited resources to pursuing highly relatable news stories.

Media scholars have studied how media corporations operate through a mixture of corporate filters that heavily constrict societal discourse (Chomsky & Herman, 1988). Such filters also induced television networks to refrain from airing politically-subversive shows that might turn off advertisers. As a result, the types of social issues that people rallied for and against were by and large weighed by corporate concerns and filtered through agendas set by a class of elite journalists and political leaders. Structural limitations of the media have historically constrained the scope of democratic participation for the average citizen.

What did the Internet Change?

Gradual technological improvements and a fall in the costs of computer parts ushered the advent of the Internet. Computers and digital devices became a commonplace household item in the 21st century. The reduced costs in technological infrastructure are now widely decentralised and controlled by end-users, rather than owned exclusively in the hands of wealthy conglomerates. With that, the Internet had eroded the centuries-old "one-to-many" communication channel that existed since the days of Gutenberg's printing press.

The mass media business model saw the plummet of physical print consumption and with it an upheaval of its established media production practices. The great transformation of the media industry was how the digital era swept away the business model of news production that was characterised by its high fixed costs and low marginal costs into a low fixed costs, low marginal costs model (Benkler, 2006, p. 32).

This simple change in communication spaces was of great significance. The shackles that previously constrained societal discourse were now removed. The once-muffled voices of a democratic citizenry — previously relegated to the confines of the local community and household — could now be heard by a far wider audience. In the place of the "one-to-many" communication model was born the "many-to-many" communication model that allows for an archipelago of conversations to take place simultaneously (Shirky, 2008).

A crucial difference today is that news consumers can react. News consumption today is akin to joining a conversation rather than being passive recipients of information from the newspaper or television set (Gilmor, 2004). Social media users can take to their platforms to share news articles, interact with like-minded users, and actively opine — the result of which spontaneously determines what topics goes viral. A politically-conscious class of citizenry and amateur opinion writers, eager to weigh in on the politics of the day, can now easily publish their thoughts on an independent blog or social media platform to anyone who will listen.

Production of information goods in the arts and media witnessed a wave of mass amateurisation (Reynolds, 2006). This represents a stark divergence from the old media model where opining was simply exclusive to full-time professional journalists and expert talking heads. The average person interested in being politically-informed had to rely on the professional judgment of elite opinion leaders, with little scope for voicing an opposing view, let alone scrutinising their source claims. The media's role as a gatekeeper has largely diminished today as amateur writers, bloggers, and journalists on the net now enjoy an unprecedented power to supersede this gatekeeping duty.

In some ways, new media supports old media. The lower entry barrier enables amateur journalists and online commentators newfound freedom to explore or persistently pursue news topics on digital weblogs and social media. This practice was structurally incompatible with the 24-hour newspaper cycle standards of a professional newsroom. Such news stories, if lacking a sufficiently "new" news angle, would have been deemed outdated, unfit-for-printing, and therefore not revisited. Citizen journalism of this form has supplemented mainstream journalism in the way that it garners traction to revive previously "dead" stories (Shirky, 2008, p. 62).

The great democratisation of societal modes of communication has resulted in a surplus of information.[1] The lower costs of media production have drastically raised the supply of informational goods. As such, where the standard model of media production was to filter out "newsworthy" topics for news consumers, media production today is better characterised as a landscape of "publish-before-filtering" (Shirky, 2008). A wide variety of social media mechanisms such as hashtags allow users to filter out the topics they seek from noisy clutter easily. Internet entrepreneurs have offered an array of digital services such as Del.icio.us (now defunct), Pinboard, or Pocket to bookmark, organise, and label web content. Indeed, the core product of Google — search engine indexing — is to provide the fundamental service of informational organisation.

To be sure, mainstream corporate media still maintains significant power to influence public opinion. But it is unquestionably true that the hierarchical institutional set-up of 20th-century media institutions has been dramatically flattened. Mass media power has diminished in the social media era where journalistic falsehoods and inaccuracies are subject to harsher scrutiny of the public (see the infamous 2004 Rathergate scandal). Today, the "standard operating procedures" of professional newsrooms is to regularly scan and report on trending and viral topics that emerge spontaneously from social media spaces. It is no longer able to dictate the news to the public exclusively. Instead, the corporate media "tests" its news narratives, subject to scrutiny and questioning by reactive news consumers.

Big Media has not been upended. But insofar as it still exists, there is a great democratisation of Big Media's old hierarchy. Its supreme privilege of unchallenged authority it enjoyed through the 20th century has now been forever, thanks to the World Wide Web, relegated to the dustbins of history.

The Internet's Impact on Singapore Civil Society

When Singapore gained independence in 1965, its political institutions were enshrined in democratic ideals that were inherited from the British.

---

[1] One of the earliest and most popular critiques of the Internet was known as the Babel Objection. Critics feared that when everyone on the Internet had a voice, it might lead to a society burdened with a surplus of information, and people being trapped in their own echo chambers (Benkler, 2006).

Half a century after its independence however, politics in Singapore under the People's Action Party (PAP) has diverged from the Western democratic ideals of freedom of expression. While the regime welcomes constructive criticism, its degree of tolerance for statements that might be defamatory or racially sensitive has maintained a low threshold. Bloggers, netizens, politicians, and journalists (both domestic and foreign) who have wandered astray from these rules are promptly punished by the law or sued in court with multi-million dollar lawsuits.

It is no surprise then that Singapore scores notoriously low in the Press Freedom Index, ranking at 151 of 180 countries (Reporters Without Borders, 2019). Through the 1974 Newspapers Printing and Presses Act (NPPA), the government has been able to insert its own political actors onto the board of directors and dictate the appointment of chief editors, thereby including its distinct brand of meritocracy and technocratic elitism even into the media sphere.[2]

In Chapter 2 of this book, we dissected the discourse on "Asian values". This political hegemony of "Asian values" too is reflected in the state's governance of the media. In a 1988 address to the American Society of Newspaper Editors in Washington, DC, Lee Kuan Yew tried to carve out a distinct model for the type of journalism he believed would be ideal for Singapore:

> "We allow American journalists in Singapore in order to report Singapore to their fellow countrymen. We allow their papers to sell in Singapore so that we can know what foreigners are reading about us. But we cannot allow them to assume a role in Singapore that the American media play in America, that of invigilator, adversary and inquisitor of the administration. If allowed to do so, they will radically change the nature of Singapore society, and I doubt if our social glue is strong enough to withstand such treatment" (TODAY, 2015).

In 2005, newly inaugurated Prime Minister Lee Hsien Loong echoed a similar refrain, as he warned against Western news journalism that was

---

[2] Having said that, it would be inaccurate to typify Singapore's media as a fully state-controlled ecosystem for the reason that media companies remain in private hands, and is subject to some modicum of market forces, commercial pressures, and for-profit incentives (George, 2012).

grounded in a confrontational and questioning style, what he characterised as "crusading journalism" (Lee, 2005). The government's significant control over the media has historically restrained much of local discourse and civil society. Indeed, empirical research finds that countries with higher restrictions of media tend to have citizens that are less politically active and more ignorant of politics (Leeson, 2008). This section briefly considers how the rise of new info-communications technologies have liberated civil society from some of these constraints.

The Battle for Singapore's Hearts and Minds

Digital technologies have enabled a heightened level of democratic participation and public consciousness in Singapore by allowing a wider diversity of conversations to take place. There are at least two significant impacts on civil society.

Firstly, the Internet and social media have dramatically amplified the voice of the Singaporean public. Before the digital era, Singapore's hybrid state-private media had been able to control and set the national agenda for political discourse. The PAP government's ability to control the media apparatus has long been criticised by civil society for its marginalisation of voices on the margin (Lee, 2002). This has given birth to the term "out-of-bounds markers" or "OB-markers", used to denote forbidden areas of political discussion such as racial and religious issues due to its sensitivity, or accusations of political corruption.

With the arrival of digital tools saw a newly-empowered Singaporean civil society that can collectively decide what issues should belong in the limelight as opposed to merely joining conversations that have been predetermined within the OB-markers (Soon *et al.*, 2015). More than that, citizens now enjoy an unprecedented ability to question and undermine the dominant narratives produced by the state media. Where the public used to be a passive news consumer with little scope for democratic retaliation beyond the ballot box, politically active citizens are now empowered to scrutinise government blunders and be an active participant in ongoing democratic discourse. Calls for accountability have become a common concern as government failures, and mismanagements are now a frequent centrepiece of political discourse that cannot be easily brushed under the rug.

A new wave of news platforms and weblogs that is willing to challenge the government's narrative has emerged on the Internet over the past decades. Given the state's control of the mainstream media, the loudest voices opposing the government tend to cluster and mobilise on social media platforms, using social media as its main channel of engaging politically-conscious Singaporeans.[3] Opposition politicians use Facebook to make announcements, question the incumbent government, and maintain an active digital presence with citizens. Elsewhere in the Singapore blogosphere exists a collective of alternative editorial outlets, blogs, and political players that take a centrist lean or pro-PAP stance.[4] While not seen as professional news publications, their social commentary on issues like culture and race receive widespread traction with the tech-savvy youth demographic (Salleh, 2015).

Many of the actors that populate this wave of internet journalism operate as citizen journalists rather than full-time professional journalists. Yet, citizen journalists, even if unable to conduct original reporting, possess the capacity to challenge the prevailing consensus and introduce unique and fresh perspective angles into current affairs. It is hard to understate what social media platforms have done toward equalising the political scales in Singapore. Political commentators — both pro- and anti-government — have successfully built fairly large and active social media followings by opining on topical issues of the day.[5]

Just as significant is the way by which new digital technologies too have enabled the ability of civil society to raise awareness outside of direct politics on issues such as poverty, the environment, the rights of LGBT (lesbian, gay, bisexual, transgender) individuals, sex workers, migrants, and various other previously undermentioned topics. With cheap video technologies and social media today, it is convenient for marketing communication and public relation firms to post short documentaries and features of society's most oppressed and underprivileged. Activists similarly make use of chat

---

[3] The most prominent example of such publications includes *The Online Citizen, The Independent Singapore, TR Emeritus,* and *State Times Review.*

[4] These publications include, but are not limited to, *Rice Media, Mothership,* and *Critical Spectator.*

[5] An extensive list of such anti-government political commentators is documented in "The Naysayer's Book Club" by Simon Vincent (2018).

platforms such as WhatsApp and Telegram to maintain a broadcasting platform to their followers. From a classical liberal perspective, this diversity of voices and thought has been a great boon to civil society in Singapore. The Internet avails a broader range of communication platforms and has reduced the concentration of communication channels in the hands of a few.

The second way by which the Internet has expanded the functioning of civil society is the subtle way by which it has expanded the cognitive boundaries of the activist public. Increased access to international news and global politics has changed the standards, benchmarks, and expectations by which Singaporeans assess and judge the performance of their government. More than that, they are now fully cognisant of previously underemphasised or suppressed issues. Martin Gurri puts it succinctly: In the technological web of modern politics, "[t]he simplicity and perfect fit between the public's perception of the world and the regime's story of legitimacy are gone forever" (2018, p. 75). A networked public realises that alternative explanations and contradictions exist.

Scholars have argued that the governance model of the PAP does not solely rely on overtly coercive forms of legislative power, but also on creating a sense of public legitimacy around its lawmaking processes (George, 2007; Lee & Lee, 2019). Despite the control of a parliamentary monopoly that allows its political decision-making to go unopposed, the PAP subjects its legislative processes to an open public consultation process that seeks feedback and open debate. This is evidenced during the passing of a recent slew of highly controversial bills such as the 2018 Films Act, the 2018 Public Order and Safety Act, and the 2019 Protection From Online Falsehoods and Manipulation Bill (POFMA) where the government mounted robust defences to justify the necessity of the laws (Lee & Lee, 2019, p. 3-4). Another prominent sign of the government's willingness to seek public feedback was the Nominated Member of Parliament (NMP) scheme that was introduced in 1990 to allow non-elected citizens to participate and vote in certain parliamentary issues. Finally, the government has also launched its own fact-checking website "Factually" to present its own version of truth against news pieces by netizens that it perceives as false.

Is the mainstream media in Singapore a slavish and unquestioning mouthpiece of the PAP government? This stereotype of the media is certainly not true in its entirety, but it contains some element of truth. Polls

show that a significant number of Singaporeans believe their government has too much control over professional media (Tan *et al.*, 2015).

The crucial point, however, is this: Insofar as the PAP seeks to preserve its political hegemony by commanding public legitimacy through the state media apparatus, social media platforms deter this monopolistic control by providing an alternative communication space for public discourse to take place. In the past decades, the only sources of information were through the mediated narratives on the state media. Today, the average Singaporean can access different viewpoints from online media that deviates from mainstream media narratives.

In the Singapore 2011 General Election, the PAP saw its lowest count of the popular vote since independence. Much of this was attributed to the impact of new information and communication technologies, digital platforms, and social media:

> "In 2011, the PAP's control of communication fell apart as soon as the election campaign started. Although the mainstream media led by the Straits Times continued to echo partisan biases and prescribed agendas in favour of the ruling PAP right up to the nomination day, many Singaporeans sought their versions of 'truth' via the Internet and by communicating about politics at the community/grassroots level. The Internet was a major factor, not so much in transmitting new information, but in facilitating the search for corroborating facts and also signifying that there can be an alternative" (Lee, 2019, p. 238).

Social media, in effect, creates a radical equalisation of the political playing ground in Singapore. The overall impact of digital communication platforms in Singapore is an *informal* liberalisation of communication spaces in Singapore. However, the *formal* legal institutional framework of the media had not been liberalised by the government. Insofar as out-of-bound markers exist in political discourse, digital platforms have allowed the public to venture into these previously obscured areas of discussion. These new spaces in the digital ecosystem have disrupted the carefully calibrated narratives of legitimacy that the state media offers to Singaporean hearts and minds.

In sum, this is a welcome change from a classical liberal viewpoint. A plurality of voices now populates popular sociopolitical discourse, a noticeably dramatic change from when the state's print media was the dominant medium for public outreach. That dissenting viewpoints can enter the political consciousness is consistent with the classical liberal view that no one institution possesses a monopoly on knowledge, necessitating the need for some form of "competition" in political discourse. This competitive logic is true for consumer goods or banking services, and no different for freedom of expression in the realm of ideas.

Concluding Remarks

This chapter has briefly sketched out why media liberalisation is desirable from a classical liberal perspective. The analytical lens is rooted in the value-free tradition of classical liberalism where a competing multiplicity of decentralised rules are preferred for epistemic reasons as described in the first chapter. This is in stark contrast to grounding the argument in a system of inherent democratic human rights as is typically advocated by left-leaning progressives, although both approaches generally reach similar outcomes in the context of media policy.

While the Internet has had a liberating effect on Singapore's politics, the government has, in recent years, proceeded to ramp up regulation in the sphere of digital communication. The most prominent example of which is the *2019 Protection from Online Falsehoods and Manipulation Act*, which does not technically censor information but requires that the offender append a link to the government's counterargument alongside the "fake news" in question. This is worrying considering that digital media is an invaluable avenue for societal discourse in Singapore. We conclude with a poignant quote by the classical liberal John Stuart Mill, who recognised the epistemic role of freedom of expression:

> "… if any opinion is compelled to silence, that opinion may, for aught we can certainly know, be true. *To deny this is to assume our own infallibility* (emphasis our own)… though the silenced opinion be an error, it may, and very commonly does, contain a portion of truth; and since the general or prevailing opinion on any object is rarely or never the whole truth, it is only by the collision of adverse opinions that the remainder of the truth has any chance of being supplied" (Mill, 2009, p. 88).

6

Political Economy of Inequality and Redistribution in Singapore

The Challenge of Inequality

Classical liberalism is motivated by scepticism of state power and a belief in institutional diversity. Logically, a classical liberal society is one that accords a high premium on private property, which allows individuals to freely pursue their own plans without central direction. A market-based economy, in the classical liberal vision, facilitates the use of individual knowledge and, coincidentally, is also one that leads to a high degree of welfare and prosperity. Indeed, since the expansion of global capitalism in the 19th century, which accelerated after World War II, many have been lifted out of insidious and intergenerational poverty.

The market economy has, however, come under criticism on a global level due to the concern of socio-economic inequality. There is a growing concern that economic globalisation has left many behind. Coupled with the resentment against what seems to be a rigged economic system in favour of elites, it is believed that the neoliberal order is unsustainable. This has been manifested in the form of large-scale protests, and a realignment of political systems in favour of populist politicians. Related to this trend is the rise of democratic socialist sentiments amongst the youth, who have lost confidence in the market economy; the *Economist* magazine accordingly explored what they felt was a worrying trend of the rise of "millennial socialists".[1]

---

[1] The Economist. (2019, February 14). *Millennial socialism*. Retrieved from: https://www.economist.com/leaders/2019/02/14/millennial-socialism.

Closer to home, socio-economic inequality has also captured attention in Singapore. The People's Action Party (PAP) government has been criticised for not paying enough attention to a growing economic divide between the haves and the have nots. Critics have increasingly called for more active welfarist and redistributive measures, nudging the PAP towards the centre-left. A large part of this trend has been due to the work of academics and public intellectuals, who have called attention to inequality as a policy concern. Such individuals include Donald Low, Teo You Yenn, Yeoh Lam Keong, and Kenneth Paul Tan, who have raised concerns about the unsustainability of Singapore's neoliberal economy and the increasing class divides it has caused.

Not coincidentally, the discussions of inequality in Singapore are followed closely by policy recommendations that advocate the state to pass a minimum wage, engage in heavier redistribution — be it through wealth, capital or income taxes — and to increase social spending, which are all policies that define the progressive left. Such a policy orientation is fundamentally at odds with the PAP's long-standing aversion to a welfare state, and their preference for a society that prizes self-reliance and economic growth.

Accordingly, we take seriously some of the arguments that are made by critics of the political establishment, especially those who have called attention to inequality and advocated social democratic policies. A prominent advocate of more significant state redistribution in Singapore, Donald Low, has on numerous occasions pointed to the necessity of the wealth tax as a policy instrument based on the recommendations of Thomas Piketty.[2] In a significant essay in his major book, he criticised what he deems as the four "myths" that have been perpetuated by the PAP government, myths that prevent Singapore from implementing a

---

[2] Daud, S. (2019, February 21). Economist Donald Low explains why wealth taxes are needed for a fairer society. Retrieved from: https://mothership.sg/2019/02/donald-low-wealth-tax/; Low, D. (2019, February 20). The curious case of missing wealth taxes in Singapore. *TODAY Online*. Retrieved from: https://www.todayonline.com/commentary/curious-case-missing-wealth-taxes-singapore; Low, D. (2019, March 11). Why Hong Kong and Singapore should tax wealth more. *South China Morning Post*. Retrieved from: https://www.scmp.com/week-asia/opinion/article/2189237/why-hong-kong-and-singapore-should-tax-wealth-more.

much-needed transition to a welfare state (Low & Vadaketh, pp. 17–30). They are:

1. Inequality is a necessary counterpart of economic dynamism and competitiveness
2. The best way to help the poor is to help the rich
3. Inequality is not really a problem as long as there isn't extreme poverty and incomes are rising across the board
4. Since pay is tied to ability, rising inequality is simply the result of increasing differences in people's ability

Through a refutation of these myths, Donald Low and his colleagues proceed to recommend a "greater welfare state".[3]

Classical Liberalism and Inequality

Our chapter engages with this ongoing conversation on inequality and the appropriate policy response. We do so, however, from a classical liberal perspective. We present examples and evidence from around the world, to assess the nature and severity of inequality, and evaluate whether social democratic policies are justified. We believe that this global perspective is essential, because research done by overseas scholars, especially that of Thomas Piketty, is influential. Additionally, many have also looked to the model of Scandinavian welfare as worthy of emulation in Singapore.

In this chapter, we push back against the recommendations made by the social-democratic advocates in Singapore for a "greater welfare state", and make the following claims:

1. Much of the discussion involving socio-economic inequality obscures the fundamental difference between inequality and poverty; the former measuring relative disparities between classes and the latter being a measure of absolute living standards.

---

[3] Smith, C. J., Donaldson, J. A., Mudaliar, S., Kadir, M. M., & Lam, K. Y. (2015). A handbook on inequality, poverty and unmet social needs in Singapore. *Social Insight Research Series,* 1–86. Retrieved from: https://ink.library.smu.edu.sg/cgi/viewcontent.cgi?article=1009&context=lien_reports.

2. The unfortunate conflation between inequality and poverty prevents us from emphasising the importance of pro-growth policies, which generate income mobility even at the cost of relative disparities.
3. Income and wealth redistribution is not a good idea, considering the unintended consequences and problems where they have been tried.

We do not argue that the free market, which classical liberals favour, is devoid of problems, and neither are we making a blind, faith-based defence of "neoliberalism" as has been practised around the world. We acknowledge that concentrations of wealth and power do exist in the world and that many economic systems are not working for the ordinary people on the street. Markets are indeed imperfect institutions.

Our purpose, in contrast, is to highlight some key classical liberal political economy insights that are worth considering for Singapore policy discourse. These are insights, we believe will enable the reader, the media professional, graduate student and even a policymaker to understand the phenomenon of "inequality" in a more careful and nuanced fashion, before rushing into a set of policy responses.

The principles we introduce here, from the discipline of political economy, are as follows. First, we show the conceptual distinction between poverty and inequality, and the dangers of conflating both. We also highlight the importance of dynamic, rather than static analysis, i.e. focusing on income mobility rather than snapshot comparisons of income differences. We also point out that the *process* through which inequality arises, whether by voluntary exchange or by rent-seeking, is equally, if not more, important than the actual level of inequality itself. These principles are unfortunately not much discussed in the Singapore discourse, which has one camp calling for egalitarian state interventions and the other resisting them.

Inequality is not the Point, Rising Living Standards are

Most critics of the market system notoriously and conveniently conflate inequality and poverty when substantiating their findings. Income inequality simply means the existence of a gap between those who earn the most and those who earn the least. The mere presence of an income gap, even if it is widening, says nothing about the actual income levels of those who make the least. In other words, an income gap does not necessarily mean that those at the lowest income brackets are poor. Just because Jeff Bezos owns ten bungalows and has liquid cash on hand does not, by itself, suggest that I am "poor" in an absolute sense. A society with a very uneven distribution of income can still be one with high levels of absolute prosperity. It is indeed often the case that a prosperous society is an unequal one, and the pursuit of equality may lead to everyone becoming equally poor.

This conflation leads observers to focus on inequality statistics overwhelmingly, and use that as evidence that people are suffering. Often, the GINI coefficient, which measures the statistical dispersion and distribution of incomes in societies, is used to portray the severity of inequality, which then merits government redistribution.

The key problem with this statistic, and many others like it, is that they capture snapshot data, rather than dynamic changes in the people who comprise the "poor" and the "rich" across multiple years of comparison. What this means is that narratives concerning inequality, citing statistics like GINI, usually omit the question of *income mobility*. It is problematic to make static comparisons of how much each quintile of income earners have gained as a percentage of the total income, as it tells us nothing about whether specific households are getting richer over time.

It has often been the case that despite a high GINI coefficient, which suggests severe inequality, income mobility has occurred, but which is unfortunately obscured. The classical liberal political economist Steve Horwitz (2015) has made this argument about the United States, showing that despite what official inequality statistics portray, the United States has experienced significant income mobility. This reasoning by Horwitz helps illustrate why the common concern about the shrinking American middle class is but a statistical artifact. Google's Chief Economist Hal Varian similarly argues that it is hard to believe that economic productivity is in a slump when America's powerhouse tech sector has created positive revolutionary changes in the way the ordinary person lead their lives.[4]

---

[4] Aeppel, T. (2015, July 16). Silicon Valley Doesn't Believe U.S. Productivity Is Down. *The Wall Street Journal*. Retrieved from: https://www.wsj.com/articles/silicon-valley-doesnt-believe-u-s-productivity-is-down-1437100700.

Thanks to Big Tech, we spend less time looking for taxis (Uber), directions (Google Maps), information (search engines), like-minded people (social media), and consumer goods (Amazon). Conventional accounts show a shrinking middle class despite this empowerment of the average person, but research shows that many of the poorer households are moving up the income ladder, causing the middle to hollow out (American Enterprise Institute, 2018; Moore, 2019).

This causes us to consider the real possibility that even if snapshot statistics like GINI portray a significant income gap between the rich and the poor, the material standard of living of specific households, regardless of whether they are poor or rich, improve over time. In other words, people do not stay poor, especially when economic opportunities are created in a healthy market economy. This is well supported on a global level, which is typically said to be rife with inequalities. Research by Christoph Lakner from the World Bank and Branko Milanovic from the Luxembourg Income Study Center shows us that inequality when measured on a *global* rather than national level, has *declined* across the board.[5] This is, according to the authors, mainly due to dramatic growth in incomes in previously under-developed regions, especially China and India. This result was independently verified by another competing study by Paolo Mauro and Tomas Hellebrandt (2015). They showed how global inequality fell for 14 years — driven mainly by economic growth in emerging countries like India and China — at the turn of the new millennium in 2000 and is projected to further decline till 2035. Citing such evidence, the influential economist Tyler Cowen warned against the sentiments of egalitarians to push for policies to redistribute income within nations, because they threaten to halt the economic progress that has lifted so many out of poverty in the first place.[6]

A broader look at history will show the importance of focusing on economic growth rather than equality. This begins by realising that poverty is and has been the natural condition of human society. It is only from the

---

[5] Lakner, C., & Milanovic, B. (2016, July 1). Global Income Distribution. Retrieved from: https://openknowledge.worldbank.org/handle/10986/29118.

[6] Cowen, T. (2014, July 19). Income Inequality Is Not Rising Globally. It's Falling. *The New York Times*. Retrieved from: https://www.nytimes.com/2014/07/20/upshot/income-inequality-is-not-rising-globally-its-falling-.html.

19th century onwards have human beings enjoyed real economic growth, and since then, this progress has been tremendous. The economic historian Deirdre McCloskey (2011) has shown that there has been an increase in global wealth by a factor of 30. When we realise the scale of this "Great Enrichment" and how it has lifted billions out of poverty, we conclude that gaps between the haves and have nots become less relevant.[7]

Overly fixating on inequality is to miss the forest for the trees.

Are Singaporeans Better Off Today?

If the present authors are indeed claiming that inequality should not be a serious concern as long as income mobility lifts people out of poverty, then the next logical question one would ask is: does income mobility exist in Singapore? This is a question worth asking because the Singapore government is criticised for perpetuating the "myth" that "inequality is not really a problem as long as there is not extreme poverty and incomes are rising across the board" (Low & Vadaketh, 2014, p. 23).

There is limited evidence to prove the positive. Given Singapore's short history, empirical data documenting income mobility is limited, but that which exists does suggest that poor people in Singapore do not stay poor. The most comprehensive study on this to date was conducted by the Singapore Ministry of Finance, which calculates intergenerational income mobility through a correlation between measures of fathers' incomes and that of their sons' incomes (Yip, 2015). The author finds that there was moderately high intergenerational income mobility in Singapore, "higher than as found in similar studies for the US" (Yip, 2015).

While there is no reliable evidence tracking the socio-economic status of the same households over time, available evidence does show that the poorer families in Singapore experience high growth in incomes, often at higher rates than the wealthier households. As mentioned, what we should care about is not the gap between the rich and poor, but to ask about whether or not the poor are experiencing economic progress. Data analysis tells us that the lowest income households have experienced constant growth in

[7] McCloskey, D. (2014, August 12). Equality lacks relevance if the poor are growing richer. *Financial Times.* Retrieved from: https://www.ft.com/content/4c62ddaa-e698-11e3-9a20-00144feabdc0.

Table 1:   Analysis of percentage change of household income of different classes

	Average Household Income in 2009	Average Household Income in 2019	Percentage Change Over the 10-year Period
Top 10% of households in Singapore	$22,909	$31,289	36.58%
Top 50% of households in Singapore	$12,629	$18,838	49.16%
Bottom 10% of households in Singapore	$1,361	$2,045	50.26%
Bottom 50% of households in Singapore	$3,760	$5,935	57.85%

Source: Department of Statistics, Singapore

income over the years. Additionally, average household income growth for the lowest 50% of households have increased faster than the top 50% of households (Table 1).

The present authors also provide some further evidence in favour of this positive outlook. We do so by introducing the political economy concept of "nirvana fallacy", which is the all-too-common error of comparing an imperfect situation with a utopian ideal; many economists typically commit the error of identifying a market failure and proceeding to recommend a government intervention, failing to realise that the same imperfections they allege in the market also apply in the political process (Pennington, 2011, ch. 3). Political economists avoid the nirvana fallacy by engaging in institutional comparisons on a similar basis.

On this note, we make some brief comparisons of Singapore's living standards with other neighbouring countries in the region. Singapore is not a perfect society, but these points strongly suggest that low-income Singaporeans still enjoy a relatively better lot in life when compared to neighbouring countries.

The first piece of evidence for this stems from a comparison of the growth of household incomes for the least well off in Asian countries. The present authors have collated income statistics from various Asian countries to track the increase in average household incomes over time — from 2010 to 2018 — focusing on the bottom quintiles. From Table 2, we note several points. First, the average household income of the bottom 20% in Singapore in 2010 (USD 1716.75) was already much higher than in other countries, second only to

Table 2:   Comparison of change of household income for the bottom 20% across Asian countries

	Average Household Income of the bottom 20% in 2010 (USD)	Average Household Income of the bottom 20% in 2018 (USD)	Percentage Change Over the Eight Years
Singapore	1716.75	2175.95	26.75
China	664.90*	937.35	40.98
Malaysia*	465.52*	685.85*	47.33
Brunei	1227.80	1385.16*	12.82
Vietnam	18.93	40.18	112.26
South Korea	1049.40*	1109.44	5.72
Cambodia	6.95	27.31*	292.95
Thailand	62.91*	80.73*	28.33
Japan	2704.91	1919.53*	−29.04
Philippines	1194.27*	2445.75	104.79

Source: Official household income statistics from various countries[8]

---

[8] For Malaysia, data was only available for the bottom 40% instead of the bottom 20%. Those numbers marked with an * are estimates of previous years' figures since current years' figures were unavailable. The currency was standardised by using 2010 and 2018 USD exchange rates. Government sources:

Singapore: Resident Households by Household Characteristics and Deciles, 2000–2019, Department of Statistics Singapore

China: China Statistical Yearbook 2013–2019, National Bureau of Statistics of China

Malaysia: Household Income, Expenditure and Basic Amenities Survey (HIES/BA) 2019, Department of Statistics Malaysia

South Korea: Household Income & Expenditure Trends in the Fourth Quarter 2011–2018, Statistics Korea

Japan: Yearly Average of Monthly Disbursements per Household by Yearly Income Quintile Group, and by Number of Household Members (Two-or-more-person), Statistics of Japan

Vietnam: Monthly average income per capita at current prices by income quintile and by province, General Statistics Office of Vietnam

Thailand: Household Socio-Economic Survey (Whole Kingdom), 2011–2017, National Statistics Office Thailand

Cambodia: Cambodia Socio-Economic Survey 2011–2017, National Institute of Statistics Cambodia

Philippines: Family Income and Expenditure Survey 2009–2018, Philippines Statistics Authority

Brunei: Brunei Household Expenditure Survey 2010/11, 2015/16, Department of Statistics Brunei

Japan (USD 2704.91). However, over 8 years, there was a 26.75% increase in the average household income of the poorest households in Singapore, such that in 2018, the least well-off Singaporeans were much better off than most of their Asian counterparts.

This is a relevant comparison because it highlights the need to avoid the nirvana fallacy. Even if one points out the need for further improvements in Singapore's social security system, it is difficult to deny that the least well-off in Singapore are still much better off than in neighbouring countries.

Aside from household income, the authors also sought to gather other indicators of standard of living across the Asian region. In Singapore, it is found that 24.85% of the bottom 20% of households (according to income levels) own at least one car. Contrast this with Cambodia in 2017, only 5% of households nationwide owned cars. Consider this with the fact that there are only 29.7 automobiles owned per 100 household units in China. Singapore is also ranked first in the Global Food Security Index in 2018 and 2019, which measures affordability, availability, and nutrition quality of food in the country. This means that Singapore is not just one of the most well-nourished populations in Asia, but in the world.

Those looking for a more holistic comparison of standard of living across countries might prefer looking at the Global Social Mobility Index instead, which looks not at specific income levels or social outcomes, but the policies, practices, and institutions of a nation, and whether they drive social mobility for all (Table 3). The ten pillars in this index cover areas such as healthcare quality, educational opportunity, and also the presence of socially inclusive institutions. A comparison of selected Asian countries' performance shows that Singapore scores well, second only to Japan in this region.

Significantly, it has outstripped other Asian nations such as Malaysia, Indonesia, and even fast-growing China. To the extent that this indicator is an accurate measure of social mobility in a nation, Singaporeans arguably enjoy greater levels of social mobility than other residents in Asia.

What about Singapore's standard of living more generally? There are numerous standard of living indicators used to compare nations across space. Still, some have been criticised for being overly narrow, or focused on material factors only, or being excessively comprehensive and thus lacking any meaningful basis for comparison. The authors believe that economic wealth remains a key foundation of overall standard of living, since material wealth, rather than corrupting our morals, liberates people

Table 3:   Comparison of selected Asian countries' performance on the Global Social Mobility Index

Country	Raw Score on Global Social Mobility Index in 2020 (or Latest Available Year)	Global Rank
Japan	76.1	15
Singapore	**74.6**	**20**
South Korea	71.4	25
Malaysia	63.0	43
China	61.5	45
Vietnam	57.8	50
Thailand	55.4	54
Philippines	51.7	61
Indonesia	49.3	67
Laos	43.8	72

Source: Global Social Mobility Report 2020, World Economic Forum

to experience other non-material values. Thus, a meaningful index should include economic wealth as a key component and encompass secondary considerations such as other essential and non-material aspects.

With this in mind, the authors identified the Prosperity Index by the Legatum Institute as a meaningful index for comparison (Table 4). It recognises that material wealth is an integral part of a good life, but also looks at other indicators simultaneously. Crucially, it reflects the authors' convictions that open and inclusive institutions are the basis for a progressive society. According to the Legatum Institute, "a nation is prosperous when it has effective institutions, an open economy, and empowered people who are healthy, educated, and safe".[9]

Significantly, Singapore is only 1 of 3 Asian countries to be featured in the top 20 positions in 2019. When it comes to healthcare achievements, Singapore ranks first globally. It is also worth pointing out that Singapore's top healthcare achievements eclipse that of other Western European nations who have more comprehensive state coverage of healthcare provisions, such as the welfare states of Australia, United Kingdom, and

---

[9] Legatum Institute Foundation. (2019, November 14). About: Legatum Prosperity Index 2019. Retrieved from: https://www.prosperity.com/about/summary.

Table 4:   Top 20 countries ranked on the Legatum Institute's Prosperity Index

Country	Global Rank on the Legatum Prosperity Index 2019	Global Rank on the Health Sub-indicator on the Legatum Prosperity Index
Denmark	1	8
Norway	2	5
Switzerland	3	3
Sweden	4	15
Finland	5	26
Netherlands	6	9
New Zealand	7	22
Germany	8	12
Luxembourg	9	19
Iceland	10	7
United Kingdom	11	23
Ireland	12	20
Austria	13	10
Canada	14	25
Hong Kong	15	6
Singapore	**16**	**1**
Australia	17	18
United States	18	59
Japan	19	2
Malta	20	14

Source: Legatum Prosperity Index 2019

Canada. Not only has Singapore achieved excellent healthcare outcomes, it has done so at a fraction of the cost, hence its equally high ranking on the Bloomberg Healthcare Efficiency Index and her label as a paragon of "affordable excellence" (Haseltine, 2013).

Economic Liberty is the Key to Rising Living Standards

If rising living standards for all should be the objective of economic policy, and if Singapore has generally achieved a higher standard of living, it is intuitive to ask: what kind of government policies do we need to generate and maintain this trend of economic progress?

Classical liberal political economists have shown that when nations maintain inclusive, market-based institutions that protect private property, enforce contracts, and which keeps state interventionism minimal, economic growth happens (Hanke & Walters, 1997; Gwartney *et al.*, 1999). A free economy provides a conducive environment for entrepreneurs, firms, civil society groups, and individuals to engage in economically productive activities. The link between economic freedom and growth is also accompanied by its positive contributions to a host of other qualitative aspects of standard of living (see Heritage Foundation, 2019).

Critics have labelled these policies as "neoliberal". Whatever label that we use, there is much evidence showing the positive benefits generated by the extension of market freedoms since the end of the Second World War. On a macro-level, the world now has the lowest number of people living in poverty than ever before,[10] and for the first time, more people are now middle class or richer (Kharas & Hamel, 2019). As the influential economist Andrei Shleifer (2009) has shown, these developments coincided with the "Age of Milton Friedman" since the 1980s.

The expansion of "neoliberalism" is of course, not a recent phenomenon but has been a progressive trend since the turn of the 19th century. Classical liberal economic historians have documented the stunning reversal of mankind's natural condition of poverty to one of prosperity, a process that began with the commercial revolutions in Europe starting in the 17th century, which are in turn a product of intellectual and policy shifts towards capitalism, freedom, and individualism (North, 2005; McCloskey, 2011; Mokyr, 2016). This realisation alone should give us reason to be cautious when "neoliberal ideology" is denounced by the leading scholars in Singaporean policy discourse.

Responding to Criticisms of Market-driven Growth

We anticipate potential objections to having society be guided by market forces. We first explore the influential research of Thomas Piketty, which

---

[10] CNBC. (2018, September 19). Global poverty rate drops to record low 10%: World Bank. Retrieved from: https://www.cnbc.com/2018/09/19/world-bank-global-poverty-rate-drops-to-record-low.html.

has increasingly entered Singapore policy discourse. We debunk the fallacy that market-driven growth is fundamentally pro-rich or based on the fantasy of "trickle-down economics". We make the important caveat that inequality, to the extent that it reflects the distribution of special privileges and political power, is much more problematic.

What about Thomas Piketty?

At this juncture, it is worthwhile to examine the research on inequality done by Thomas Piketty, and other scholars who have built on his earlier work. This is essential concerning local policy discourse in Singapore because most of the proponents of a greater welfare state in Singapore are inspired by the arguments of Thomas Piketty and his colleagues. Both Donald Low[11] and Sudhir Vadaketh,[12] for example, make a case for greater wealth taxes based on Piketty's research. Teo You Yenn similarly cites Piketty in her influential ethnographic study of inequality in Singapore.[13] An important handbook on this issue also cites the work of Piketty, going on to recommend "a greater welfare state".[14]

The problem with this heavy dependence on Piketty is that Piketty's scholarship suffers from several theoretical problems that have not withstood scrutiny. The first problem with Piketty's position is that it focuses entirely on physical capital to the exclusion of human capital. This is not a distinction without a difference. Human capital, and not just

---

[11] Vadaketh, S. T. (2014, March 13). *Should Singapore tax the wealthy more?*. Retrieved from: https://www.ipscommons.sg/should-singapore-tax-the-wealthy-more/; Vadaketh, S. T. (2016, September 9). *GE2015: Final thoughts (1 of 4)*. Retrieved from: https://sudhirtv.com/2015/09/10/ge2015-final-thoughts-1-of-4/.

[12] Low, D. (2019, February 20). The curious case of missing wealth taxes in Singapore. TODAY online. Retrieved from: https://www.todayonline.com/commentary/curious-case-missing-wealth-taxes-singapore; Daud, S. (2019, February 21). *Economist Donald Low explains why wealth taxes are needed for a fairer society*. Retrieved from: https://mothership.sg/2019/02/donald-low-wealth-tax/; Low, D. (2019, March 11). Why Hong Kong and Singapore should tax wealth more. *South China Morning Post*. Retrieved from: https://www.scmp.com/week-asia/opinion/article/2189237/why-hong-kong-and-singapore-should-tax-wealth-more.

[13] Teo, Y. Y. (2018, April 27). Step 1: Disrupt the Narrative. Retrieved from: https://www.ethosbooks.com.sg/blogs/epiphany/step-1-disrupt-the-narrative-inequality-singapore.

[14] Smith, C. J., Donaldson, J. A., Mudaliar, S., Kadir, M. M., & Lam, K. Y. (2015). A handbook on inequality, poverty and unmet social needs in Singapore. Retrieved from: https://ink.library.smu.edu.sg/cgi/viewcontent.cgi?article=1009&context=lien_reports (p. 58).

labour and physical capital, is a significant factor of production generating economic growth, especially in economies at the innovation frontier. Piketty's omission of human capital — which he strangely justifies by equating a measurement of human capital with human slavery[15] — allows him to reach his conclusion easily which is that "capital [is] always more unequally distributed than labor." This is simply untrue if one considers the prevalence of human capital. What gives workers their value is not just their physical body, but the skills, talents, and experience they possess. As McCloskey expresses in her critique of Piketty,

> "If human capital is included — the ordinary factory worker's literacy, the nurse's educated skill, the professional manager's command of complex systems, the economist's understanding of supply responses — the workers themselves in the correct accounting own most of the nation's capital, and Piketty's drama from 1848 falls to the ground (McCloskey, 2014, p. 89).

Additionally, the narrative constructed by Piketty is one that also omits the "Great Enrichment" explained above. Ordinary people today enjoy a higher standard of living. Interestingly, this "Great Enrichment" has *decreased* other forms of inequalities, i.e. inequalities in access to consumption, education, and healthcare, which were all facts excluded from Piketty's singular focus on income and wealth gaps (Delsol, 2017; Eberstadt, 2017). This is not including how people today enjoy better quality consumer products that make lives more convenient, which are typically left out of conventional economic indicators.

Piketty's empirical findings have also been criticised. Critics have shown that his measurement of wealth inequality, based on tax returns, omits the way tax rules have evolved (Feldstein, 2017) and that his measurement of income inequality also does not take into account income redistribution and the way household sizes have changed over time (Burkhauser, 2017). In an important contribution, Phil Magness and Robert Murphy also spot inaccuracies not only in the statistics gathered but in the historical

---

[15] According to Piketty, "Attributing a monetary value to the stock of human capital makes sense only in societies where it is actually possible to own other individuals fully and entirely — societies that at first sight have definitively ceased to exist" (Piketty, 2014, p. 63).

interpretations by Piketty of the case study countries he focuses on. They find both glaring factual errors, such as date inaccuracies, and data selection bias, which allowed them to misrepresent facts to buttress their preferred narrative (Magness & Murphy, 2015). These same criticisms are extended to even Piketty's collaborators, such as Emmanuel Saez and Gabriel Zucman, who have built on his later work with contributions of their own. The highly contested nature of their claims has even been highlighted in a feature by the Economist Magazine.[16]

Finally, if Piketty's overarching thesis were true, why is it that the wealthiest people today are very different people from those that were featured in *Forbes* top billionaires 20, 30 years ago? After all, Piketty's enthralling argument is that the returns to the wealthy's capital far exceed the growth rate of the economy. In other words, while the masses nibble away at a slowly but surely growing pie of wealth, the wealthiest of the world merely have to sit on their golden laurels lazily and watch their assets multiply. Yet, as Juan Ramón Rallo (2017, p. 31) points out, the super-rich of the 80s and 90s were Japanese businessmen and investors whose wealth has since collapsed. Today, the richest are Jeff Bezos, Bill Gates, Mark Zuckerberg, Larry Page, and Sergey Brin, men who did not inherit their wealth but earned them from creating innovations that uplifted the average person's lives.

Is economic growth pro-rich?

Even though most can agree that market-based policies raise living standards, some will push back by insisting that market-driven growth is not shared equally by all. Critics of our position might go even further by suggesting that market-driven growth works by concentrating benefits on the rich. It is charged that "trickle-down economics" does not work. It has been suggested that the PAP's economic orientation is based on a "myth" that "the best way to help the poor is to help the rich", prioritising growth over equity (Low & Vadaketh, p. 21).

---

[16] The Economist. (2019, November 28). Economists are rethinking the numbers on inequality. *The Economist*. Retrieved from: https://www.economist.com/briefing/2019/11/28/economists-are-rethinking-the-numbers-on-inequality.

It is important to consult the academic literature. Numerous economists have acknowledged that the best way to help the poor is to create institutions that reward productive, entrepreneurial behaviour. This usually comes in the form of inclusive institutions, whereby private property protections, the rule of law, and contract enforcement release the entrepreneurial talents of peoples. Such an environment is not "pro-rich", but have an *indirect, uplifting impact on the poor*, who in many cases have a latent wealth-creating ability that is otherwise repressed by poor governance. Interested readers should check out Emily Chamlee-Wright's (2002) important ethnographic study on female entrepreneurs in Ghana benefitting from better institutions and Hernando de Soto's (2003) study on how indigenous capitalists benefit from clearer property titles in Peru. Market-driven growth works not because it is pro-rich. It works because it harnesses the wealth-creating potential latent in *every* individual.

There is one point of clarification, however. In some sense, the rich do indeed benefit the poor. Most new products and services, as well as technological inventions, are usually first luxuries enjoyed by the rich, before being commercialised for mass consumption. The role of the rich as the "first-users" of novelties has an important function, for it makes possible the consumption by everyone else. Hayek reminded us of this simple logic when thinking about inequality:

> "If today in the United States or western Europe the relatively poor can have a car or a refrigerator, an airplane trip or a radio, at the cost of a reasonable part of their income, this was made possible because in the past others with larger incomes were able to spend on what was then a luxury. The path of advance is greatly eased by the fact that it has been trodden before... What today may seem extravagance or even waste, because it is enjoyed by the few and even undreamed of by the masses, is payment for the experimentation with a style of living that will eventually be available to many" (Hayek, 2014, p. 40).

Additionally, William Baumol's (2004) research finds that corporations and big firms are a big source of economic innovation, and policies that support them can lead to developmental benefits for larger society. On a more philosophical level, the existence of inequality (provided that they occur in the absence of state-created privileges) provides a basis for mutual learning in society, as individuals copy and learn from the more successful amongst us, leading to progressive improvements on a whole (Pennington, 2011).

Of course, this is not to imply that pro-business policies like tax cuts and minimal regulation are a panacea for society. These policies should come together with a larger pro-market package of solutions that collectively empower all citizens, not just corporations.

How inequality arises is important

Our defence of market freedoms does not imply an uncritical embrace of all forms of inequality. We acknowledge that inequality may sometimes be undesirable and worthy of state correction. This is based on the efforts of political economists to distinguish between different forms of inequality that result. In other words, the issue of *how inequality comes about* is as critical, if not more critical than, the very existence of inequality itself.

This distinction is a critical one to draw in the local policy context because progressive-liberals have criticised Singapore's policies for paying insufficient attention to inequality and obsessively focusing on economic growth. According to this line of argument, the PAP government has maintained this pro-growth orientation by perpetuating a myth that "inequality is a necessary counterpart of economic dynamism and competitiveness" (Low & Vadaketh, 2014, p. 18). Accordingly, this creates the wrong impression that Singaporeans should simply accept inequality if they are to experience a growing economy.

The critical error committed by this perspective is its failure to distinguish between different forms of inequality and its insistence in condemning *inequality per se*. Additionally, a review of Donald Low and colleague's "four myths" will reveal that they fail to consult the larger political economy academic literature surrounding the variations of inequality and only lifts one quote by Prime Minister Lee Hsien Loong before trying to refute the idea. A careful understanding of political economy will reveal that inequality is not necessarily a counterpart of economic dynamism and competitiveness; it is only so if inequality arises through unhampered free exchange.

Political economists have made a critical distinction between various forms of inequality, specifically, the natural inequality that emerges through the free exchange of individuals in an unhampered economy, and the inequality that arises due to state privileges. In an influential account, Robert Nozick (1974) had shown, through a compelling thought experiment, how free and uncoerced transactions made by individuals can lead to, on a macro-level, large disparities in incomes and wealth. If individuals vote with their wallets for Bill Gates to become a billionaire, why should the resulting inequality be condemned?

Accordingly, inequality is, to a large extent associated with individual effort and enterprise. This stems from the basic economic premise that "incentives matter". When individuals are not allowed to enjoy unequal rewards, they have no incentive to invest greater effort at the margins and will instead be incentivised to shirk. This is why communist systems throughout history have suffered from very poor outputs and a lack of worker motivation, despite forced attempts to the contrary (Boettke, 1990a). This, in turn, means that inequality is a "necessary counterpart of economic dynamism and competitiveness" (Low & Vadaketh, 2014, p. 18) only to the extent that such inequality arises from the free exchange of individuals in an unhampered economy.[17]

On the flip side, political economists have also noted that inequality may not always result from the free exchange of individuals in an unhampered market economy, but may instead reflect special advantages gained via the political process. Firms or individuals may benefit from subsidies, tax breaks, regulatory loopholes, or favourable grant terms, owing to their ability to influence the political process to their advantage. The inequality that arises from what political economists call "rent-seeking" does not create value for society (Rowley *et al.*, 2013; Holcombe, 2018). The resources expended on such privileges represent a welfare loss, and a diversion of productive effort into unproductive channels (Baumol, 1996).

In simple words, if Bill Gates became a billionaire through his provision of attractive products that consumers voluntarily purchased, such

---

[17] It is granted here that while some level of natural inequality is a necessary part of a dynamic economy, it is not a sufficient condition.

inequality reflects the value Gates created for ordinary people. The disparity that results from this exchange is praiseworthy. Gates did not steal, kill, or defraud anyone. However, when corporations enrich themselves through political activities, there is a loss of economic welfare. A famous case of this sort is that of Archer Daniels Midland. This American conglomerate has enjoyed agricultural subsidies and protectionism, which have altogether cost Americans tens of billions of dollars in higher prices (Bovard, 1996). Much of the inequality in the United States is arguably a result of crony capitalist activities (Lewis, 2013). This is another reason to question the use of conventional inequality statistics like the GINI coefficient because it lacks a political economy framework allowing one to distinguish between different forms of inequality.

Is inequality in Singapore artificially created through state-granted privileges? This question is difficult to answer definitively, considering the mixed nature of Singapore's economy. While Singapore has largely embraced market forces in resource allocation, the state is nonetheless heavily involved in key sectors of the economy and plans industrial policy very proactively. Considering this, it is not a stretch of imagination to hypothesise about how the existence of government-linked corporations (GLCs) and other state-linked entities allow some to maintain a higher socio-economic status than they otherwise would enjoy in a more laissez-faire environment.

What this means is that economists have not necessarily claimed simplistically that "inequality promotes economic growth or competitiveness". They have, however, argued that economic freedom promotes growth and competitiveness, *with wealth inequalities emerging as a by-product*. While some inequality is a necessary corollary of economic freedom, it is not the causal agent that brings about economic growth. Thus, the insistence that "there is little evidence to show that more unequal countries do better economically" (Low & Vadaketh, 2014, p. 20), is true, only because no serious economist has ever made this claim.

While there may be no evidence suggesting that inequality promotes economic growth, there is tremendous evidence showing that economic freedom is non-negotiable when one seeks a strong, healthy, and dynamic economy. This is true on multiple levels. Most fundamentally, economists have done statistical analyses and cross-country comparisons to identify the link between economic freedom and economic growth and competitiveness (Gwartney *et al.*, 1999; Hanke and Walters, 1997). It is shown that when a society generally has lower taxes, government spending, minimal regulations, and market institutions that protect private property and uphold the rule of law, a market economy flourishes (Boettke, 1994). These outcomes are also closely related to higher performance on social indicators like gender equality, income distribution, and environmental quality. This is why Singapore needs to maintain the pro-business, pro-market economic environment that has been established since its independence. This is the very engine of economic progress that has also enriched other developing nations.

Should Singapore Implement a "Greater Welfare State"?

Progressive liberal critics of the Singapore PAP government advocate for the establishment of a "greater welfare state".[18] This includes a minimum wage law, higher redistributive taxes, and more generous social provisions. Such a preference goes against the PAP's preference for a pro-business climate, which is why the minimum wage policy has been rejected in favour of Workfare. Additionally, a welfare state approach is antithetical to the PAP government's belief in individual self-responsibility. Such an approach breeds government dependency and fiscal problems further down the line. In a revealing statement, Low & Vadaketh (2014, p. 20) argue that "the claim that Europe's fiscal mess is the result of overly generous social welfare systems simply cannot be substantiated". Notwithstanding the mounting evidence of financial unsustainability and ruin associated with the model, Singapore's welfare state advocates remain steadfast.

Unfortunately, both sides have not adequately substantiated their positions. The claim by Low is not substantiated by an academic reference, nor has the government, to our knowledge, produced any political economy evidence to substantiate their claim to reject the welfare state, but have

---

[18] Smith, C. J., Donaldson, J. A., Mudaliar, S., Kadir, M. M., & Lam, K. Y. (2015). A handbook on inequality, poverty and unmet social needs in Singapore. Retrieved from: https://ink.library.smu.edu.sg/cgi/viewcontent.cgi?article=1009&context=lien_reports.

rather made ad hoc statements in policy speeches and pronouncements in favour of their stance.

Since both the minimum wage and universal welfare have never been implemented in Singapore before, we present evidence of other countries' experiences.

Problems of Minimum Wage

The prominent economist Lim Chong Yah had recently recommended the use of minimum wage legislation, and expressed his hopes that the "government would change its mind" on it.[19] This was understandably echoed by progressive figures in Singapore, such as Mr Yeoh Lam Keong, who believes that if properly implemented, would "make poverty history in Singapore".[20] It is also supported by prominent opposition politicians, such as Jamus Lim and Chee Soon Juan, whose party had recommended it in successive elections.[21]

It is generally understood that a minimum wage adds to labour costs for firms, which then leads to unemployment effects, especially for those of lower incomes and skills. This is based on the basic economic principle that incentives matter, i.e. if workers are to be paid more, then employers will reduce their demand for them and even quicken the pace of automation. This line of argument, which the PAP believes in, is of course disputed by some economists, who present evidence of the reverse.

We acknowledge that there are indeed studies out there showing how the minimum wage, after being implemented in various settings, does not necessarily lead to unemployment. How does one make sense of all the contradicting evidence? It should first be noted that up till the 1980s, the consensus amongst the economics profession was that indeed the

---

[19] Jagdish, B. (2017, June 10). Singapore should have minimum wage, says economist Lim Chong Yah. *Channel NewsAsia*. Retrieved from: https://www.channelnewsasia.com/news/singapore/singapore-should-have-minimum-wage-says-economist-lim-chong-yah-8928862.

[20] Lam, K. Y. (2017, June 11). *Why Singapore should have minimum wage*. Retrieved from: https://www.facebook.com/lamkeong.yeoh/posts/1544533408955054?pnref=story.

[21] Daud, S. (2019, June 9). *SDP proposes 'S'poreans First' policy for hiring & retrenchment, S$7 per hour minimum wage*. Retrieved from: https://mothership.sg/2019/06/sdp-population-singaporeans-first/.

minimum wage would lead to higher unemployment.[22] It was only in the 1990s when contrary research, such as the well-known Card & Krueger study, started to form, saying the opposite.[23] Additionally, it should also be noted that not all studies are equally credible. Arguably the most credible and comprehensive study of the minimum wage to date is the one conducted by David Neumark and William Wascher, which looks beyond the usual employment effects to other effects such as the acquisition of skills and longer-term labour market outcomes.[24] This study, published by the MIT Press, comes to an unambiguous conclusion:

> "A comprehensive review of evidence on the effect of minimum wages on employment, skills, wage and income distributions, and longer-term labor market outcomes concludes that the minimum wage is not a good policy tool".[25]

Economic theory says that when an asset becomes more expensive, its quantity demanded will fall. To argue that the minimum wage does not lead to unemployment is a strong claim that amounts to questioning the law of demand itself. This would require clear and unambiguous evidence, yet, based on what is presented above, this high bar has not been met by the advocates of the minimum wage.

Additionally, economic theory also sheds some light as to why there are contrary opinions on the minimum wage's employment effects. The warnings against the minimum wage are not simply based on the prediction of higher unemployment for low-wage workers, but also that employers may adjust for higher labour costs in other unseen ways. Even if workers are not laid off, employers may reduce workers' fringe benefits and non-wage elements of their remuneration package (Clemens *et al.*, 2018). Employers

---

[22] McConnell, L. E., & Miller, R. J. (1981, May 24). *Report of the Minimum Wage Study Commission*. Retrieved from: https://cpb-us-e1.wpmucdn.com/blogs.rice.edu/dist/f/3154/ files/2015/11/Minimum-Wage-Study-1983-Carter-Administration-1hkd1cv.pdf.

[23] Card, D., & Krueger, A. B. (1994). Minimum Wages and Employment: A Case Study of the Fast-Food Industry in New Jersey and Pennsylvania. *The American Economic Review,* 84(4), pp. 772–793. Retrieved from: http://davidcard.berkeley.edu/papers/njmin-aer.pdf.

[24] Neumark, D., & Wascher, W. L. (n.d.). *Minimum Wages.* Retrieved from https://mitpress.mit.edu/books/minimum-wages.

[25] Ibid.

might also work their workers harder to maximise the returns on the wages paid. In the long-run, employers may also shift towards automated processes (Lordan & Neumark, 2018) and resort to more self-service by customers (Basker *et al.*, 2015). These are unseen costs that take time to manifest themselves in the economy. For these reasons, it is eminently possible that some researchers do not detect a rise in unemployment and thus prematurely portray it in a benign light.

It has also been suggested by some, for example, economist Lim Chong Yah, that if the minimum wage were set at the right level, i.e. benchmarked to productivity, then its negative side effects may be avoided. This is plausible at face value. However, given the knowledge problem that policymakers face, it is difficult to expect them to be able to set the wage level that isn't too low for it to be ineffective, and not too high for it to be costly to employers. If productivity levels are indeed an important factor to be considered, then it is not clear why a better policy shouldn't directly aim for productivity improvements as a means to improve the welfare of workers; which is already a policy the PAP government has pursued.

Problems of Universal Welfare

Comprehensive welfare states are also beset with problems, giving us cause for concern when considering its applicability in Singapore. There are numerous negative impacts experienced by countries that have implemented welfare states, lessons that we would be wise to heed.

Even though it seems like some local advocates of welfare states have dismissed it, there is a serious problem of government over-spending when they embark on the path of universal welfare. High government spending, regardless of what it is used for, at its root, means less money in the hands of the value-creating, private sector (Mitchell & Debnam, 2010). An increased presence of the state saturates the private sector, leaving small-, medium-, and micro-enterprises to compete for resources with larger, state-based counterparts (Low, 2001). Additionally, there is no guarantee that just because large amounts are spent by the government that they are spent effectively and efficiently. There is waste inherent in government spending, and financing the spending requires taxation and slowing down growth by lowering work incentives; a process made worse in bigger governments (Caporale & Poitras, 2017).

There are several lines of argument demonstrating why universal welfare entitlements is not a good policy approach and something that Singaporean policymakers have good reason to be cautious of. First, state provision of welfare can involve massive inefficiency. This is exactly what has plagued Britain's National Health Service (NHS), which wastes an approximately "£7.6bn a year on overpriced loo rolls, lost crutches and wheelchairs and management consultants" (Gornall, 2017). This a predictable result of the misplaced incentives inherent in public sectors, which are shielded from competition and where bureaucrats tend not to suffer penalties for poor performance. This is further reflected in a comparative study of European healthcare systems. The NHS ranks almost always in the bottom third on health system performance internationally. The study concludes that "despite some relative improvements in the last 15 years, the NHS remains an international laggard in terms of those health outcomes that can be attributed to the healthcare system" (Niemietz, 2016).

Second, welfare programmes in Western countries have prolonged poverty and led to unintended social outcomes. Amity Shlaes produced an influential study analysing US government policies in the aftermath of the Great Depression. New Deal policies not only prolonged the Depression's effects, she found, but also created welfare dependency amongst the families receiving the new social provisions (Shlaes, 2007). In her second book, she investigated the Great Society welfare programmes by Lyndon Johnson that were meant to end poverty. She points out its dramatic consequences: an increase in black unemployment, family breakdowns, a loss of competitiveness in firms, and an overall inflationary climate (Shlaes, 2019). More fundamentally, her work exposes the folly of overambitious social engineering, even if directed to a good intention of ending poverty, a point that epistemic liberals have previously emphasised.

The work of Amity Shlaes is echoed by other scholars too. Charles Murray's (1985) ground-breaking study documented the perverse incentives created by welfare programs and how they made it more difficult for people to break out of poverty. Murray had also shown that poverty was on the decline prior to the 1960s, but this happy trend was reversed with the onset of the "Great Society" programs of the 60s. Not only did welfare have a negative economic impact, it also hurt the family structure, as individuals were incentivised to avoid marriage in order to claim handouts.

It should also be noted that the work versus welfare trade-off is not only seen in the United States, but is also found in European welfare states (Tanner & Hughes, 2015). There is substantial evidence of the similarities between both America's and Europe's welfare states and the fiscal mess that both have created (see Tanner, 2013). These points clearly contradict Donald Low's poorly substantiated claim that "Europe's fiscal mess is the result of overly generous social welfare systems simply cannot be substantiated" (p. 20).

Attempts to close inequality through standard welfare-state policies such as redistributive taxes, subsidies, minimum wage laws, price controls, and the public provision of "free social goods" like health care can, and often have, slowed down economic growth, thus stifling the generation of wealth that the least-well-off depend on (Booth, 2016). Put another way, policy attempts to fight inequality retard economic growth, slow down poverty reduction at best, and exacerbate poverty at worst.

Third, welfare does not only involve economic costs, measured in dollars and cents. It has a profoundly *human* cost. This is because welfare programmes reduce recipients to the status of being a dependent, one who is beholden to the goodwill of the state (Norberg, 2018). Human beings want to be in-charge of their lives, be able to support themselves and their families, and create value for society through work. As Singapore Minister Ong Ye Kung had recently pointed out, "making *handouts* easy and unconditional is *not dignity*. Self-reliance is".[26] This point has been widely developed by classical liberal scholars. Arthur Brooks (2010) specifically, has called this "earned success", which is the fulfilment one enjoys when given the opportunity to, and eventually, succeeding in the world of work.

Encouraging Self-Responsibility and Up-Skilling

The direct, resulting implication, therefore, is that government social policy should encourage work, even if they involve limited social assistance. A

---

[26] CNA. (2018, May 15). *Minister for Education Ong Ye Kung on tackling inequality*. Retrieved from: https://www.facebook.com/ChannelNewsAsia/posts/video-making-handouts-easy-and-unconditional-is-not-dignity-self-reliance-is-say/10155589582962934/.

testament to its pro-work orientation, Singapore's main "welfare" scheme is titled "Workfare". One of its components is the Workfare Income Supplement, which provides a cash payment to low-income individuals who are working.[27] It is not a "free handout" but essentially an incentive to encourage work.

Singapore has also deliberately rejected a national minimum wage law. In its place, it has instead introduced a targeted "Progressive Wage Model" in several low-wage sectors such as cleaning, security, and landscaping. Employers in these sectors are expected to pay their workers a minimum wage and are also incentivised to send them for retraining to increase their productivity.[28] Where typical minimum wage legislation simply expects employers to pay the mandated wage, Singapore's take on it goes further in its encouragement of productivity improvements.

Subsidies are also provided, but only in a limited and targeted fashion. In the healthcare sector, for example, individuals are expected to make copayments for their medical expenses and cannot rely on government subsidies to simply cover 100% of their bill. More aid is in fact given to the neediest individuals who cannot afford even essentials, but the operative principle of self-responsibility looms heavy in the Singapore system. Not surprisingly, health outcomes in Singapore far exceed those of the United States, even though it spends only a fraction of its gross domestic product (GDP) on healthcare in comparison to the USA.[29]

A further illustration of Singapore's pro-work orientation is its insistence on productivity improvements as a basis of increasing one's earning potential. In fact, Singapore's Workfare has a training support component, which incentivises workers to upgrade their skills in order to increase their productivity and thus their earning potential.[30]

It is worth mentioning that this productivity thrust in Singapore's socio-economic policy is criticised by progressive-liberals. Another "myth"

---

[27] Retrieved June 18, 2020, from Workfare Singapore: http://workfare.gov.sg.

[28] Ministry of Manpower. (n.d.). *What is the Progressive Wage Model*. Retrieved from: http://www.mom.gov.sg/employment-practices/progressive-wage-model/what-is-pwm.

[29] Callick, R. (2008, May 27). *The Singapore Model*. (2008, May 27). Retrieved from: https://www.aei.org/articles/the-singapore-model/.

[30] Workfare. (n.d.). *Workfare Training Support (WTS) Scheme*. Retrieved from: https://www.workfare.gov.sg/Pages/WTS.aspx.

is the notion of "since pay is tied to ability, rising inequality is simply the result of increasing differences in people's ability" (Low & Vadaketh, 2014, p. 26). Low takes issue with this idea because he feels that the Singapore government's effort to improve wages by merely raising productivity is insufficient, and points out how wages can stagnate, even apart from reasons due to productivity.

This point has to be understood in a wider context of how people's earnings are determined. It should be granted that productivity is not the only factor that determines how much a person earns, and a whole host of factors go into it. Someone could earn more perhaps due to rising demand for the skills he offers, or simply due to pure luck; many entrepreneurs stumble upon profit opportunities and capitalise on them at the right time and at the right place. Bringing in the role of entrepreneurship into economic analyses helps us realise the place of such contingencies (see Kirzner, 1997). Hence, it is superficially true that "wages are not just a function of one's productivity levels" (Low & Vadaketh, 2014, p. 26).

Yet, this does not mean that productivity improvements are not important, because higher productivity does reflect, to some extent, the efficient use of resources, which is an important goal of economic policy. Additionally, one should also note the many unseen factors which could have contributed to low productivity in Singapore. One could point to cultural factors of risk-aversion in Singapore society. Others could allude to the generous grants and subsidies doled out by government agencies, which could have stifled the entrepreneurial spirit of individuals, who grow dependent on state largesse.

There is no one magic solution to raising productivity or even to raise income levels, and certainly, the solution cannot rely only on "reducing our intake of low-skilled foreign workers" (Low & Vadaketh, 2014, p. 27). Although populist politicians on the left often use foreign workers as a bogeyman for domestic wages, restricting foreign labour itself will bring about other costs, especially higher labour costs on businesses.[31] While firms' dependence on cheap foreign labour is indeed a concern, one

---

[31] Ling, S. (2020, March 20). *SDP chief Chee Soon Juan urges government to focus on local employees' interests over bringing in more foreign workers.* Retrieved from: https://www.theonlinecitizen.com/2020/03/20/chee-soon-juan-urges-government-focus-on-local-employees-interest-rather-than-bring-in-more-foreign-workers/.

should still acknowledge the widespread benefits of open immigration policy across the globe (Clemens, 2011). Most immigrants that enter a nation are either very highly-skilled or are low-skilled, suggesting that they complement rather than substitute local workers. Immigrants at the low-end usually take up jobs that locals do not favour, and those at the high-end create jobs and transfer knowledge (Powell, 2015).

A better solution to raise productivity and, more generally, incomes would be to raise the innovative capacity in the economy. In this new phase of economic development, societies will need to compete not purely based on cost, or labour, but on how well they innovate. This is especially so for Asian economies, which have not reached the stage of capitalist development characterised by Schumpeterian creative destruction (Sally, 2015). On this note, one should realise that it is a market-based enabling environment that is necessary to spur indigenous, bottom-up innovation, which has so far been lacking in Singapore.

Conclusion

Economic inequality is an issue that has been increasingly featured in local policy discourse, and one that progressive figures have used to press for greater state intervention. Even the PAP government has inched towards the left in recent years, though it retains its pro-growth core. Unfortunately, in the current discourse, the distinction between inequality and economic progress has not been adequately pointed out, and the contributions of market freedoms to material empowerment of the poor have been similarly neglected. Economic inequality does not always require state action, and in any case, redistribution may not itself be the suitable policy response.

7

What Does Economic Mobility Look Like?

The People's Action Party's (PAP) consensus of governance in Singapore has been increasingly challenged in recent years. Leading this charge is a group of academic scholars who may be described as adhering to a "progressive" ideology that emphasises the injustices of socio-economic inequality, and which necessitates a greater role for state policy. Accordingly, policies like universal provision of welfare, minimum wage legislation, and higher taxes on high-income earners and corporations are believed to be legitimate in achieving greater equality.

Chapter 6 has provided reasons for why such a sentiment should be tempered. This chapter will do so in a different light. It will discuss the novel argument made by Nanyang Technological University (NTU) sociologist Teo You Yenn, author of *This is What Inequality Looks Like* (henceforth referred to as "*TIWILL*"). Not only has it achieved widespread acclaim, public intellectuals have acknowledged it as the 2018 "Book of the Year", and it has ranked among the top non-fiction bestsellers in local Singaporean bookstores (Singapore Unbound, 2018). Specifically, it has been considered a "masterfully crafted text", "probably the year's single most valuable intervention in Singapore's public discourse, in any medium", and one that challenges the dominant state narrative regarding social policy (George, 2018; Sinha, 2018). The success of this book has also led to Teo being considered the 2019 "Woman of Insight" by the gender-equality group Association of Women for Action and Research (AWARE) Singapore.

Additionally, Teo's book is consciously anti-establishment and seeks to "disrupt the narrative" (Teo, 2018). It challenges the incumbent PAP government's approach towards social policy. She shows that current policies are inadequate and require reform. Moreover, she shatters the popular image of Singapore as a place of affluent prosperity by uncovering the hidden realities of the underprivileged. It exposes a side of Singapore that is seldom seen in public: ordinary people struggling to make ends meet, those who may have fallen through the cracks in a society that prizes meritocracy, self-reliance, and individualised welfare assistance.

For these reasons and more, her book is worth paying attention to. This chapter examines both the methodology used by Teo in *TIWILL* and the policy conclusions that she makes in it. We believe that her account is a welcome contribution to local policy discourse, mainly because she writes in an atypical manner distinct from other scholars who engage in policy issues. Her unique style, combined with her ethnographic method, restores dignity to the subject under study, especially involving a topic such as inequality.

While we welcome Teo's unique methodological approach, she nonetheless makes use of problematic political economy assumptions in her account, which influences the policy conclusions she eventually arrives at. First, she conflates inequality with poverty. She also commends the Scandinavian welfare state system. Both steps in her analysis lead her to recommend the same universal entitlements based system for Singapore. We argue that Teo's ethnographic method may be harnessed in service of diametrically opposite policy conclusions, such as the classical liberal model of governance we present in this book.

Economists Should Study Culture

What sets Teo's *TIWILL* apart is its unique methodological approach applied to studying inequality. *TIWILL* is different from conventional investigations of the same topic in that it consciously treats inequality not "primarily as a question of numerical trends", or as "an objective fact, a question of numbers" (Teo, 2018, pp. 11 & 33). Instead, Teo chooses to explore inequality as a lived, everyday reality. Specifically, it draws from "three years of conversations, observations, and in-depth interviews with people who live with very limited income" (Teo, 2018, p. 10).

Teo employs a sociological approach to her research. In an important methodological appendix, she explains how she avoided not only typical quantitative methods, but even usual surveys and formal interviews, which she believes are unable to shed light on certain questions that "we do not understand well, where there are phenomena that are hidden, stigmatized, sensitive, or complicated" (Teo, 2018, p. 276). She resorted instead to informal conservations and direct observation to better get at what goes on in everyday life. As a sociologist, she rightly declares that such an approach is not value-neutral, but an inherently subjective enterprise (Teo, 2018). Far from being a weakness of the approach, this provokes critical reflection on any hidden biases and norms taken for granted. This is in line with how post-modern scholars and critical theorists expose multiple avenues by which claims of value-neutrality may obscure oppressive values and the exercise of domination.

TIWILL has great methodological value for researchers. This is particularly relevant for economists, who overwhelmingly employ a positivist framework that focuses on mathematical modelling and statistical empirical work, while generally eschewing qualitative data. Indeed, almost every academic investigation on questions on socio-economic inequality relating to Singapore has worked within such a paradigm (see Low & Vadaketh, 2014; Mukhopadhaya, 2014; Yahya, 2015). The technocratic nature of Singaporean public administration arguably privileges the policymaker to think like a social engineer and justify policies based on their supposed objective contributions to public welfare (Barr, 2006a, 2006b). In such a world, the ethnography in *TIWILL*, and the larger interpretive wing of social science, seems quaint or unproductive.

Yet, there is no particular reason why investigations of socio-economic phenomena (including inequality) should be conducted in a purely positivistic fashion. Qualitative methods capture verbal expressions — or in Chamlee-Wright's (2010) words: privilege 'talk' — that are crucial for explaining economic behaviour beyond a standard self-interest model. Archival-historical studies, ethnographies, and survey interviews are examples of qualitative methods that can investigate cultural beliefs in richer detail and provide a 'thick' account of ideology. By listening to what is being said and the background context by which these thoughts are expressed, the researcher can access the mental constructions of his respondents. This access lets the researcher understand an individual's beliefs, biases, and prejudices (as well as the dynamic interplay between them) that play a crucial role in shaping their interpretative processes of the world and influence action. Through narrative forms of knowledge in qualitative research, the researcher can make his own subjective interpretations of the respondent's thoughts.

In a now-classic paper, Geertz (1973, p. 412–455) studied the popular cockfighting games in Balinese culture. While on the surface Balinese men seem to gamble exorbitant amounts of money on a simple game, Geertz argued that cockfights were a social space where cultural values such as honour, respect, and social status were vigorously contested. The Balinese interpreted cockfighting not merely as money gambling, but more importantly as 'status gambling'. For instance, a man could never bet against a fighting cock owned by his own community, while he would have a higher obligation to bet for a cock owned his own kin. By situating himself up close in the community of the Balinese, Geertz's ethnographic work observed how informal rules and customs structured the cockfighting games.

While quantitative methods provide a 'thin' explanation, qualitative methods go beyond and try to offer a 'thick' description of the research question at hand. The cultural economist Don Lavoie argued for such 'thick' explanations in economics when he warned against the obfuscation of insights through excessive formalism in economics. By using only quantitative and econometric tools, the economics profession could not provide rich details to important historical questions (Lavoie & Chamlee-Wright, 2001, p. 21–22).

As Friedrich Hayek famously argued, "the facts of the social sciences are what people think and believe"; the social sciences should be rightly concerned with the subjective thoughts, assessments, and values of human beings, even if they are "irrational" (Storr, 2010). Studying economic behaviour like a natural scientist would leave economic science bereft of an understanding of social meanings, which shape human action (McCloskey, 2008). Economists have good reason to expand their methodological paradigm and embrace the theories and practical approaches inspired by the "interpretive turn" in social sciences, which are already commonplace within the field of cultural studies (see Rabinow & Sullivan, 1987).

Teo You Yenn Makes Policy Recommendations

TIWILL is not merely a work of descriptive ethnography but makes policy recommendations involving the proper relationship between state and market. In other words, Teo's work is not value-neutral but has clear normative undertones. This is because she does arrive at policy conclusions, though they are, admittedly, not the central focus of her book.

Teo's policy suggestions are in turn based on two major political economy assumptions, which we have investigated further in the preceding chapter. The first assumption she makes is that socio-economic inequality is an "urgent" problem that requires addressing but one that remains, unfortunately, "bleak" in the global economy (Teo 2018, p. 22). This is a clear normative statement which sets the stage for policy conclusions to be recommended. Her value judgement that inequality is an "urgent problem" to be solved is then linked with her second assumption, which is that the neoliberal, market-based, and individualised welfare system is defective and ought to be replaced by something akin to the Swedish universal welfare state model (Teo, 2018).

These premises reveal the author's political orientation in the social democratic tradition, one that is sceptical of the role markets play in society and one which favours greater state intervention for redistribution purposes. *TIWILL* is not merely a sociological, ethnographic account, but one which makes progressive, democratic socialist political recommendations.

We question these assumptions being made, considering research by political economists. As we have explained in the preceding chapter, inequality has actually decreased on a global level. While inequality may have increased in specific countries, that itself is a static snapshot which may obscure dynamic changes in income mobility over time. The expanding economic freedom in both developing and developed countries have led to economic progress (Gwartney *et al.*, 1999; Shleifer, 2009; Norberg, 2016), which may in turn be hampered if egalitarian policies are implemented.

The possibility that absolute income growth has occurred on a global level while income inequality exists within nations suggests that Teo has made a problematic conflation at the heart of her work. She had explicitly chosen to study poverty and inequality in conjunction. Teo is right to look at both, so as to investigate the structural forces that harm an individual's material position, and the desire to avoid "research devoid of humanity" (Teo, 2018, p. 11).

Our criticism is different. The problem is how both poverty and inequality are conceptually conflated, considering that inequality measures relative material positions between individuals, while poverty is an absolute concept. Simply put, a given society can have a highly egalitarian distribution of income while remaining in a general state of material poverty. Conversely, just because a society is unequal does not mean that its people must be poor.

As explained previously, some level of inequality is unavoidable if we are to live in an economically prosperous society. This is because individuals require the incentive to save, investment, work hard, and contribute to output, which will unavoidably mean that some will end up ahead than others. On a deeper level, the products of technological progress are always necessarily going to be initially concentrated in the hands of a few before being widely disseminated through mass production. Such inequality is even critical to the way human beings learn in society. Without the opportunity for people to make interpersonal comparisons and learn from the "more successful" amongst them, human progress is not possible (Pennington, 2011).

The resulting implication is that policymakers should accord a wide degree of economic freedom, and an institutional framework of private property protection, the rule of law, and contract enforcement — a combination that rewards productive wealth-creating behaviour (de Soto, 2003; Leeson & Coyne, 2004; Baumol *et al.*, 2007). In turn, this suggests that for Singapore policymakers, it would be counterproductive to establish a universal-entitlements welfare system of the sort Teo suggests. Such welfare states, as practised in Europe and the USA, have shown to have hurt economic growth, the very basis of wealth creation the poor require (Tanner, 2013; Murray, 2016). The Scandinavian countries, including Teo's choice of Sweden, have not, contrary to popular opinion, escaped the trade-off between high growth and equal incomes. The Swedish economic success is predicated on decades of market-based policies and economic freedom and preceded the establishment of the welfare state (Sanandaji, 2015).

We Arrive at a Different Conclusion with the Same Method

In an interesting twist, the policy conclusion that Teo favours does not necessarily flow from the methodological approach taken. The explicit preference for a universal welfare system is contingent upon the political economy assumptions highlighted above. The ethnographic, interpretive research approach, and even the larger cultural studies literature that she works within, may support an opposite conclusion if these assumptions are relaxed.

Cultural political economists, mixing their traditional toolkit with insights from cultural studies, have generated a large body of work positing how markets are not just a realm of endless material acquisition involving atomistic individuals, but also a moral space. These new lines of inquiry contribute to the burgeoning social economy research paradigm, which demonstrates how market actors shape, and are in turn shaped by, social bonds (see Lavoie & Chamlee-Wright, 2001; Storr, 2009; Langrill & Storr, 2015; Storr & Choi, 2016). Recognising the pervasiveness of social norms, these scholars show how trust, reciprocity, and mutual respect are fundamental sociological ingredients that lubricate the market process (Heinrich *et al.*, 2001; Zak, 2011). Additionally, markets are also portrayed as training grounds for people to learn and develop virtues (Storr & Choi, 2017).

This different conception of the market brings with it an appreciation of economic liberty and the role of meaningful work in an individual's life. According to the political theorist John Tomasi, economic liberty allows ordinary people to "think of themselves as in some sense the central causes of the particular lives they are leading" (Tomasi, 2014, p. 59). In other words, they get to develop their self-esteem as they engage in personal projects and create value for others through meaningful work. Conversely, an individual loses the fulfilment of 'earned success' when cut off from work opportunities.

The sociological, ethnographic approach that Teo has utilised may be used to pursue a slightly different line of inquiry. Rather than investigating what inequality looks like, cultural political economists might instead conduct an ethnography of ordinary individuals taking advantage of the

opportunity that economic liberty affords. One might interview, converse with, and observe Singaporeans launching entrepreneurial ventures and small business, for instance, and how they attain upward social mobility in the everyday context of market exchange. Rather than asking what inequality looks like, a more fruitful approach may be to ask: How does social mobility look like? How does economic progress look like? How does free-market entrepreneurship look like?

It is with this in mind that we have followed the methodological lead of Professor Teo You Yenn in the next section, where we present some new research findings. While we do not conduct a full-fledged ethnography, which would pose considerable logistical difficulties that would require us to go beyond the scope of our volume, we have done a series of direct interviews with individual Singaporeans. This second-best alternative has allowed us to go up close and personal just as *TIWILL* has, but also allowed us to tell a different story.

Our Conversations

We conducted a series of interviews with local Singaporeans to find out their personal views and experiences with the system of meritocracy. Specifically, we wanted to know from their own experience whether meritocracy has enabled them to achieve social mobility in Singapore, and understand any barriers that hindered them. We identified these individuals after approaching local grassroots leaders in Singapore familiar with social work. We conducted interviews with anyone keen without preference for their educational background, career status, or income levels.

What we found from these interviews was that indeed, meritocracy in Singapore has had a positive effect. Everyone we interviewed admitted that throughout their educational journey, early career, and growing up in Singapore, they enjoyed the equal opportunity to succeed. These interviewees also attested to the importance of self-reliance and working hard in their quest for a higher socio-economic status in life. A general attitude shared amongst all the subjects was that a positive, resilient attitude was necessary to overcome any familial or personal disadvantages, and with that, success was possible.

Significantly, none of these individuals ever confessed to benefitting from state welfare entitlements, nor did they express its necessity in guaranteeing social mobility in Singapore. A significant number of them achieved the current level of success they have despite not receiving government benefits, such as a young Malay podiatrist who was rejected by a government scholarship. A fair number of our interviewees also confessed to living a rather happy and meaningful life even if they did not fall within the highest income group or socio-economic strata.

It should also be pointed out, however, that another theme which emerged from these conversations we conducted was their criticism of the Singapore education system, which, despite its meritocratic foundations, systematically picked winners and losers. It was admitted that the education system generally rewarded students who are academically inclined, and those who fit within a particular notion of "merit" defined by the PAP-state. This aligns with the argument made in Chapter 3 of this book about how the parameters of meritocracy in Singapore are state-defined, precluding a pluralist form of meritocracy from being pursued.

A significant interview was the one conducted with Dr Zuhairah, a young lady in her twenties training to become a podiatrist. Admitting that she hailed from an "average household family", she took it upon herself to enter a university course of her choice, believing it to be integral to her career aspirations. She eventually joined a podiatry course in Australia, which she has since graduated from successfully.

She, however, spoke frankly about the general perception of Malays in Singapore as being "lazy". Admitting that this perception existed, she had instead chosen to turn this pessimism into personal motivation: "Race I don't think is a factor, more of a pushing factor to me" (*sic*). She believes that her success story today stands as an encouragement to fellow members of the Malay community. Her message was "Come on guys, you don't have to be part of the crowd, you can be out of the crowd, you can do something about yourself" (*sic*).

Race has indeed been a topic of discussion in Singapore society recently, with concerns that racial minorities are underprivileged as compared to the Chinese community.[1] Indeed, Dr Zuhairah also shared how she was turned

---

[1] CNA. (2016, 16 August). *Regardless of Race*. Retrieved from: https://www.channelnewsasia.com/news/video-on-demand/regardless-of-race/regardless-of-race-7827236.

down for a job offer due to the employer's policy against the wearing of the Muslim headdress. Her testimony suggests that while such imbalances do exist, they can be overcome with personal effort. She had overcome the scepticism of members of her community who questioned her decision to pursue postgraduate studies, and also personal family circumstances when she was younger.

Education is typically seen as a pathway to social mobility around the world, and hence, education financing is crucial. This is another challenge that some of our interviewees had to overcome in their educational journey. Dr Zuhairah herself was rejected from a government scholarship despite scoring 4 points for her O Levels and being from National Junior College. This meant that she had to fund her overseas education on her own, relying on her personal grit all the way. This suggests that while scholarship financing can help, they do not necessarily benefit all students, due to the stringent qualifying criteria.

Dr Zuhairah's sharing is related in part to another interview with Mr Glen Lim, who is the founder of an education-based start-up company XL Meets. Glen had initially failed to be accepted to university. He overcame this setback by putting in extra effort in his National Service, and with a recommendation from his Army Commander, obtained an admission interview which he then succeeded.

This indirect path to university also helped him realise the extra difficulty that polytechnic students in Singapore face when applying for university. Apparently, there are specific quotas that limit the number of university places available for polytechnic students, something that Glen, who was in favour of a fairer and more transparent system for accepting students, felt strongly about.

Glen's experience with Singapore's education system is, however, generally positive. He believes, as expressed in the interview, that due to the meritocracy principle, there is no lack of opportunities to succeed in Singapore, and it's ultimately up to each individual what to make of their circumstances. He expressed this articulately: "Life is not fair, but you can make it fairer with your efforts"; for all its shortcomings, Singapore's education system offers a good chance at success. It is thus unsurprising that he is a firm believer in self-responsibility, rather than outwardly projecting blame for one's circumstances. As he eloquently pointed out,

"If you want change to happen, you have to be part of the change or be the change", recalling his concern with Singaporeans tending to blame government without taking the effort to help.

His appreciation for Singapore's meritocratic education system was strengthened by his overseas experience and encounters with international students, both in his time on an exchange programme in university and also in his current work. Being a co-founder of XL Meets, he has a social mission to improve education and career mobility for youth. His work, motivated by his conviction that education is essential for social mobility, has seen him organising study missions for local youths as well as those in the wider Asian region, giving them an international exposure they may otherwise lack.

These two interviews relate closely with the case of Mr Adrian Phoon, who now runs an interior design company after working for Keppel Corporation for several years, and who also actively volunteers in his community. He had received a government scholarship with Keppel in the first year of his polytechnic studies to study naval architecture with a 3-year bond to the company. These few years in Keppel had given Adrian exposure to the corporate world and also revealed to him the importance of a positive learning attitude in the workplace. This is an especially important insight, especially in light of reports about millennial workers behaving like an "entitled generation".[2] Adrian had recounted a case of a National University of Singapore (NUS) intern working for him in Keppel, who had repeatedly asked for a testimonial. Such behaviour, according to Adrian, reflected a poor working attitude, whereby youth should prioritise learning opportunities even if given menial tasks.

The experiences he gained, coupled with his desire for greater aspirations, eventually gave Adrian the confidence to pursue the path of entrepreneurship, which he admits is not easy in Singapore, given the general preference for a safe job. It was ultimately his desire to "fight for what you want" that made the difference for him.

---

[2] The Straits Times. (2015, January 26). *Singaporeans have a misplaced sense of entitlement, says SICC Head Victor Mills*. Retrieved from: https://www.straitstimes.com/opinion/singaporeans-have-misplaced-sense-of-entitlement-says-sicc-head-victor-mills.

While Adrian did benefit from a government scholarship, he also did admit that the local education system suffered from structural rigidities, which perhaps could have contributed to the sense of risk aversion amongst Singaporeans. He shared frankly about how lower-level education is good at teaching structured curricula and fundamentals (rubrics and checklists) but fails to encourage critical thinking or support alternative talents. It was this insight that Adrian now has a preference to send his children, if he has any, to primary and secondary school education locally, but overseas for tertiary education.

Even as Adrian managed to achieve social mobility for himself through the government scholarship he received in his polytechnic years and currently through entrepreneurship. This is akin to the story of a separate individual, Mr Tng Bing Rong, who is now the Chief Operating Officer of Theo10, a local small- and medium-size enterprise (SME) specialising in organic skincare products.

In our interview with Bing Rong in his own office, he shared how he hails from a low-income family, which he felt had restricted his life options previously. Having limited access to private tuition, and also experiencing the untimely demise of his grandmother in secondary school, he had struggled with secondary school. The neighbourhood school that he was in meant that he found himself "hanging out with gangsters who had 'no ambition, no vision'".

He did not allow his circumstances to get the better of him, fortunately. Applying himself hard, he eventually entered polytechnic, where he ultimately graduated with a diploma. He candidly shared with us that it's important to remain resilient in all circumstances. Using a rather graphic metaphor, he said, "It's like being a cockroach; wherever you go, you will never die".

Bing Rong also provided further points about how he was inspired to go beyond his station in life, to dream big. When considering his career path, he had put a large premium not just on having an income, and how "I don't want just to be a small part of a system, just doing things automatically". With his distinctive English-Mandarin expression, Bing Rong expressed his mindset with an idiom: '人以梦想为大' (people should always have big dreams to give them purpose). This is what led him to take up entrepreneurship, a rewarding but high-risk endeavour.

Today, Bing Rong not only runs his company but also contributes back to society by engaging in various forms of social entrepreneurship and civil society activities, believing that those who have received much should also give back. He seems to have come full circle. We ended our conversation by asking him to distil for us what meritocracy in Singapore meant to him personally. He recounted to us how in the early stages of his entrepreneurial journey, no one believed he could make it: "At the start, others will not believe that you can do so much". But eventually, he persisted, and realised that "success doesn't come from people who are wealthy or in power" but "can be achieved by anyone as long as they put in hard work, which will, in turn, give them the rewards".

Our conversations with Adrian and Bing Rong prompted us to think further about how the education system may reward talent, but in a narrow academic lens. Dr Zuhairah had managed to climb this ladder, achieving her current doctoral status, despite certain difficulties she faced. But not everyone, as the testimony of Adrian or even Bing Rong attests, would have the same academic pedigree to do likewise.

The narrow focus of the local education system was made real in a separate interview with Mr Christopher John, who never pursued academic success, at least in the conventional sense the way Dr Zuhairah did. He hails from Bishan Park Secondary, what Singaporeans would classify as a "neighbourhood school", and did not pursue any further studies after retaking his O Levels.

However, this did not stop Christopher from making meaningful decisions later on, especially after encountering at-risk youths in his National Service days, some of whom had, in his words, "dropped out of school in primary school, joined gangs", with "tattoo everywhere, some 21 years old and having a son or daughter" (*sic*). Graduating with 4 O Levels, Christopher had initially assumed he "would be the worst", but ended up realising "I was the most educated there". His time in National Service was formative, helping him realise that there were others more unfortunate than him. "I don't want to be the best. If I see the person running last and I'm an average or better runner, I will run with the last person and I will push the last person."

Christopher has since made a career out of helping others, rather than pursuing, what for many Singaporeans, is a more "usual", or "conventional" path to socio-economic success, which usually entails graduating with a degree from a top university and earning a high income from a corporate job. Today, his mission is to "give greater dignity to the forgotten". He does this mainly through his cleaning company, an entrepreneurial venture he embarked on after years of doing youth-related counselling work. Through his work, he provides opportunities and help to the cleaners working for him.

Christopher John's unique story suggests that there are indeed many pathways to "success", and that one can be entirely happy, or content in life, without having gone through the Singaporean pathway of educational, meritocratic, excellence. The question, however, is whether the system adequately caters for students who do not fit the cookie-cutter model.

Whether the education system is a cookie-cutter model may sometimes depend on arbitrary factors unique to each child. Some might succeed, some might fall through the cracks. Some of the limitations of the local education system were also reflected in a separate interview with Mr Zulqarnain, an early childhood teacher at PCF Sparkletots. His role affords him the unique position to interact not only with young students, but their parents, and understand their educational aspirations for their children. Through his teaching experiences, he arrived at the belief that the education system today in Singapore is mostly rigid, to the point of curtailing critical thinking. This is why he prepares engaging lessons for his young charges, encouraging them to question assumptions and think out of the box. An endearing story he recounted was how he asked his students to wonder why they would always draw the sun at the top of the drawing block (a standard practice). When his students replied with "Can ah?", he responded, "Why not?".

Aside from thinking out of the box, Mr Zulqarnain has also emphasised the importance of teaching empathy and respect in schools. This is because to him, "Schools don't teach you how to talk to people... how to be nice to people... treat people with respect... it's what you learn in life". This point relates to the general concern that in Singapore society, the pursuit of wealth and academic success is too much of a preoccupation that other virtues are neglected, a concern that general commentators have raised before.[3] Mr Zulqarnain shares frankly that "You can have money... you can have wealth... your IQ very smart but at the end of the day if you don't have the EQ, you

---

[3] Teng, A. (2016). Exam stress among the young: When grades define worth. *The Straits Times*. Retrieved from: https://www.straitstimes.com/singapore/when-grades-define-worth.

don't have the basic communication with people, then half of the battle is gone, especially if you are dealing with people on the ground" (*sic*).

Race is often discussed in relation to Singapore's system of meritocracy nowadays, specifically whether being part of the minority constitutes a significant hindrance. Besides race, class has also been recently considered, with the concern that class divides are increasing in Singapore. If this is true, it means that youth from upper-class backgrounds benefit more from family resources, connections, and experience in ways that those from lower-class backgrounds don't.

With this in mind, we found the next interview with Dr Faisal, a dentist. Dr Faisal is a practising dentist who graduated from Dentistry in King's College London in the United Kingdom (UK), and who actively gives back to the community by engaging with the elderly and also through volunteerism at the grassroots level.

He has admittedly come a long way from what he has frankly shared, is his humble middle-class origins. Sharing that he comes from a "typical middle-class family", he also went to a "neighbourhood school", Bedok South Secondary School. Slowly but surely, through his educational journey, he realised his dream of becoming a dentist, even though he had once initially thought of medicine as a career. He had also done well in the O Levels and qualified for junior college, but for some reason was not allowed to do science as a subject. This led him to pursue his A Levels in the UK in a private setting, before his degree studies.

We questioned Dr Faisal about whether race was ever a hindrance for him. Admittedly, he confessed that there are a smaller proportion of Muslim professionals in Singapore, and some may have a harder time getting their foot through the door or getting internships. What is crucial, however, is that such disadvantages are not insurmountable, the same realisation Dr Zuhairah came to: "As a minority it is a bit more difficult because your access to social capital is lesser... but it is not impossible". Ultimately, it was about the unique value that one brings to the table. If someone in Singapore hails from a minority background and had talent and hard work, social mobility is possible. Dr Faisal's own experience is testament to that.

Dr Faisal, however, made an important caveat, which is that while social mobility is possible under Singapore's meritocracy, social connections do matter as well. Dr Faisal's own father is a party activist, which arguably provided him with the social capital he needed in the nascent stages of his career. This is, of course, not available to everyone in society, which can sometimes cause an unequal playing field. This point made by Dr Faisal suggests that "social capital" is significant and gives an unfair advantage to some as compared to others on the lower rungs of the system. While meritocracy does generally work in Singapore, this is not to say that everyone starts from the same starting point.

The limits of meritocracy are seen in the way the education system may not have adequately integrated people from different social classes. Dr Faisal admits, through his ongoing engagement with schools in a voluntary capacity today, there remains a stark difference in the quality and type of opportunities between neighbourhood and elite schools. This, of course, was the motivation he needed to succeed personally, which he did. But in addition to that, it raises the question of how much the education system is perpetuating existing divides rather than bridging them.

The emphasis on social connections (which some enjoy but others don't) does not invalidate, but coheres with the classical liberal argument made by the present authors, which is that class divides often stem from state-privileges, rather than from any inherent feature of the market economy. Those who benefit from close connections to state officials may understandably experience more socio-economic success than those who don't (Hart *et al.*, 2017). If connections to high ranking party officials or establishment elites in Singapore matter for social mobility, that constitutes a case for the removal of said privileges.

Concluding Remarks

Some may criticise the present authors on the grounds of selection bias, that these individuals were arbitrarily selected to depict meritocracy in a more benign light. It is true that none of these interviewees, at least to our knowledge, struggle with dire financial constraints, or are in poverty. They indeed live much more comfortable lives than those engaged by Professor Teo You Yenn in her ethnographic study.

But this only reinforces the point we make: that anyone employing a similar ethnographic method can tell a different story, and indeed arrive at a different policy conclusion than Professor Teo, despite using roughly similar qualitative approaches to get up close and personal with ordinary people. Ethnography is a double-edged sword that cuts both ways. If the present authors had proceeded to conduct a more extensive ethnographic study with these interviewees here, focusing on the theme of social mobility and economic progress, we would come to a conclusion that is less critical of Singapore's meritocracy than Teo.

8

A History of Singapore's Environmental Policy Through A Classical Liberal Lens

In recent years, the environment has been a growing issue of concern in local policy discourse. The People's Action Party (PAP) government is increasingly criticised for paying insufficient attention to the environment, with new voices calling for stricter policies to transform our economic system in environmentally friendly directions. Invariably, these environmentalist voices reflect the global ascendancy of progressive ideas, which condemn the excesses of neoliberalism and its negative ramifications on environmental health. Understandably, these voices find themselves at odds with the PAP's capitalist orientation and emphasis on economic growth.

Thus, local policy discourse, with regards to the environment, is grappling with how best to navigate the trade-off between economic growth and environmental conservation, as well as the proper role of the state in environmental policy. Much of the calls for environmental policy reform are driven by local activists, who are in turn part of a larger group of progressive voices challenging the "Singapore Consensus".

This chapter provides a new classical liberal perspective on the ongoing discourse on the Singapore government's role in environmental conservation. We acknowledge from a classical liberal perspective that activists' concerns have a legitimate moral claim and should not be outrightly dismissed. However, we find it regrettable that much of the new activist rhetoric surrounding environmentalism in Singapore wrongly diminishes economic concerns and fails to recognise the essential contributions of market-based mechanisms in achieving positive environmental outcomes.

What is needed is a competitive market order that helps to bridge the gulf between economic growth and environmental quality. We provide insights from classical liberal political economy to show that this approach to environmental policy would embrace bottom-up forces rather than a central top-down blueprint.

Rise of Environmental Consciousness

Contemporary policy discourse around the world has featured greater attention towards environmental concerns. Due to the efforts by scientists, environmentally conscious political figures and celebrities, and most recently youth climate activists, protecting the environment and fighting against climate change has risen as an urgent policy priority. The United Nations has called climate change the greatest threat to global security, and a 26-country survey by the Pew Research Center shows countries agreeing that climate change is the biggest international threat (Rosane, 2019).

This increased attention on the environment has also trickled into local policy discourse in recent years. Considering the globalised nature of Singapore's economy, it is unsurprising that global concerns are also deeply felt by the local population. Nowhere is this truer than in local civil society involving youth activists, who have taken the lead to champion a range of issues such as the environment. Millennial activists in Singapore achieved a milestone in 2019, which saw Singapore's first-ever climate rally being held at Hong Lim Park in September, with a turnout of approximately 1,700 people. This rally featured a mass "die-in", which aimed to raise awareness of the loss of biodiversity and human lives in the global fight against climate change. These activities were spearheaded mainly by youth-oriented environmental organisations inspired by the work of Greta Thunberg and the global wave of environmental initiatives.

What is significant to note is that the environmental activists at this rally opposed the Singapore government's policies towards the climate, on the basis that they did not go far enough. They had objected to the PAP's announcements in the earlier National Day Rally involving S$100 billion worth of funds to protect Singapore against the adverse effects of higher sea levels because these were "adaptive" rather than "preventive" measures (Wong, 2019). In other words, the government should take steps to mitigate climate change, rather than simply put in place measures to minimise its negative side effects. This "mitigation" paradigm is reflected in calls for the government to "decarbonise the economy", "divest fully from polluting industries", and raise the carbon tax to even higher levels. Activists urge the government to take even bolder steps to achieve the aim of net-zero emissions by 2050 (SG Climate Rally, n.d.).

The rise of youth-led environmental advocacy in Singapore is closely associated with the increasing suspicion against the market economy. This is already true on a global level, where environmental activists make radical calls for an overhaul of the capitalist system. Locally, youth climate activists express a similar scepticism against markets, believing that since "capitalism helped create the climate crisis", "we should not look to it as a solution".[1] Thus, the rise of environmental consciousness has a political element to it. Environmentalism, globally and locally, is typically associated with an anti-market ideological orientation.

Singapore's Environmental Policy and Its Critics

A Pro-growth Environmental Policy

To a large extent, Singapore's environmental policy adopts an anthropocentric approach, i.e. the role of environmental policy is ensuring a higher standard of living for humans rather than to protect the intrinsic value of the natural environment. Conservation efforts to preserve the environment is not conducted for the sake of the environment in and of itself, but rather for the twin purposes of helping the economy grow and to keeping Singapore clean and green for residents (Chang, 2016). This is unsurprising, given Singapore's pragmatism when it comes to policymaking. Environmental policy by the PAP has not been influenced by radical ideologies in the wider environmental movement, which have emphasised the intrinsic value of the natural world,[2] and the concomitant

---

[1] Seah, B. (2019, October 9). Capitalism helped create the climate crisis. We should not look to it as the solution. *TODAY Online*. Retrieved from: https://www.todayonline.com/commentary/capitalism-helped-create-climate-crisis-we-should-not-look-it-solution.

[2] Radical environmental philosophers, such as the prominent Arne Naess, have agitated for environmentalists to go beyond "shallow" thinking which merely tinkers at the margins, and to question the very basis of the industrial capitalist system which has wrought such havoc to the natural environment.

necessity for radical and structural overhauls to the present-day industrial system that we live in.

Instead, much of the government's justification for its carbon-intensive industry has been built on a familiar narrative: that Singapore is small in size, resource-poor, and geopolitically vulnerable. These natural circumstances, it is argued, implies that economic supremacy becomes Singapore's only way of survival. Its continued economic growth is ensured only by its premier position as an international hub that in turn is secured insofar as it remains an attractive business and capital-friendly tax-free haven. Therefore, its fossil fuel-intensive activities, while remaining under harsh scrutiny and condemnation by local environmentalists, continues to be regarded by the government as a necessary evil for maintaining the prosperity of Singapore. In a recent conference, Trade and Industry Minister Chan Chun Sing echoed the same economic justification for Singapore's continued use of fossil fuels, despite being a developed nation:

> "Singapore is a data hub. Many Internet companies, many digital companies, would like to set up their data centres in Singapore. But data centres require huge amounts of energy; huge amounts of energy require huge amounts of carbon budget. Are we able to attract these companies? If we are unable to attract them, what does it mean for our economy, our position as a global hub for the digital services?" (The Straits Times, 2020)

However, it would be remiss to claim that the environment has been neglected in Singapore. It is in vogue for politicians to tow an environmentalist line today, but the PAP government has long committed efforts to improving the natural environment since the early days of the country's independence. Indeed, the 2018 Environmental Performance Index that measures environmental health across 180 countries ranks Singapore as the third best in air pollution and second in water pollution (Wendling *et al.*, 2018).

Singapore's environmentalist initiatives date as far back as the 1960s, as seen by its very early tree-planting efforts in its vision to develop Singapore as a "Garden City" (Yuen, 1996). Over just a few decades, at least 55,000 trees were planted by 1971, tripled to 158,000 in 1974, and reached

1.4 million trees by 2014 (National Library Board, n.d.). Environmental policy was designed not only to introduce tree planting as part of community practice, but also mandated by formal legislation for the Housing Developing Board (HDB) to allocate space wherever possible for tree planting. Development of roads ensured that sufficient space was allowed for tree planting along roads. Within the same timeframe of a few decades, parks in Singapore grew from a measly 13 to an astounding 330, making the total area of green spaces 9,707 ha — approximately 7.4% of Singapore's entire geography. The Garden City vision had been undisputedly achieved, and Singapore enjoyed the international reputation of a lush and green city, a promotional marketing tactic that was synonymous with Singapore's tourism sector.

Singapore was also an early signatory to the 1989 Montreal Protocol and its subsequent amendments. This intergovernmental agreement that sought to phase out the usage of ozone-depleting substances (ODS) was entered into despite the economy's heavy dependence on the import and manufacture of chlorofluorocarbons (CFCs). Although Singapore contributes to only 0.11% of global carbon emissions and has a lack of energy alternatives due to physical constraints, its commitment to climate change was apparent as early as 1997 when it ratified the United Nations Framework Convention on Climate Change (UNFCCC), and in 2006 when it signed the Kyoto Protocol, albeit under less stringent criteria than most developed nations that would have meant sharper fossil fuel reductions.

In line with its pro-growth orientation, the Singapore government's environmental policy has also placed much emphasis on the importance of achieving energy efficiency through at least two thrusts.[3] Public education campaigns on electronically efficient technologies are done to nudge households towards the purchase of more energy-efficient appliances. In the private sector, government grants are offered to

---

[3] This was one of the primary goals of the Inter-Agency Committee on Energy Efficiency (IACEE) formed in 1998, today assimilated into the National Climate Change Secretariat (NCCS). Today, these initiatives are pushed out by various government agencies such as the National Environment Agency (NEA) and the Energy Efficiency Programme Office (E2PO).

incentivise companies towards the early adoption of energy-efficient infrastructure, and energy management training programmes are also offered to engineers and managers. By making the right investments in infrastructure and the adoption of new technologies to reduce emissions, the government's goals to drive energy efficiency have been unquestionably successful — all without incurring the costs to economic growth. While Singapore's TOE (tonnes of oil equivalent) per capita has consistently increased, energy intensity per gross domestic product (GDP) has been on a steady decline (Jadhav *et al.*, 2016). This means that Singapore has not only been able to sustain economic growth but at an economised rate of energy usage (See Chart 1). This trend is corroborated by longer trend data shown in Chang (2016), where Singapore's energy usage per unit of GDP has been on a constant and gradual decline since the late 1960s. Chart 2 shows that in addition to reducing emission output, Singapore has managed to deliver on GDP growth at the same time. In other words, Singapore has managed to simultaneously have their cake and eat it too.

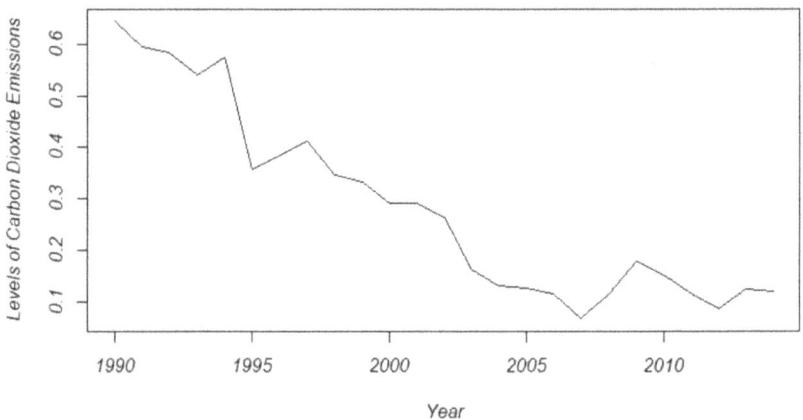

Chart 1:   Singapore's carbon emissions per PPP$ of GDP (kg per PPP$ of GDP), 1990–2014

Source: The World Bank.

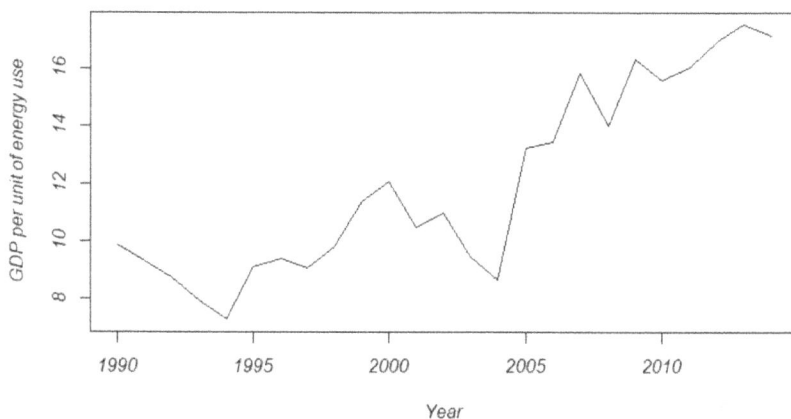

Chart 2:   Singapore's GDP per unit of energy use (constant 2017 PPP$ per kg of oil equivalent), 1990–2017

Source: The World Bank.

Critics of Singapore's Environmental Policy

Due to the PAP government's strong commitment to economic growth, it eschews not only the policy proposals of radical environmentalists who advocate an overthrow of the capitalist system at its most extreme, but even much of the moderate proposals made by climate activists and environmentally-conscious political parties elsewhere. Consequently, it is easy to understand why, given the pro-business stance of the PAP government, they seem to be resisting higher carbon taxes and policies to decarbonise the economy and divest from fossil fuels — policies that leading mainstream environmentalists around the world advocate.

Yet, it is unquestionably true that Singapore's third to first world industrialisation has come at considerable cost to the rich forestry that hitherto existed on the island. Economic development in Singapore meant a radical restructuring of land use in a way that has made agricultural land obsolete but also with significant impacts on its natural reserves. This impact, however, dates back to long before British colonialism. As O'Dempsey (2014) documents, Singapore's once common dipterocarp and mangrove forests were largely felled during the period of colonialism.

Modern industrialisation in the 21st century has accelerated this deforestation. Today, less than 7% of Singapore's original mangrove forests remain. The 2018 Environmental Performance Index scores Singapore as one of the lowest in preservation of its biodiversity and habitats, although the same report acknowledges that this is largely due to its small geographic size and the necessity of state industrialisation (Wendling *et al.*, 2018).

Critics of Singapore's approach to the environment often take issue with the government's prioritisation of economic growth (Neo, 2007). The government's approach is also accused of being conducted in an authoritarian top-down fashion that excludes the democratic participation of local civil society (Han, 2016). It is argued that the conservationist appeals of local environmentalists, although considered in a consultative process, ultimately takes a backseat to the government's overarching policy goals of growth. This was demonstrated in the clash between the state and environmental non-governmental organisations (NGOs) in northern Singapore Senoko. When the government announced its plans in 1993 to clear the area for the development of housing estates, the Nature Society of Singapore (NSS) started a petition to protest the government's plans to clear the forest and construct new housing estates, arguing that the forest was a rich natural habitat to at least 180 species of birds. Although the petition gathered the popular support of 25,000 Singaporeans, the government overrode this consensus and went ahead with its plans.

Even when environmental civil society groups have successfully lobbied the government to preserve its nature reserves, these actors are largely subordinated to the state and operating within a constrained political arena (Francesch-Huidobro, 2008). This was highly apparent in the contestation of the Lower Peirce Reservoir catchment area. In 1990, when the NSS learnt of the plans to construct a golf course over a designated "nature reserve" area, it began lobbying in opposition to the state, albeit in a highly restrained manner. In reaction to the Public Utilities Board's (PUB) decision not to make its Environmental Internal Assessment (EIA) public, the NSS produced its own EIA. Yet, the NSS was cautioned by a separate government agency (National Parks Board [NParks]) not to make its EIA public because they were making use of information in NSS's document to refute PUB. Making the information public would mean making it harder for PUB to reverse its decisions and make a graceful exit, as it would be common knowledge that an environmental NGO had successfully combatted the planning of a major state agency. At around the same time, a popular petition campaign by the NSS that garnered 17,000 signatures was promptly thwarted by the Internal Security Agency (ISA) when the head of NSS was investigated for ties to a Malaysian environmental NGO. Although the construction of the golf course was eventually tabled and the nature reserve preserved, this saga is a telling example of how the state ultimately disciplines local environmentalist efforts.

The Contribution of Classical Liberalism

Classical Liberalism Applied to Environmentalism

What does classical liberalism have to contribute to local discourse on environmental policy? It should be clear that classical liberalism does not aim to settle the normative debate between industrialists and conservationists.

Classical liberalism accepts that both sides have a legitimate claim to the use of environmental resources. In the context of Singapore, local environmental activists like the NSS have a legitimate moral claim to preserving the rich biodiversity of Singapore's mangrove forests. From their perspective, the construction of new housing estates and shopping malls in the pursuit of economic growth matters naught to them. An increase in national GDP is not a justifiable cost for the continual pillage of Mother Nature and what scarce environmental resources Singapore has remaining.

However, just as there might be environmentalists who hold deeply passionate views about the preservation of nature, classical liberals recognise this view is not representative of everyone. Singaporeans may place a stronger desire for industrialisation, economic growth, and the accompanying higher standards of living. Unlike environmentalists, these Singaporeans — let's call them economic pragmatists — do not place as high a premium on the environment. Indeed, this is demonstrably clear by the desire of Singaporeans in political elections for more residential estates and commercial projects. They see alternative uses for environmental resources, be it in the form of manufacturing plants, housing estates, or recreational activities. In the eyes of the economic pragmatists, lush greenery and clean air might be desirable, but not to the extent by which it impedes modern industrialisation.

Whose right to the environment triumphs? The classical liberal approach does not aim to settle this debate in normative values. We agree with the traditional environmentalist opinion that the PAP's approach to environmentalism has tended to privilege developmental goals in a way that assumes development is "necessary" and value-free (Neo, 2007). At the same time, we acknowledge too that preserving environmental resources at the costs of economic development is not a granted assumption. Just as a parent might sacrifice family time in pursuit of a high-paying corporate position, or certain cultures give up the material benefits of a globalised economy for a slower, laidback pace of life, we should not assume that economic priorities are ex-ante given and considered "essential". It matters who is asking the question and what they subjectively prefer.

The philosopher David Schmidtz (2000) makes the point clearly that all environmental disputes can be boiled down into one of three categories: a conflict in environmental values, conflicting usage of environmental resources, or conflicting economic priorities. Although environmentalists tend to frame the debate as a primordial battle between "a love for nature" versus "a relentless quest for economic profits", the reality is that conflicts are often grounded in a disagreement in priorities. Even when two parties might regard the environment with equal concern, it is a mistake to assume that both parties are in an equal position to treat the use of environmental resources as equally pressing.

For example, weaning off the use of carbon-intensive fossil fuels towards expensive renewable technologies may be a luxury for those of us lucky enough to live in the developed world, but it is not one that people living in developing nations can afford. It is not hard to see why. People living on the edges of poverty desperately need the cheap and reliable energy supply that once propelled developed economies to the heights of economic prosperity they enjoy today. In fact, many remain poor because of a lack of access to cheap and abundant energy, which at the moment remains fossil fuels.[4]

---

[4] Lomborg, B. (2013, December 3). The Poor Need Cheap Fossil Fuels. *The New York Times*. Retrieved from: https://www.nytimes.com/2013/12/04/opinion/the-poor-need-cheap-fossil-fuels.html.

In this light, the punitive environmental regulations that many environmentalists champion would cripple economic growth at the expense of the least well-off, with little regard for a difference in values and priorities that they are privileged enough not to have to consider. Even in more developed countries like the United States, environmental regulations have led to negative outcomes on standards of living.[5] The United States' economy has particularly suffered from an overdose of regulation (including those by the United States Environmental Protection Agency), which has led to a trickling down of harmful effects on middle-class households.[6]

It is from this premise that environmental values and priorities are difficult to resolve that classical liberals recognise a decentralised regime of free markets as the solution to reconciling these disagreements. Insofar as people have differing opinions on how best to treat environmental resources, we need an economic system that coordinates conflicting values and priorities. To a significant extent, the Singapore government has recognised the value of incorporating market forces in environmental policy. Privatisation of key industries was allowed to enable the competitive allocation of scarce resources. Privatisation also introduced market incentives to penalise wasteful behaviour through the price mechanism. The next section considers how free-market mechanisms have been used in Singapore's environmental management.

Market Institutions in Singapore's Environment Policy

The argument for market prices, as Hayek (1945) famously stated, is that they enable conflicting goals over scarce resources to be resolved in a process of mutual adjustment. Without having to know the reason for why

---

[5] O'Toole, R. (2013, October 28). *Reducing Livability: How Sustainability Planning Threatens the American Dream*. Retrieved from: https://www.cato.org/publications/policy-analysis/reducing-livability-how-sustainability-planning-threatens-american; Bruegge, Christopher D., Deryugina, Tatyana, & Myers, Erica. (2018). The Distributional Effects of Building Energy Codes. *NBER Working Paper Series*, Working Paper 24211. Retrieved from: https://www.nber.org/papers/w24211.pdf.

[6] McLaughlin, P., Ghei, N., & Wilt, M. (2018). *Regulatory Accumlation and its Costs: An Overview*. Retrieved from: https://www.mercatus.org/publications/regulation/regulatory-accumulation-and-its-costs.

it is that the price of a certain resource has gone up, capitalists can depend on the price system as a knowledge signal to look for cheaper alternatives. As the economist Alex Tabarrok puts it, a price is a signal wrapped up in an incentive. Capitalists competing for the same resources in a market economy are required to evaluate the justification of its costs, driving scarce resources to entrepreneurs that have the highest demand for it. Without private property and market prices, it is difficult for policymakers to know the relative value of scarce resources according to what different actors in the economy want to use them for.

A large body of research in free-market environmentalism has applied Hayekian price theory analysis towards this end of understanding how market institutions resolve environmental conflicts (Anderson & Leal, 2015). A market system that allows prices to function, profits to be made, and respects property rights enables environmental actors to evaluate the opportunity costs of their activities. This theoretical lens allows us to study an economy that is enabled to move towards a positive-sum game of environmentalism where both economic development and environmental preservation can coexist, as opposed to political regulations of the environment that pits a negative-sum game of "winner takes all" (we elaborate on this in the next section).

Although the shape and form of traditional environmentalist case studies do not necessarily apply to Singapore's context due to its small size, understanding how the government has allowed market forces in environmental policy provides a useful stepping stone to understand how market institutions can drive pro-environmental outcomes.

Privatisation of waste collection was rejected initially but finally began initiation throughout the 1990s. Competitive market pricing was introduced into the waste industry, where consumers are expected to internalise full costs as with any other good. Although the government initially subsidised waste disposal, the rapidly growing Singaporean economy created an increasing amount of waste that would require the construction of new facilities. This increasingly unsustainable situation prompted the government to react by shifting the pecuniary burden for private disposal companies to absorb, which was inevitably passed on to Singaporean residents (Tan *et al.*, 2016). Private waste disposal companies saw fit to charge higher rates for larger volumes of waste. This in turn

created a strong incentive for industrial sectors producing large volumes of waste to not only curb reckless disposal but also to pragmatically consider a cost-benefit analysis on the potentials of recycling waste. By 1999, the waste collection industry achieved free-market competition among nine different sectors, subject to licensing criteria by the government. Licenses to construct waste incineration plants and NEWater plants were also awarded to privatised entities. The structure for these industries evolved toward a public-private partnership where the government remained as an overall regulator while operational risks are internalised by the corporation.

Price mechanisms were also introduced in the areas of air and water pollution. To combat air pollution due to increasing vehicle usage in the 1980s, the government introduced a differential tax rate to price leaded petrol at 10 cents per litre more than unleaded petrol, which was more environmentally friendly, to encourage the shift in consumption. In the case of water pollution management, the Trade Effluent Tariff Scheme was enacted to allow the discharge of liquid waste or sewage (of a certain limit) into public sewers for a fee. These fees in turn go towards paying off the extra costs of treating the extra loads of pollution at water reclamation plants. Both of these cases stand in contrast to standard environmentalist command-and-control style policies that might have outrightly banned the usage of leaded petrol or discharge of trade effluents.

In 1998, Singapore also became one of the first early adopters of market-based quotas to regulate the discharge of chlorofluorocarbons (CFCs) and other ozone-depleting substances (ODS) in commercial activity. The decision to slowly phase out ODS stemmed from the pragmatic recognition that Singapore's economic development was highly dependent on the development of its domestic electronics and chemical industries. Limited quotas therefore induced producers to consider the opportunity costs of emitting ODS and explore alternative options. The Tender and Quota Allocation System (TQS) allowed manufacturers to trade ODS permits and allocate it to its most economically desired ends, facilitating a more environmentally friendly outcome. Again, rather than taking the easy option of legislating a ban on the release of CFCs, market mechanisms were used to carefully allow moderate amounts of pollution and at the same time deter its usage towards environmentally superior alternatives over time.

From a classical liberal viewpoint, market-based policies are preferable to political bans for the way that it allows economic development to continue while at the same time incentivising market innovation to pave a path toward a greener economy. At its heart is a recognition that innovation is the key to solving environmental problems. Such market innovation occurs when economic actors (energy producers specifically) are allowed to make profits and encouraged to reinvest revenue toward cleaner and more efficient energy production techniques.

Tensions with Command-and-Control Environmental Regulations

While market forces have been harnessed upon effectively for the environment in Singapore, it is unlikely to satisfy green political theorists and activists who favour command-and-control forms of environmental regulation that are imposed from the political arena by the state, henceforth referred to as "political environmentalism". The contradictory tensions between a classical liberal, market-oriented approach and political environmentalism are obvious. The classical liberal approach emphasises that environmental problems are best addressed by encouraging the process of market innovation to spur green technological development. Lured by profits and guided by price signals, entrepreneurs play an essential role in driving investment.

Political environmentalism, on the other hand, would introduce mandatory bans and regulations across-the-board in pursuit of short-term policy goals. The case for political environmentalism comes in different variants, but a common denominator is its theoretical grounding in collective-action-problem-type market failures. The argument is that because individuals in the private sector lack incentives to behave in an environmentally friendly manner, their carbon footprints represent economic externalities that leave society in a suboptimal environmental outcome. For example, energy corporations reap the full profits of burning fossil fuels but fail to pay the full social costs since carbon emissions deteriorate the environmental public good. As such, a central authority of some kind is needed to rearrange incentives and curb such behaviour to the ideal alignment private and social costs, typically involving coercive measures such as a Pigouvian carbon tax or the suppression of carbon emissions through intergovernmental agreements.

In the following section, we offer two arguments from a classical liberal perspective to be sceptical of political environmentalism.

Democratic failures

Our first contention is that political environmentalism is overly optimistic of the political democratic process, and does not take the potential of "democratic failures" seriously. Regulating carbon emissions, in effect, is a proposal to mitigate environmental problems by transferring it into the realm of democratic politics, rather than relying on market innovation and technological growth. In theory, policymakers will produce environmental legislation, the effectiveness of which is subject to democratic check and accountability by voters.

But while collective action problems may exist in markets, the same problems exist within the political process. Democratic polities function efficiently when voters are sufficiently well-informed to hold politicians accountable. Yet a wealth of research finds that despite educational improvements in the 21st century, the average voter is hopelessly misinformed and lacks basic social science training, let alone be able to assess complex public policy (Somin, 2013; Achen & Bartels, 2016). Caplan (2006) finds that voters are often systematically biased against the market, foreign trade, immigration, and economic developments that might destroy jobs, and are overly pessimistic in political affairs.

It is not that voters are "stupid", but that being informed in politics is a high-cost endeavour with low reward. Reading 20 books on environmental policy might make you an expert, but it does not change the reality that your one vote come election day is almost unlikely to make any difference. Therefore, people are "rationally ignorant" and would rather channel their time productively toward their careers and family. This widespread voter ignorance and poor quality of voter decision-making make democracies highly vulnerable to exploitation by politicians and corporatist lobbying. In short, collective action problems, too, exist in politics for the simple reason that most voters do not live up to a lofty "democratic ideal".

Moreover, even relatively well-informed voters will find it fiendishly difficult to vote for the "right" political party due to the institutional structure of democratic politics. Consider that in a market setting, resource values are reflected in the price system. Prices allow consumers to make easy comparisons across their many competing needs, *without having to understand the underlying production methods* of the consumer good they are shopping for.

In politics however, voters lack market prices and therefore cannot make such easy comparisons at the ballot box (DeCanio, 2014). To assess the effectiveness of competing policies, voters must be able to know whether financial budgets and tax dollars are going to its most optimal use. But how do voters compare if a politician's decision to reallocate funding from environmental protection to healthcare is well-spent? Absent market prices, there is no common metric for calculating a trade-off between voting for different political candidates. The complexity of this mental exercise is only further aggravated by the fact that voters are not choosing between two policy options, but *bundles* of policies that politicians advertise across healthcare, environment, social welfare, education, etc. Without the clear epistemic function of market prices, it is unsurprising that political competition tends to be driven by alarmist and moralist claims that appeal to popular voters, rather than sound evidence grounded in fiscal prudence and scientific research.

Further to that, political environmentalism underestimates the pervasiveness of externalities in politics. Although the case for political environmentalism usually stems from a diagnosis of economic externalities, political environmentalism itself also imposes heavy externalities on taxpayers and the less well off. These externalities are most pronounced in the case of renewable energy technologies which have yet failed to achieve economies of scale but continue to enjoy disproportionately huge state subsidies and tax cuts. In the context of the US, cleaner energy forms received 65% of energy subsidies despite only contributing to 7% of energy output (Scarborough, 2015). Solar and wind — heralded by environmentalists as ideal — received 28% of government subsidies while contributing a measly 1.4% of energy. A New Zealand study that estimated the costs of complete decarbonisation and running solely on renewables found that the economic bill would be greater than the entire current national budget, paid on an annual basis.[7] Similarly, the European Union's proposal to drastically reduce emissions by 2050 would externalise about $1.4 trillion annual to the taxpayers.[8]

Political externalities can be seen in the persistence of state subsidies in public projects that have proved environmentally damaging. There are many such examples, but perhaps the most well-known is the European Union's Common Agricultural Policy (CAP) that generously subsidises domestic European farmers. By eliminating market incentives of farmers to be cost-efficient and produce according to market demand, this has resulted in widespread environmental degradation due to intensive farming from unecological use of chemicals (Souchère *et al.*, 2003). Further to that, the policy's practice of heavily subsidising imports has had the effect of undercutting smaller local farmers to the advantage of big farming corporations, resulting in less market competition that would otherwise have lowered costs for European consumers, manifesting in another form of political externality. On this view, collective action problems exist in markets, but it is not at all clear that the democratic process of politics will resolve this problem, and may even exacerbate the problem.

A negative-sum game

Secondly, political environmentalism is a negative-sum game that does not aim at reconciliation between conflicting environmental values. Instead, it insists on a paternalistic one-size-fits-all rule that ignores pre-existing priorities. This differs from market institutions which facilitate a positive-sum game in the way that it allows for both environmental goals and economic growth to be pursued simultaneously. States possess

---

[7] New Zealand Institute of Economic Research (2018). *Economic impact analysis of 2015 emissions targets: A dynamic Computable General Equilibrium analysis.* Retrieved from: https://www.mfe.govt.nz/sites/default/files/media/Climate%20Change/NZIER%20 report%20-%20Economic%20impact%20analysis%20of%202050%20emissions%20 targets%20-%20FINAL.pdf.

[8] Knopf, B., Chen, H. Y.-H., De Cian, E., Förster, H., Kanudia, A., Karkatsouli, I., Keppo, I., Koljonen, T., Schumacher, K., & Van Vuuren, D. P. (2013). Beyond 2020 — Strategies and Costs for Transforming the European Energy System. *Climate Change Economics,* 4(1), 1–38. Retrieved from: https://www.worldscientific.com/doi/abs/10.1142/S2010007813400010.

an exclusive authority to produce or regulate goods, while markets do not. Indeed, even environmentalists are free to pay off energy producers to pollute less, or even purchase market tradable carbon quotas to tear them up!

For left-leaning environmentalists in Singapore advocating government regulation of carbon producers, their advocacy ironically bears little difference from the government's traditionally high-handed and paternalistic style to override the conservation of nature in favour of economic development despite public opposition, as seen in the aforementioned case of Senoko. After all, they merely seek to influence the institution of government in their favoured direction. Just as the state imposes intangible and non-pecuniary costs on environmentalists when they ignore their pleas, the types of political regulations that environmentalists champion such as carbon taxes would similarly enforce high opportunity costs on those who wish to undertake commercial activities.

This is brought into clear view when one considers the significant economic costs of environmental regulations. Carbon taxation, a staple of many environmentalist policy platforms, involves costs that disproportionately fall on the shoulders of the less well off, as Singapore policymakers have themselves acknowledged (Min, 2017). Countries with higher carbon taxes experience higher energy prices (Institute for Energy Research, 2018). This is especially true in seasonal countries that depend on winter heating and where tens of thousands of people still perish from cold-related illnesses; carbon taxes have led to households struggling with higher energy prices.[9] Cheaper heating helps reduce winter mortality, and to the extent carbon taxes raise energy prices, more people die (Chirakijja et al., 2019).

To offset this disproportionate tax burden on the low income, some governments rely on tax cuts and rebates to citizens in order to achieve "revenue neutrality".[10] The problem with the proposal of revenue neutrality

---

[9] This has been reported in Britain. Fraser, N. (2013, 28 March). It's the cold, not global warming, that we should be worried about. *The Telegraph*. Retrieved from: https://www.telegraph.co.uk/news/health/elder/9959856/Its-the-cold-not-global-warming-that-we-should-be-worried-about.html.

[10] The Singapore government's version of this are the GST Voucher U-Save rebates.

lies in a little-known concept called the tax interaction effect, pioneered by Stanford economist Lawrence Goulder.[11] Goulder shattered the simplistic idea that governments can compensate workers from the economic damage of a carbon tax through simple rebate schemes or tax deductions. Simply put, the economic impact of carbon taxes is not equal to other types of taxes. Carbon taxes are targeted at a much narrower tax base (energy producers) in comparison to broad-based taxes like labour and consumption. Therefore, carbon taxes create a distortionary effect that ripples through the economy in a larger magnitude.

A carbon tax first penalises high energy consumption activities. In Singapore, this would apply to the bulk of the economy since 79% of total electricity consumption comes from industrial and commerce-related activities, while households make only 14.7% (Energy Market Authority, 2018). The rise in energy costs would then trickle down to local businesses who will inevitably react in other cost-cutting measures.

Economists who study the tax interaction effect find that the impact of carbon taxes on wealth creation is far more destructive to a worker's earnings than the amount that is compensated in tax rebates (Goulder, 2000). Supporters of revenue neutrality believe it is possible to reduce a dollar in other taxes for every other dollar raise in carbon taxes, when in fact the overall effect of carbon taxes is the retardation of wealth creation and economic productivity.

Top-down environmental policies may actually do more harm than good. According to an Oxford study, environmental regulations can lead to statistically significant negative impacts on trade, employment, and productivity (Dechezleprêtre & Sato, 2017). While some feel that this may be a necessary sacrifice in order to induce innovation in clean technologies, the resulting benefits may not be large enough. Economic effects like these

---

[11] A second problem with political promises of revenue neutrality is that they are often anything but neutral. In 2008, the government of British Columbia implemented a carbon tax on the unprecedented political campaign of revenue neutrality, then considered a big deal for local Canadian voters and businesses due to the competition it faces from nearby North American jurisdictions. Not long after the carbon tax went into effect, the revenue neutrality commitment was quickly forgotten and abandoned for various political reasons, hanging the lower and middle classes up to dry (Taylor, 2017). The British Columbian government's tax revenues soared as the tax started at 10 CAD in 2008, rose to 30 CAD in 2012, and is projected to reach 50 CAD by 2021 (Jackson & Eisen, 2019).

are not just statistical abstractions, but impact ordinary people and affect their livelihoods. This gives us cause for concern when considering political environmentalism, which imposes high human costs.

The economic costs of leading environmentalist proposals are seen on the global level as well. Estimates have shown that the Paris Climate Agreement of 2015 is highly expensive, considering that it makes sweeping calls to divest from fossil fuels. A recent study argues that the Paris Agreement would lead to a 4% increase in poverty in developing countries (Campagnolo & Davide, 2019). This is a significant insight considering that much of the developing world requires affordable and reliable energy for their economies to grow, which at this point remains fossil fuels — the very same forms of energy that first world countries today depended on historically.

In light of the high costs that political environmentalism would impose on economic development, there is good reason to ask of political environmentalism's most broad-sweeping regulatory proposals: "What if you're wrong?" It is on this note that we argue the institutional plurality of classical liberalism is desirable. When different competing solutions to the environment are allowed to be developed concurrently, the risks and harmful impacts of being wrong are reduced.

The pluralistic approach to environmental problems that classical liberals favour finds its fullest expression in environmental entrepreneurship. Globally, this is already solving many intractable environmental problems, such as conservation of endangered animals, the creation of alternative energy sources, and also the management of scarce natural resources (Huggins, 2013). Interestingly, these market-driven processes help to bridge the gap between economic objectives and environmental goals, achieving a reconciliation that political environmentalism is unable to achieve.

With this, we encourage greater environmental entrepreneurship in the Singapore context. Such bottom-up solutions are unfortunately seldom proposed, or even discussed, by environmental activists, who have advocated policies such as fossil fuel divestment, carbon taxes, and even government regulations on private business. Of course, environmental entrepreneurs already abound in the local context.[12] An abundance of tech

---

[12] See for example such student-led efforts. https://blog.smu.edu.sg/undergraduate/soa/joline-tang-eco-minded-entrepreneur/

companies such as Olio, FoodCloud and Karma have developed apps to reduce food wastage by connecting grocers and local restaurants with the homeless and needy. Moreover, much of entrepreneurship tend to emerge in environmentally friendly outcomes without explicitly intending to be. Take for example new clothing fashion companies (such as Style Theory) whose business model allows consumers to rent rather than purchase apparel, mitigating a longstanding problem in today's consumerist culture where clothes are infrequently used in its shelf life.

It is our sincere hope that the policy discourse surrounding the environment may give greater attention to these bottom-up efforts, and for continued attention to be paid to developing a conducive climate for business and entrepreneurial ventures. Some of these ventures will undoubtedly fail, but the whole point of institutional plurality is precisely the trial-and-error learning process it facilitates to discover new solutions to environmental problems as different firms, individuals, and organisations try out different approaches of their own.

Conclusion

The present authors do not wish to give the impression that governments have no role to play in the environment. Our view is simply that government action should be limited to situations where there are no obvious market solutions. For example, Singapore's geographic limitations would make it difficult for nuclear facilities to be built, implying some scope for the state to spur these efforts on. As much as possible however, market competition and profit incentives should be relied upon, as are common in many of Singapore's public-private partnerships.

Classical liberalism has much to offer to the burgeoning debate in environmental policy by recognising the shortcomings of the political process comparative to the market process. Unfortunately, mainstream opinion tends to lambast the latter while glorifying the former in idealised states. Yet, Singapore's environmental achievements today have succeeded in no small part due to the introduction of market forces and being highly cognizant of economic realities. Market capitalism is a friend to the environment, rather than an enemy.

9

Why (Classical Liberal) Political Philosophy?

We have presented a classical liberal perspective on governance in Singapore that is deeply rooted in scepticism of central political authority and national economic planning. This is a new paradigm that has not been considered thus far in local policy discourse, which has until now been characterised by a binary choice between the People's Action Party (PAP) status quo and its anti-establishment critics.

We anticipate that our book may strike some as guilty of partisan ideology. After all, Singapore's governance, at least that which is defined by the PAP, is built on considerations of pragmatism which transcend the narrow dictates of any political ideology. The argument here is that the Singapore state should, and does in fact, pursue policies simply based on "what works best" for the welfare of Singaporeans, and that consequently, leaders should be ready to discard old practices if they are found wanting. This implies that PAP policymaking is "rational" and purely "evidence-based", rather than adhering to any ideological sacred cows.[1] Lee Kuan Yew himself expressed it best:

> "We are pragmatists. We don't stick to any ideology. Does it work? Let's try it, and if it does work, fine, let's continue it. If it doesn't work, toss it out, try another one. We are not enamored with any ideology".[2]

---

[1] The Straits Times. (2015, March 30). Keep pragmatism as guiding principle. *The Straits Times.* Retrieved from: https://www.straitstimes.com/opinion/keep-pragmatism-as-guiding-principle.
[2] Interview with the New York Times, 29 August 2007. Retrieved from http://www.nytimes.com/2007/08/29/world/asia/29iht-lee-excerpts.html?pagewanted=all

This pragmatic, non-ideological approach to governance is what many have explained as the basis for Singapore's socio-economic success. Take the Central Provident Fund (CPF), Singapore's social security system, which is said to be crucial to Singapore's successful healthcare policy. While CPF provides the basis for the government to provide universal access to healthcare, a goal that most progressives emphasise, it nonetheless is based on an underlying belief in individual self-responsibility, a fundamental conservative principle. Singapore's model of governance thus does not align with any one narrow ideology but is a unique hybrid synthesising varied elements. While Singapore is largely a market-based capitalist economy, the government has never shied away from intervening proactively in society when it deems fit.

In political economy terms, Singapore is not a Western-style liberal democratic, free-market capitalist society, nor a Scandinavian-style democratic socialist society, and definitely not a socialist, command economy in the image of Mao's China. It may most accurately be described as a semi-authoritarian developmental state-capitalist government, which is a unique, historically contingent system that emerged in the late 20th century (Low, 2001; Haggard, 2018). This unique hybrid is said to be the source of Singapore's stunning socio-economic success. In short, Singapore's pragmatic leaders have borrowed bits and pieces from various models where relevant, jettisoning others which are not appropriate.

Aside from the ostensibly pragmatic nature of Singapore's policymaking, Singaporeans in general also seem to not care much about political ideology, i.e. abstract political values such as justice, freedom, and democracy. It is mostly accepted that Singaporeans vote and form political preferences based on "bread and butter" issues, tangible benefits relating to material well-being.[3] To such Singaporeans, thinking about politics philosophically might seem anathema. Why care about political *ideas*? Why bother about the liberalism outlined in this book?

In this last chapter, we highlight the value of political philosophy in Singapore. Political philosophy here can be understood in two ways: first, it may refer to the specific political *ideologies* — whether egalitarianism,

---

[3] Ortmann, S. (2015). Singapore 2011–2015: A Tale of Two Elections. *Asia Maoir, 26,* 197–212. Retrieved from: https://www.asiamaior.org/the-journal/08-asia-maior-vol-xxvi-2015/singapore-2011-2015-of-two-elections.html.

socialism, or liberalism — in making policies and discussing politics. Some individuals may be more ideological than others, seeing the world of politics in a way that is very aligned to a consistent set of maxims. It may also refer more generally to the *discipline* of political philosophy, which explores deeper normative questions and moral commitments relating to various political arrangements.

We think that the first is inescapable in, and the second, very constructive for policy discourse. We should be honest enough to admit that we are all to some extent motivated by a specific political ideology, an interrelated set of ideas influencing how we see society and what we envision to be the ideal form of government. When we consider political philosophy more generally, it helps us think more critically about the trade-offs inherent in policymaking, helps us imagine a better future, and more importantly, makes us aware of our own human limitations.

We Cannot Escape Political Ideology

Policymaking that is purely non-ideological and conforming to the neutral dictates of reason is impossible. The PAP itself has some core principles they are motivated by and have also perpetuated ideological hegemony over society. Besides, many critics of the PAP's brand of governance are themselves also situated in their own ideological position. The influence of ideology is always present. As John Maynard Keynes succinctly put it,

> "The ideas of economists and political philosophers, both when they are right and when they are wrong are more powerful than is commonly understood. Indeed, the world is ruled by little else. Practical men, who believe themselves to be quite exempt from any intellectual influences, are usually slaves of some defunct economist".[4]

The PAP has exercised ideological hegemony over Singaporean society, something acknowledged by various scholars. It is said that the PAP leaders believe in the principles of meritocracy, elitism, and multi-racialism — principles that have translated into a discernible pattern in policymaking. Not only are these principles present, there is a strong consensus within

---

[4] Keynes, J. M. (2016). *The General Theory of Employment, Interest and Money*. Stellar Classics.

Singapore society of their legitimacy; the state has socialised Singaporeans into accepting these values (Mauzy & Milne 2002, ch. 5). Kenneth Paul Tan and Teo You Yenn (2013) have also argued that the ideology of neoliberalism holds sway over Singapore's governance. Tan specifically explains that "pragmatism" is largely a rhetorical device used in service of larger neoliberal aims to forge an alliance with global capital (Tan, 2012).

We add an argument: the notion of pragmatism, far from being a form of value-free approach to policymaking, actually legitimises a very specific form of governance with its own assumptions of how government should act. Pragmatism in Singapore entrenches the practice of technocratic paternalism, which is where political leaders are believed to know what's best for Singaporeans and that they should proceed to impose their designs on us. This is not a "neutral" approach to governance, but a value-laden one. Significantly, it exaggerates the capacity of enlightened individuals to capture all the necessary knowledge needed to do what's best for people and elevates the hyper-rationality of our supposedly impartial political masters.

While the PAP political establishment is motivated by some core principles of governance, its critics are similarly bound by their own ideological shackles. The most discernible line of criticism that has emerged in recent years is led by academic scholars such as Teo You Yenn, Donald Low, Yeoh Lam Keong, and P.J Thum. Concerned about the excesses of neoliberalism, these scholars emphasise the importance of greater state provision of social welfare to resolve the injustice of inequality, and state action to solve climate change. Their academic works and commentaries are a reflection of the ascendancy of leftist, democratic socialist political ideas in the wider world, media, and academic institutions.

We cannot escape the power of ideas, however neutral or impartial we claim to be. The inescapable limits of the human cognitive faculty mean that we must resort to mental heuristics and shortcuts to navigate the world (North & Denzau, 1994), and this explains why much of our political choices and preferences are shaped by some form of ideology or set of values. Whether we are pro-establishment (PAP supporters), or anti-establishment (critics of the PAP), we will be lying if we claimed to be "above" ideology.

Some may be concerned that the introduction of "partisan ideologies" may make Singaporean politics more divisive, such as that which we observe in the United States. Surely it would be better if citizens and politicians can achieve consensus and work together for the betterment of Singapore, rather than adamantly defend their ideology at all costs and fail to compromise. Would we want Singaporeans to be politically divided just like Americans, i.e. "big government" versus "small government", "pro-choice" versus "pro-life"? PAP versus anti-PAP? Prime Minister (PM) Lee Hsien Loong himself warned against ideological partisanship evident in American politics: "If Singapore had a blue constituency and a red constituency, I think Singapore will be in trouble".[5] The implication is that the PAP, and Singapore politics more generally, must strive for "consensus".

But why should we see this pessimistically? Singaporeans may become even more engaged democratic citizens when they are more ideologically conscious. The Yale-NUS political scientist Bryan Garsten (2009) had written about how political persuasion, rightly understood, is part and parcel of a healthy deliberative democracy. This is helpful. Political ideology does not exist on an abstract, mental plane, but is regularly communicated in political discourse. It is part of the way we persuade others in politics. We frame our political arguments in ideological terms like "to achieve equality of opportunity". Persuasion in turn is "worthwhile because it requires us to pay attention to our fellow citizens and to display a certain respect for their points of view and their judgments. The effort to persuade requires us to engage with others wherever they stand and to begin our argument there, as opposed to simply asserting that they would adopt our opinion if they were more reasonable" (Garsten, 2009, p. 3). Rightly executed, our practice of ideological persuasion can enrich political discourse, and strengthen our democracy.

Why Political Philosophy is Valuable

We do not claim that political ideology should always motivate our political choices, or even be the main factor. What we suggest is that Singaporeans

---

[5] Chan, R. (2012, November 27). PAP can't afford to be just a note taker of people's views, PM tells party activists. *The Straits Times*. Retrieved from: https://www.asiaone.com/print/News/Latest%2BNews/Singapore/Story/A1Story20121126-385749.html.

should think more philosophically about politics. In simpler words, we should, in our everyday discourse, academic debates, and public forums, consider the deeper values that undergird certain policies, and whether they should be maintained, reformed, or even abolished.

Political philosophy, understood in a more general sense, refers to the systematic and logical reflection of the fundamental values of political society. Political philosophers ask fundamental ethical questions such as: What is the best form of society? What rights do people have and what should the government do, or not do? What is the nature of an individual's relationship with wider society? Not only do political philosophers ask these questions, they also critically approach them, applying careful reflection, sifting through these ideas, and making coherent and informed conclusions.

This is a constructive exercise for both policymakers and ordinary citizens. For one, it helps us **think critically about the deeper trade-offs** between competing ends in political society. Let's consider this in the context of immigration policy in Singapore, in which the dominant position articulated expresses the importance of welcoming foreigners for the larger goal of economic competitiveness. The value of economic growth, however, conflicts with other social ends that Singaporeans may cherish. PM Lee himself acknowledged in a recent 2015 interview that when managing immigrants and foreign workers, "there are no easy choices". He clarified, "There are trade-offs. If we have no foreign workers, our economy suffers, our own lives suffer. We have a lot of foreign workers, the economy will do well, (but) we have other social pressures, other problems…".[6]

Policy questions are complex, because values and ends that people cherish conflict. Should economic growth in Singapore come first? Or should it be sacrificed for the sake of social objectives? PM Lee is right when he mentioned that there are "no easy answers". These questions are, by nature, philosophical questions, and not technical ones. Hence, they must be confronted in the realm of philosophy. Political philosophy, by equipping one with the tools to navigate such questions of value, enables

---

[6] Chang, R. (2015, August 3). No easy choices on foreign worker, immigrant policies: PM Lee. *The Straits Times*. Retrieved from: http://www.straitstimes.com/singapore/no-easy-choices-on-foreign-worker-immigrant-policies-pm-lee.

policymakers — and the public at large — to think more critically when facing such challenges, and make better choices, both in policymaking and at the ballot box. Political philosophy provides these tools because it involves applying reason and logic to carefully evaluate various moral claims, helps to reveal any potential contradictions that may exist, and provides one with justifications to accept some as superior to others.

When political philosophy becomes the stuff of everyday politics, it helps Singaporeans become more politically intelligent. The value of political philosophy is that it helps us determine the ethical standards with which we can judge whether policies are good or bad, just or unjust. Before we can just do "what works", we need to determine what counts as "working". Without such standards, our public debate will lack critical depth. Some Singaporeans will shout "we want fewer foreigners", only to be shouted down by others who insist "we welcome them", with both sides talking past each other since the deeper normative assumptions of both parties are left unexamined. Why do some insist on restricting immigration? What are their deeper moral assumptions? Let's work them out, let's talk, let's deliberate together.

Political philosophy also **inspires us to imagine a better future**. The danger of an approach that excludes all political-philosophic reasoning altogether is that it closes off consideration of new moral possibilities that may be much needed in society, and the world at large. Using the same example of immigration cited above, it is important for policymakers, in fact, for Singaporeans in general, to think beyond the tangible concern of economic growth. The question of immigration touches on whether human beings possess a fundamental and universal right of movement, and whether, as citizens, we have an obligation to strangers. This consideration cannot be avoided, especially when the Rohingya refugees, facing a dire humanitarian crisis, tried to enter Singapore waters in 2009. The official reason for Singapore's rejection of these migrants was due to our small size.[7] This is certainly a valid reason, but we have to wonder if the moral considerations raised above were considered. Even if they are ultimately rejected in favour of a "pragmatic" position, there are good reasons for more

---

[7] The Straits Times. (2015, May 19). Singapore can't accept refugees: MHA. *The Straits Times*. Retrieved from: http://www.straitstimes.com/singapore/singapore-cant-accept-refugees-mha.

robust value-based debate to be conducted in the first place, where moral considerations of justice, duty, and obligation are raised and questioned.

To the extent that political entrepreneurs wish to pursue moral reform of the status quo, political philosophy helps one think of new institutions and new ways to organise our society. It does so because it reminds us that our present institutions are just one set amongst many variations, and are contingent on time and place. Things could change, as they always have in history.

Why Classical Liberal Philosophy?

The classical liberal perspective we present is unique in two ways. First, classical liberalism is a progressive philosophy, but at the same time a very realistic, constrained one. Second, it provides a new third way in local discourse.

It is progressive because it recognises the power of ideas to influence the course of society. Not only do political ideas, or "ideology" for that matter, guide the actions of policymakers, they also shape the future trajectory of a nation, for better or for worse. The scholars Wayne Leighton and Edward Lopez (2014) have provided a framework showing how political change is affected by the actions of intellectuals (the second-hand dealers of information in mass society, like journalists) and academic scribblers (academics in universities). This is a serious matter. The prosperity that humanity enjoys in the modern world today may itself be traced back to a shift in the intellectual climate of opinion in the 16th century towards greater liberty and dignity for commerce and markets (McCloskey, 2011). Conversely, the rise of 20th-century totalitarian ideologies triumphed over liberal ideas which were ascendant just one century before, an unfortunate turn of events which led to global upheavals between the two World Wars (Mises, 2011).

However, we do not advocate naïve utopianism. Political philosophy, rightly practised, is also sensitive to the real-world circumstances that limit our ability to redesign society from scratch. Good philosophy pays attention to the insights from social sciences, especially the discipline of political economy (Schmidtz, 2016; Pennington, 2017). On this note, the authors have emphasised how market outcomes, while imperfect, may made worse by equally, if not more, imperfect political actors, who lack the incentive and knowledge to do what's right. State intervention may not be the proper solution to the alleged ills of market societies commonly pointed out by its critics, i.e. inequality (Chapters 6 & 7) environmental damage (Chapter 8).

Classical liberalism is also a new third way in Singapore policy discourse. Our perspective accords a high premium on market-based mechanisms since economic freedom is an important engine of welfare. This is why we have expressed scepticism regarding the rising chorus of voices in Singapore calling for egalitarian policies such as wealth & income redistribution, and state regulation for the purposes of environmental protection.

Given that progressive, democratic socialist ideas are in the ascendancy all around the world, we are also concerned about how the new generation of youths in our universities are intellectually influenced to condemn the global capitalist order we currently live in.[8] While there is indeed much room for reform in global economies, it is of concern if young people are oblivious to the way markets have facilitated tremendous socio-economic progress in history and how they remain much needed for millions more in under-developed regions.

Importantly, we are not political conservatives defending the PAP establishment. While the PAP's brand of governance has much to be admired, given its widespread use of market-mechanisms in policymaking, the emphasis of resource efficiency in delivering public goods, and the emphasis on meritocracy as a guiding principle, it nonetheless falls short of what we offer as the classical liberal ideal. The authoritarian controls on civil liberties and political freedoms are a concern, which other liberals have pointed out before. The government's strong role in the economy through government-linked corporations and sovereign wealth funds also pose a substantial barrier to market competition.

On a deeper level, beyond any specific policy implementation, epistemic liberalism also provides a counterpoint to the PAP government's strong belief in their ability to rationally plan for Singapore's future. Central

---

[8] The Economist. (2019, February 14). Millennial socialists want to shake up the economy and save the climate. *The Economist.* Retrieved from: https://www.economist.com/briefing/2019/02/14/millennial-socialists-want-to-shake-up-the-economy-and-save-the-climate.

planning works mainly for well-defined policy areas with very clear-cut solutions and where high compliance is necessary. This is why vaccinations for infectious diseases (eg. smallpox, Covid-19), for instance, should be subject to command-control. There is a well-known, clear cut solution to the problem (contagious diseases), and there is a need for high compliance (no immunisation means contagion & death). However, many of the tasks that governments regularly engage in have unclear, even complex, means-ends relationships. Planning the economy, for instance, is one of the most complex tasks one can ever conceive, especially given the challenge of disruptive innovation and global supply chains today. Socially engineering outcomes to achieve a harmonious, perfect society risks systemic and unintended consequences. Epistemic liberalism warns us against a fatal conceit, the dangerous presumption that we have the knowledge needed to engineer outcomes as we wish. Evolution, not intelligent design, is the preferable path.

From Philosophy to Policy

We hope that through this book, Singaporeans, *for the first time*, are presented with an alternative, classical liberal perspective on governance, a perspective which is important, but which has never featured in any prominent way before. We also hope that academic scholars, especially those dealing with local public policy concerns, take seriously the contributions of market principles, especially implications of incentive and knowledge problems. Such insights, arguably, are lost in the current political landscape which either prizes technocratic planning by the state (PAP), or its replacement with progressive, left-leaning principles (PAP's critics).

Classical liberalism provides guidance on policymaking. On one level, classical liberalism evaluates the philosophical underpinnings of particular institutional arrangements. Models of governance may be motivated by conservative philosophical principles (Scruton, 2007), egalitarian principles (see Arneson [2013] for an overview), and communitarian principles (see Bell [2016] for an overview), amongst others. The epistemic liberalism approach presented in this book questions whether the knowledge necessary for such moral evaluation is available to a single mind, and recommends pluralistic arrangements allowing different values to coexist. It is with this understanding that we provided a critique of the way meritocracy has been operationalised in Singapore (Chapter 3), how "Asian values" have been used to disavow liberalism (Chapter 2), and how governance has overwhelmingly been structured on technocratic lines (Chapter 4).

On another level, in the realm of political economy, classical liberalism emphasises the superiority of market institutions over centralised ones, since they can better account for incentive and knowledge problems (see Haeffele [2018] for a volume on how such concepts are applied empirically in policy research). It allows us to evaluate policies by looking at the right mix of public and private allocation of resources that will lead to the best outcomes, and whether unintended consequences are likely to occur in centralised arrangements.

Are there specific policy implications flowing from our position? Indeed there are. Here are the broad areas of policy reform to be considered in Singapore, subject to further empirical research.

1. Industrial policy. The Singapore government has relied on industrial planning to restructure our economy to achieve ever-higher levels of value-add. This has involved the use of grants, incentives, and the provision of government services. It is worthwhile asking whether this top-down approach is best placed to help Singapore become an innovative global city, a task that requires a strong indigenous private sector driven by small enterprises. This is especially needful since academic economists have criticised the weak indigenous, local private sector in Singapore. Specifically, Hawyee Auyong and Donald Low (2014) highlighted the two-tier economy in Singapore, with the local business sector subject to lower productivity and innovation efficiency. Pang Eng Fong and Linda Lim (2016, p. 156) described how "domestic private enterprise…has probably been crowded out by the large state-linked and multinational sectors". Tan Kim Song and Manu Bhaskaran (2016, p. 51) echoed the same tune, saying that Singapore's economic performance was achieved "without developing the inherent production and indigenous innovation capacity". Linda Lim (2014) further added that Singapore's skills shortage is "exacerbated

by talent diversion into the large state sector", and that "the national private sector of entrepreneurial and corporate employers is much smaller, less-developed, and lower-paying than in other high income developed economies."

2. Housing and infrastructure. Singapore has managed to, through a hybrid system, provide basic housing for all since our independence. As we move on to a new phase of development, policymakers will have to think of how best to optimise limited space to meet the needs of a growing and ageing population. Classical liberal policy research will hopefully recommend ways for private actors to find creative uses of space to transcend natural limitations and envision new forms of living. Already, Airbnb, a leading private alternative to state-housing, is subject to stiff restrictions.[9] It is worth asking: is this doing more harm than good?

3. Education and learning. While the Singapore education system is recognised for its excellence, it is not without its critics, such as the concern of high stress, criticisms of rote learning, and a lack of multiple pathways to success. It is worth asking whether the centralised arrangements in local education contribute to these problems and whether market alternatives may provide more diverse pedagogical techniques for students and viable pathways to self-actualisation. Private tuition has already a big industry but is very much serving the unmet needs of families who are locked within the state system. With greater space afforded to private educators, will we see more valuable alternatives springing up?

4. Permissionless innovation. The Singapore government is known to be paternalistic and prone to the use of prohibition as a policy tool. It is worth asking if this fosters an overly precautionary approach that will stifle new innovations, which necessarily requires a disruptive, anti-establishment frame of mind.[10] It is worth asking how a change in culture, not just in rules, may be necessary for Singapore to harness

---

[9] Neo, R. W. (2019, May 8). Short-term home sharing remains illegal in Singapore; Airbnb disappointed. *TODAY Online*. Retrieved from: https://www.todayonline.com/singapore/short-term-home-sharing-remains-illegal-singapore-airbnb-disappointed.

[10] Permissionless Innovation. (n.d.) *Book*. Retrieved from: https://permissionlessinnovation.org/book/.

disruptive innovations that will enhance various aspects of society, from transportation, to healthcare, to urban living.

5. Civil society, grassroots activism, and political competition. Singapore's political system is well recognised as being closed and unfriendly to competitive pressures. Much has been said about this. It is also worthwhile to consider how media and political liberalisation in Singapore contribute not just to democratic principles, but more pragmatic considerations such as an expansion of our creative industries.

We clarify once again that this book is **not a policy manual**, giving specific, detailed guidelines for government policies in every realm. This book is not a blueprint for healthcare policy, education policy, economic policy, and so on. Such detailed policy prescriptions are beyond the scope of this book or any one single book for that matter. In fact, as classical liberals, we place great emphasis on dynamic competition that produces knowledge — *precisely because we do not always know what is best for others* (Hayek, 1968). For classical liberal ideas to be made more relevant to these specific policy areas, more empirical policy research will need to be conducted, showing the importance of competition, market principles, and the private sector in generating positive outcomes.[11] This book hopefully presents a stepping stone towards further research along these lines. Classical liberalism constitutes a progressive research programme.

---

[11] Examples of such research done may be found in pro-market think tanks such as the Mercatus Center and Cato Institute in the United States, the Institute for Economic Affairs in the UK, the Institute for Democracy and Economic Affairs in Malaysia, the Center for Indonesian Policy Studies in Indonesia, and many more.

References

Abdullah, W. J. (2017). Bringing Ideology in: Differing oppositional challenges to hegemony in Singapore and Malaysia. *Government and Opposition, 52*(3), 483–510.

Acemoglu, D., & Robinson, J. (2012). *Why Nations Fail: The Origins of Power, Prosperity, and Poverty.* Crown Business.

Acemoglu, D., & Robinson, J. (2019). *The Narrow Corridor: States, Societies, and the Fate of Liberty.* London: Penguin.

Achen, C., & Bartels, L. (2016). *Democracy for Realists.* New Jersey: Princeton University Press.

American Enterprise Institute. (2018, January 31). *Yes, the US Middle Class is Shrinking, but it's Because Americans are Moving up.* Retrieved from: https://www.aei.org/carpe-diem/yes-the-us-middle-class-is-shrinking-but-its-because-americans-are-moving-up-and-no-americans-are-not-struggling-to-afford-a-home/.

Amsden, A. (2000). East Asia's challenge. *The American Prospect.* Retrieved from: https://prospect.org/features/east-asia-s-challenge/.

Anderson, B., & Latham, A. (1986). *The Market in History: Papers Presented at a Symposium Held 9–13 September 1984 at St. George's House, Windsor Castle, Under the Auspices of the Liberty Fund.* Cambridge University Press.

Anderson, T. L., & Leal, D. R. (2015). *Free Market Environmentalism for the Next Generation.* New York: Palgrave Macmillan.

Ariely, D. (2008). *Predictably Irrational.* New York: HarperCollins Publishers.

Arneson, R. (2013). *Egalitarianism.* Retrieved from: https://plato.stanford.edu/entries/egalitarianism/.

Auyong, H., & Low, D. (2014). *Productivity Challenge: Part IV.* Singapore: Lee Kuan Yew School of Public Policy.

Bacevich, A. J. (2017). *America's War for the Greater Middle East: A Military History.* Random House.

Badhwar, N. K. (2016). Justice within the limits of human nature alone. *Social Philosophy and Policy, 33*(1–2), 193–213.

Baechler, J. (1975). *The Origins of Capitalism.* Palgrave Macmillan.

Baraka, A. (2013, September 2). The human rights hypocrisy of the west. *CounterPunch.* Retrieved from: https://www.counterpunch.org/2013/09/02/the-human-rights-hypocrisy-of-the-west/.

Barnett, R. (2014). *The Structure of Liberty.* Oxford University Press.

Barr, M. (2000a). *Lee Kuan Yew: The Beliefs Behind the Man.* Georgetown University Press.

Barr, M. (2000b). Lee Kuan Yew and the Asian Values Debate. *Asian Studies Review, 24*(3), 309–334.

Barr, M. (2006a). Beyond technocracy: The culture of elite governance in Lee Hsien Loong's Singapore. *Asian Studies Review, 30*(1), 1–18.

Barr, M. (2006b). The charade of meritocracy. *Far Eastern Economic Review, 169*(8), 18–22.

Barr, M. (2019). *Singapore: A Modern History.* I. B. Taurus.

Barr, M. (2020, April 16). *Singapore: The Limits of a Technocratic Approach to Healthcare.* Retrieved from: https://newnaratif.com/research/singapore-the-limits-of-a-technocratic-approach-to-healthcare/share/orireyl.n.q.onq/4ebd8559ced222717d3db09651225926/.

Barr, M., & Rahim, L. Z. (2019). *The Limits of Authoritarian Governance in Singapore's Developmental State.* Palgrave Macmillan.

Basker, E., Foster, L., & Kilmek, S. (2015). Customer-labor substitution: Evidence from gasoline stations. *Center for Economic Studies.*

Bauer, J. R., & Bell, D. A. (1999). *The East Asian Challenge for Human Rights.* Cambridge University Press.

Baumol, W. (1996). Entrepreneurship: Productive, Unproductive, and Destructive. *Journal of Business Venturing, 11*(1), 3–22.

Baumol, W. (2004). *The Free-Market Innovation Machine: Analyzing the Growth Miracle of Capitalism.* University of Chicago Press.

Baumol, W. Litan, R., & Schramm, C. (2007). *Good Capitalism, Bad Capitalism, and the Economics of Growth and Prosperity.* New Haven, CT: Yale University Press.

BBC. (2015, March 22). *In Quotes: Lee Kuan Yew.* Retrieved from: https://www.bbc.com/news/world-asia-31582842.

BBC. (2017, February 27). Singapore PM on free speech and trade. *BBC*. Retrieved from: https://www.bbc.co.uk/programmes/p04v5v32?fbclid=IwAR14LEMy NjxhJfvbPwrhYuBMS4adPHeXW0TmPCoQP9VFEU91dGyeat2jjto.

Beito, D. T. (2000). *From Mutual Aid to the Welfare State: Fraternal Societies and Social Services, 1890–1967*. London: The University of North Carolina Press.

Beito, D. T., Gordon, P., & Tabarrok, A. (2002). *The Voluntary City: Choice, Community, and Civil Society*. California: The Independent Institute.

Bell, D. (2006). *Beyond Liberal Democracy*. Princeton University Press.

Bell, D. (2008). East Asia and the West: The Impact on Confucianism on Anglo-American Political Theory. In J. Dryzek, B. Honig, & A. Philips, *Oxford Handbook on Political Theory*. Oxford University Press.

Bell, D. (2016). *Communitarianism*. Retrieved from: https://plato.stanford.edu/entries/communitarianism/.

Bell, D. (2018). *The China Model: Political Meritocracy and the Limits of Democracy*. Princeton University Press.

Bell, D., & Li, C. (2013). *The East Asian Challenge for Democracy*. Cambridge University Press.

Benkler, Y. (2006). *The Wealth of Networks: How Social Production Transforms Markets and Freedoms*. New Haven; London: Yale University Press.

Benson, B. (2011). *Enterprise of Law: Justice Without the State*. Independent Institute.

Berger, P. (1987). *The Capitalist Revolution: Fifty Propositions about Prosperity, Equality, and Liberty*. Wildwood House.

Berggren, N. (2012). Time for behavioral political economy? An analysis of articles in behavioral economics. *Review of Austrian Economics, 25*(3), 199–221.

Boaz, D. (1997). *Libertarianism: A Primer*. New York: Free Press.

Boettke, P. (1990a). *The Political Economy of Soviet Socialism*. Springer.

Boettke, P. (1990b). The theory of spontaneous order and cultural evolution in the social theory of FA Hayek. *Cultural Dynamics, 3*(1), 61–83.

Boettke, P. (1994). The political infrastructure of economic development. *Human Systems Management, 13*(2), 89–100.

Boettke, P., & Nicoara, O. (2015). What Have We Learned from the Collapse of Communism? In *Oxford Handbook of Austrian Economics*. Oxford University Press.

Boettke, P., Aligica, P., & Tarko, V. (2019). *Public Governance and the Classical-Liberal Perspective*. Oxford University Press.

Boettke, P., Caceres, W. Z., & Martin, A. (2013). Error Is Obvious, Coordination Is the Puzzle. In R. Frantz, & R. Leeson (Eds.), *Hayek and Behavioral Economics* (pp. 90–109). London: Palgrave MacMillan.

Boettke, P., Coyne, C., & Leeson, P. (2008). Institutional stickiness and the new development economics. *The American Journal of Economics and Sociology, 67*(2), 331–358.

Boh, J. (2017). 'Nudging' Singapore to be cleaner and greener. *Ethos* (17).

Booth, P. (2016). *Taxation, Government Spending and Economic Growth*. London: Institute for Economic Affairs.

Bovard, J. (1996). *Archer Daniels Midland: A Cast Study in Corporate Welfare*. Washington DC: Cato Institute.

Brennan, J. (2016). *Political Philosophy — An Introduction*. Washington D.C.: Cato Institute.

Brennan, J. (2017). *Against Democracy*. Princeton University Press.

Brennan, J., & Schmidtz, D. (2009). *A Brief History of Liberty*. Wiley.

Brooks, A. (2010, July 14). *The Secret to Human Happiness is Earned Success*. Retrieved from: http://www.aei.org/publication/the-secret-to-human-happiness-is-earned-success/.

Buchanan, J. M. (1999). Politics without Romance: A Sketch of Positive Public Choice Theory and Its Normative Implications. In J. M. Buchanan, *The Collected Works of James M. Buchanan. Volume 1: The Logical Foundations of Constitutional Liberty* (pp. 45–59). Indianapolis: Liberty Fund, Inc.

Burczak, T. (2013). A Hayekian Case for a Basic Income. In G. L. Nell, *Basic Income and the Free Market* (pp. 49–64). Palgrave Macmillan.

Burkhauser, R. (2017). The Rich, and Everyone Else, Get Richer. In J.-P. Delsol, N. Lecaussin, & E. Martin (Eds.) *Anti-Piketty: Capital for the 21st century.* (pp. 77–80). Cato Institute.

Camerer, C. F., & Loewenstein, G. (2004). Behavioral Economics: Past, Present, Future. In C. F. Camerer, G. Loewenstein, & M. Rabin (Eds.), *Advances in Behavioral Economics* (pp. 3–51). Princeton University Press.

Campagnolo, L., & Davide, M. (2019). Can the Paris Deal Boost SDGs Achievement? An Assessment of Climate Mitigation Co-benefits or Side-effects on Poverty and Inequality. *World Development, 122*, 96–109.

Caplan, B. (2011). *The Myth of the Rational Voter: Why Democracies Choose Bad Policies*. New Jersey: Princeton University Press.

Caporale, T., & Poitras, M. (2017). *The Trouble with a Keynesian Stimulus Spending*. Mercatus Center.

Carpenter, T. G. (2019). *Gullible Superpower — U.S. Support for Bogus Democratic Movements*. Cato Institute.

Chamlee-Wright, E. (2002). *The Cultural Foundations of Economic Development: Urban Female Entrepreneurship in Ghana*. Routledge.

Chamlee-Wright, E. (2010). *Qualitative Methods and the Pursuit of Economic Understanding. Society for the Development of Austrian Economics* (pp. 321–331). Texas: Springer.

Chamlee-Wright, E., & Storr, V. (2015). Social Economy as an Extension of the Austrian Research Program. In P. Boettke, & C. Coyne, *The Oxford Handbook of Austrian Economics.* Oxford University Press.

Chan, H. C., & Haq, O. (1987). *S. Rajaratnam: The Prophetic and the Political — Selected Speeches and Writings of S. Rajaratnam.* Singapore: Grahm Brash.

Chan, J. (2013). *Confucian Perfectionism: A Political Philosophy for Modern Times.* Princeton University Press.

Chang, Y. (2016). Energy and Environmental Policy. In L. Y. Lim (Ed.), *Singapore's Economic Development: Retrospection and Reflections* (pp. 299–319). Singapore: World Scientific.

Chia, S. Y. (2005). The Singapore model of industrial policy: Past evolution and current thinking. *Presentation at the Second LAEBA Annual Conference.*

Chirakijja, J., Jayachandran, S., & Ong, P. (2019). Inexpensive heating reduces winter mortality. *National Bureau of Economic Research.*

Chomsky, N., & Herman, E. S. (1988). *Manufacturing Consent: The Political Economy of the Mass Media.* New York: Random House.

Choo, D. (2012, December 3). PM Lee defends system of meritocracy. *Yahoo Singapore.* Retrieved from: https://sg.news.yahoo.com/pm-lee-defends-system-of-meritocracy-055639189.html?guccounter=1.

Chua, B. H. (2003). Multiculturalism in Singapore: An instrument of social control. *Race Class, 44*(58), 58–77.

Chua, B. H. (2017). *Liberalism Disavowed: Communitarianism and State Capitalism in Singapore.* Singapore: NUS Press.

Clemens, J., Kahn, L., & Meer, J. (2018). The minimum wage, fringe benefits and worker welfare. *National Bureau of Economic Research.*

Clemens, M. (2011). Economics and emigration: Trillion-dollar bills on the sidewalk?. *Journal of Economic Perspectives, 25*(3), 83–106.

Cofnas, N., Carl, N., & Woodley, M. (2018). Does activism in social science explain conservatives' distrust of scientists? *Am Soc, 49,* 135–148.

Confucius. (2001). Analects. In P. J. Ivanhoe (Ed.), *Readings in Chinese Classical Philosophy* (B. W. Van Norden, Trans.). New York: Seven Bridges Press.

Confucius. (2003). *Analects: With Selections from Traditional Commentaries.* Hackett Publishing.

Cowen, T. (2002). *Creative Destruction: How Globalization Is Changing the World's Cultures.* Princeton University Press.

Coyne, C. (2013). *Doing Bad by Doing Good: Why Humanitarian Action Fails.* Stanford University Press.

Coyne, C., & Ryan, M. (2009). With friends like these, who needs enemies? Aiding the world's worst dictators. *Independent Institute, 14*(1), 26–44.

Cromwell, D. (2012). *Why Are We the Good Guys?: Reclaiming Your Mind from the Delusions of Propaganda.* John Hunt Publishing.

Davie, S. (2015, July 4). 7 in 10 parents send their children for tuition: ST poll. *The Straits Times.* Retrieved from https://www.straitstimes.com/singapore/education/7-in-10-parents-send-their-children-for-tuition-st-poll.

DeCanio, S. (2014). Democracy, the market, and the logic of social choice. *American Journal of Political Science, 58*(3), 637–652.

Dechezleprêtre, A., & Sato, M. (2017). The impacts of environmental regulations on competitiveness. *Review of Environmental Economics and Policy, 11*(2), 183–206.

Delsol, J.-P. (2017). The Great Process of Equalization of Conditions. In J.-P. Delsol, N. Lecaussin, & E. Martin (Eds.) *Anti-Piketty: Capital for the 21st century.* (pp. 5–18). Cato Institute.

Demsetz, H. (1969). Information and efficiency: Another viewpoint. *The Journal of Law and Economics, 12*(1), 1–22.

De Soto, H. (2003). *The Mystery of Capital: Why Capitalism Triumphs in the West and Fails Everywhere Else.* Basic Books.

Dworkin, R. (2000). *Sovereign Virtue: The Theory and Practice of Equality.* Cambridge: Harvard University Press.

Easterly, W. (2006). *The White Man's Burden: Why the West's Efforts to Aid the Rest Have Done So Much Ill and So Little Good.* Penguin.

Easterly, W. (2014). *The Tyranny of Experts.* Basic Books.

Eberstadt, N. (2017). Longevity, Education and the Huge New Worldwide Increases in Equality. In J.-P. Delsol, N. Lecaussin, & E. Martin (Eds.) *Anti-Piketty: Capital in the 21st century* (pp. 19–30). Cato Institute.

Energy Market Authority. (2018). *Singapore Energy Statistics.* Singapore.

Epstein, R. (1995). *Simple Rules for a Complex World.* Chicago: Harvard University Press.

Feldstein, M. (2017). Piketty's Numbers Don't Add Up. In J.-P. Delsol, N. Lecaussin, & E. Martin (Eds.) *Anti-Piketty: Capital for the 21st century.* (pp. 73–76). Cato Institute.

Fingarette, H. (1978). Response to Professor Rosemont. *Philosophy East and West, 28*(4), 511–514.

Francesch-Huidobro, M. (2008). *Governance, Politics and the Environment: A Singapore Study.* Singapore: Institute of Southeast Asian Studies.

Freedom House. (2019). Singapore country report. *Freedom House.* Retrieved from: https://freedomhouse.org/report/freedom-world/2019/singapore.

Friedman, J. (2009). A crisis of politics, not economics. Complexity, ignorance and policy failure. *Critical Review, 21*(2–3), 127–183.

Friedman, M. (1962). *Capitalism and Freedom.* Chicago: University of Chicago Press.

Fund, J. (2015, March 27). In Singapore, Lee Kuan Yew Built a Welfare State that works. *National Review.* Retrieved from: https://www.nationalreview.com/2015/03/singapore-lee-kuan-yew-built-welfare-state-works-john-fund/.

Garsten, B. (2009). *Saving Persuasion: A Defense of Rhetoric and Judgment.* Harvard University Press.

Gaus, G. (2015). Public Reason Liberalism. In S. Wall (Ed.), *The Cambridge Companion to Liberalism* (pp. 112–140). Cambridge University Press.

Gaus, G. (2017). Hayekian Classical Liberalism. In J. Brennan, B. van der Vossen, & D. Schmidtz, *The Routledge Handbook of Libertarianism.* Taylor and Francis.

Gee, C. (2012, October 2). The educational 'Arms Race': All for one, loss for all — part 2. *IPS Commons.* Retrieved from: https://www.ipscommons.sg/the-educational-arms-race-all-for-one-loss-for-all-part-2/.

Geertz, C. (1973). *The Interpretation of Cultures.* New York: Basic Books, Inc.

George, C. (2007). Consolidating authoritarian rule: Calibrated coercion in Singapore. *The Pacific Review, 20*(2), 127–145.

George, C. (2012). *Freedom from the Press: Journalism and State Power in Singapore.* Singapore: NUS Press.

George, C. (2018, November 15). *My Book of the Year 2018.* Retrieved from: https://singaporeunbound.org/blog/2018/11/4/my-book-of-the-year-2018-1.

George, T. (1973). *Lee Kuan Yew's Singapore.* London: Andre Deutsch.

Ghai, Y. (1999). Rights, Social Justice, Globalization in East Asia. In D. Bell, & J. Bauer, *The East Asian Challenge for Human Rights* (pp. 241–263). Cambridge University Press.

Gigerenzer, G., & Todd, P. M. (1999). *Simple Heuristics That Make Us Smart.* Oxford University Press.

Giles, H. A. (2013). *Chuang Tzu.* Routledge.

Gilmor, D. (2004). *We the Media.* California: O'Reilly Media, Inc.

Global Times. (2017, June 14). *Can Big Data Help to Resurrect the Planned Economy?* Retrieved from: http://www.globaltimes.cn/content/1051715.shtml.

Goh, C. T. (1988). *Agenda for Action: Goals and Challenges.* Singapore: Singapore National Printers.

Gornall, J. (2017, April 3). *How the NHS Wastes a Staggering £7.6bn a Year.* Retrieved from: https://www.dailymail.co.uk/health/article-4377250/How-NHS-wastes-7-6bn-year.html.

Goulder, L. H. (2000). Economic impacts of environmental policies. *National Bureau of Economic Research.*

Guriev, S., & Rachinsky, A. (2005). The role of oligarchs in Russian capitalism. *Journal of Economic Perspectives, 19*(1), 131–150.

Gurri, M. (2018). *The Revolt of The Public and the Crisis of Authority in the New Millennium.* San Francisco: Stripe Press.

Gwartney, J., Holcombe, R., & Lawson, R. (1999). Economic freedom and the environment for economic growth. *Journal of Institutional and Theoretical Economics, 155*(4), 1–21.

Habegger, B. (2010). Strategic foresight in public policy: Reviewing the experiences of the UK, Singapore, and the Netherlands. *Futures, 42*(1), 49–58.

Hack, K. (2012). Framing Singapore's History. In N. Tarling, *Studying Singapore's Past: C. M. Turnbull and the History of Modern Singapore* (pp. 17–64). Singapore: NUS Press.

Haeffele, S. (2018). *Knowledge and Incentives in Policy: Using Public Choice and Market Process Theory to Analyze Public Policy Issues.* Rowman and Littlefield.

Haggard, S. (2018). *Developmental States.* Cambridge University Press.

Hall, P. A., & Soskice, D. (2001). *Varieties of Capitalism: The Institutional Foundations of Comparative Advantage.* Oxford University Press.

Han, H. (2016). Singapore, a Garden City: Authoritarian environmentalism in a developmental state. *Journal of Environment & Development, 26*(1), 1–22.

Hanke, S., & Walters, S. (1997). Economic freedom, prosperity and equality. *CATO Journal, 17*(2), 117–146.

Harris, S. (2014, July 29). The social laboratory. *Foreign Policy.* Retrieved from: https://foreignpolicy.com/2014/07/29/the-social-laboratory/.

Hart, D. M., Chartier, G., Kenyon, R. M., & Long, R. T. (2017). *Social Class and State Power: Exploring an Alternative Radical Tradition.* Springer.

Haseltine, W. A. (2013). *Affordable Excellence: The Singapore Healthcare Story.* Washington D.C.: Brookings Institution Press.

Hayek, F. A. (1945). The use of knowledge in society. *The American Economic Review, 35*(4), 519–530.

Hayek, F. A. (1952). *The Sensory Order: An Inquiry Into the Foundations of Theoretical Psychology.* Chicago: University of Chicago Press.

Hayek, F. A. (1960). *The Constitution of Liberty.* Chicago: The University of Chicago Press.

Hayek, F. A. (1968). Competition as a Discovery Procedure. In B Caldwell, *The Collected Works of Friedrich Hayek: Market and Other Orders*. Routledge.

Hayek, F. A. (2002). Competition as a discovery procedure. *The Quarterly Journal of Austrian Economics, 5*(3), 9–23.

Hayek, F. A. (2014). *The Constitution of Liberty*. Routledge.

Heinrich, J., Boyd, R., Bowles, S., Camerer, C., Fehr, E., Gintis, H., & McElreath, R. (2001). In search of homo economicus: Behavioral experiments in 15 small-scale societies. *American Economic Review, 91*(2), 73–78.

Heritage Foundation. (2019). *The Power of Economic Freedom*. Retrieved from: https://www.heritage.org/index/pdf/2019/book/chapter4.pdf.

High, J. (2017). *Humane Economics*. Mercatus Center.

Ho, P. (2010, January 1). *Thinking About the Future: What the Public Service Can Do*. Retrieved from: https://www.csc.gov.sg/articles/thinking-about-the-future-what-the-public-service-can-do.

Ho, P. (2012). *Governing for the Future: What Governments can do*. Retrieved from: https://www.rsis.edu.sg/wp-content/uploads/rsis-pubs/WP248.pdf.

Ho, P. (2015, February 10). *Complexity and Urban Governance*. Retrieved from: https://www.csf.gov.sg/files/media-centre/speeches/2015-02-10-peter-ho---vienna-conference-on-complexity.pdf.

Ho, P. (2016a, February 14). *Simulations, Exercises and Games in the Civil Service*. Retrieved from: https://www.csc.gov.sg/articles/simulations-exercises-and-games-in-the-civil-service

Ho, P. (2016b). *The Power of Games to Drive Policy Outcomes*. Retrieved from https://www.csc.gov.sg/docs/default-source/ethos/ethos_16(web).pdf.

Holcombe, R. (2018). *Political Capitalism — How Economic and Political Power Is Made and Maintained*. Cambridge University Press.

Horwitz, S. (2010). The Microeconomic Foundations of Macroeconomic Disorder: An Austrian Perspective on the Great Recession of 2008. In S. Kates, *Macroeconomic Theory and Its Failings* (pp. 96–111). Edward Elgar Publishing.

Horwitz, S. (2015). *Hayek's Modern Family: Classical Liberalism and the Evolution of Social Institutions*. Palgrave Macmillan.

Horwitz, S. (2015). Inequality, mobility, and being poor in America. *Social Philosophy and Policy*.

Hsiao, K.-c. (1979). *A History of Chinese Political Thought* (Vol. 1). (F. Mote, Trans.) Princeton University Press.

Huemer, M. (2013). *The Problem of Political Authority — An Examination of the Right to Coerce and the Duty to Obey*. Palgrave Macmillan.

Huggins, L. (2013). *Environmental Entrepreneurship: Markets Meet the Environment in Unexpected Places.* Edward Elgar Publishing.

Hundt, D., & Uttam, J. (2017). *Varieties of Capitalism in Asia: Beyond the Developmental State.* Springer.

Institute for Energy Research. (2018, June 18). *Countries with Carbon Taxes See Higher Energy Prices.* Retrieved from: https://www.instituteforenergyresearch. org/international-issues/countries-carbon-taxes-see-higher-energy-prices/.

Jackson, T., & Eisen, B. (2019). *Assessing British Columbia's Tax Competitiveness.* Vancouver: Fraser Institute.

Jadhav, N. Y., Mhaisalkar, S., & Püttgen, T. (2016). Energy Transitions — Energy Efficiency and Renewable Energy Challenges in the Tropics. In T. Y. Soon (Ed.), *50 Years of Environment: Singapore's Journey Towards Environmental Sustainability* (pp. 127–168). Singapore: World Scientific.

Johnson, N. D., & Koyama, M. (2017). States and economic growth: Capacity and constraints. *Explorations in Economic History, 64*, 1–20.

Keane, J. (2015, April 28). *Why Read Tocqueville's Democracy in America?.* Retrieved from: https://theconversation.com/why-read-tocquevilles-democracy-in-america-40802.

Kharas, H., & Hamel, K. (2019, September 2018). *A Global Tipping Point: Half the World is Now Middle Class or Wealthier.* Retrieved from: https://www. brookings.edu/blog/future-development/2018/09/27/a-global-tipping-point-half-the-world-is-now-middle-class-or-wealthier/.

Kiesling, L. (2014). The Knowledge Problem. In C. J. Coyne, & P. Boettke (Eds.), *Oxford Handbook of Austrian Economics.* Oxford University Press.

Kirzner, I. (1997). Entrepreneurial discovery and the competitive market process: An Austrian approach. *Journal of Economic Literature, 35*(1), 60–85.

Kjellberg, P., & Ivanhoe, P. J. (1996). *Essays on Skepticism, Relativism, and Ethics in the Zhuangzi.* SUNY Press.

Kling, A. (2017). *Three Languages of Politics.* Washington D.C.: Cato Institute.

Koh, T. (2000). Asian values reconsidered. *Asia Pacific Review, 7*(1), 131–136.

Kong, L. (2000). Cultural policy in Singapore: Negotiating economic and sociocultural agendas. *Geoforum, 31*(4), 409–424.

Kong, L., & Sinha, V. (2015). *Food, Foodways and Foodscapes — Culture, Community and Consumption in Post-Colonial Singapore.* Singapore: World Scientific.

Koppl, R. (2018). *Expert Failure.* Cambridge University Press.

Kukathas, C. (2000). Does Hayek speak to Asia? *Independent Review, 4*(3), 419–429.

Kukathas, C. (2003). *The Liberal Archipelago.* Oxford University Press.

Kukathas, C. (2006). The mirage of global justice. *Social Philosophy and Policy,* *23*(1), 1–28.

Lakner, C., & Milanovic, B. (2014, May 27). *Global Income Distribution: From the Fall of the Berlin Wall to the Great Recession.* Retrieved from: https://voxeu. org/article/global-income-distribution-1988.

Langbert, M. (2018). *Homogenous: The Political Affiliations of Elite Liberal Arts College Faculty.* Retrieved from: https://www.nas.org/academic-questions/31/2/homogenous_the_political_affiliations_of_elite_liberal_arts_college_faculty.

Langbert, M., Quain, A. J., & Klein, D. B. (2016). Faculty voter registration in economics, history, journalism, law, and psychology. *Econ Journal Watch,* *13*(3), 422–451.

Langrill, R., & Storr, V. (2015). Contemporary Austrian Economics and the New Economic Sociology. In C. Coyne, & P. Boettke (Eds.) *Oxford Handbook of Austrian Economics*, (pp. 547–562). Oxford, UK: Oxford University Press.

Lau, D. (2003). *Mencius.* The Chinese University Press.

Lavoie, D. (1986). The market as a procedure for discovery and conveyance of inarticulate knowledge. *Comparative Economic Studies, 28*, 1–19.

Lavoie, D., & Chamlee-Wright, E. (2001). *Culture and Enterprise: The Development, Representation and Morality of Business.* London, UK: Routledge.

Lebar, M. (2016). Virtue Ethics. In A. Powell & G. Babcock, *Arguments for Liberty.* Cato Institute.

Lee Kuan Yew School of Public Policy. (2018, November 13). Meritocracy in Singapore: Solution or problem? *Lee Kuan Yew School of Public Policy.* Retrieved from: https://lkyspp.nus.edu.sg/gia/article/meritocracy-in-singapore-solution-or-problem.

Lee, H. L. (2018, May 17). Singapore at a turning point. *The Straits Times.* Retrieved from: https://www.straitstimes.com/opinion/singapore-at-a-turning-point.

Lee, H., & Lee, T. (2019). From contempt of court to fake news. *Media International Australia*, 1–12.

Lee, K. Y. (1992, November 10). Democracy, Human Rights and the Realities. Tokyo, Japan.

Lee, K. Y. (2000). *From Third World to First: The Singapore Story 1965–2000.* New York: HarperCollins Publishers.

Lee, K. Y. (2002, February 5). Address by Senior Minister Lee Kuan Yew at the Ho Rih Hwa Leadership in Asia Public Lecture. *Singapore Government Press Release.* Retrieved from: https://www.smu.edu.sg/sites/default/files/microsites/hrh/pdf/SGP_20020205_MM-Lee-Speech.pdf.

Lee, K. Y., & Han, F. K. (2011). *Lee Kuan Yew: Hard Truths to Keep Singapore Going.* Singapore: Straits Times Press.

Lee, T. (2002). The politics of civil society in Singapore. *Asian Studies Review,* 97–117.

Lee, T. (2005). Going online. In A. Romano, & M. Bromley, *Journalism and Democracy in Asia* (pp. 15–27). London; New York: Routledge.

Lee, T. (2019). Pragmatic Competence and Communication Governance in Singapore. In L. Z. Rahim, & M. D. Barr, *The Limits of Authoritarian Governance in Singapore's Development State* (pp. 233–253). Singapore: Palgrave Macmillan.

Leeson, P. (2014). *Anarchy Unbound: Why Self-Governance Works Better Than You Think.* Cambridge University Press.

Leeson, P. (2008). Media freedom, political knowledge, and participation. *Journal of Economic Perspectives, 22*(2), 155–169.

Leeson, P., & Coyne, C. (2004). Plight of underdeveloped countries. *CATO Journal, 24*(3), 235–249.

Legge, J. (1960). *The Chinese Classics.* Hong Kong: Hong Kong University Press.

Levy, J. (2016). There is no such thing as ideal theory. *Social Philosophy and Policy, 33*(1–2), 312–333.

Lewis, H. (2013). *Crony Capitalism in America: 2008–2012.* AC2 Books.

Lim, L. (2014). What's Wrong With Singaporeans? In D. Low, & S. Vadaketh, *Hard Choices: Challenging the Singapore Consensus.* NUS Press.

Long, R. (2003). Austro-Libertarian themes in early confucianism. *Journal of Libertarian Studies, 17*(3), 35–62.

Lopez, E., & Leighton, W. (2014). *Madmen, Intellectuals, and Academic Scribblers: The Economic Engine of Political Change.* Stanford University Press.

Lordan, G., & Neumark, D. (2018). *People Versus Machines: The Impact of Minimum Wages on Automatable Jobs.* National Bureau of Economic Research.

Low, D. (2011). *Behavioural Economics and Policy Design: Examples from Singapore.* Singapore: World Scientific.

Low, D., & Vadakeh, S. T. (2014). *Hard Choices: Challenging the Singapore Consensus.* Singapore: NUS Press.

Low, L. (2001). *The Political Economy of a City-State: Government-Made Singapore.* Oxford University Press.

Low, L. (2001). The Singapore developmental state in the new economy and polity. *The Pacific Review, 14*(3), 411–441.

Magness, P., & Murphy, R. P. (2015). Challenging the empirical contribution of Thomas Piketty's Capital in the 21st century. *Journal of Private Enterprise, 30,* 1–34.

Mahbubani, K. (1993). The dangers of decadence: What the rest can teach the west. *Foreign Affairs, 72*(4), 10–14.

Mahbubani, K. (2005). *Beyond the Age of Innocence: Rebuilding Trust Between American and the World.* New York: Public Affairs.

Mahbubani, K. (2008). *The New Asian Hemisphere.* Public Affairs.

Mahbubani, K. (2018a). *20 Years of Can Asians Think?* Singapore: Marshall Cavendish.

Mahbubani, K. (2018b). *Has the West Lost it?* Singapore: Allen Lane.

Marina, W. (1998). Capitalism and the Tao. *The Mises Review, 16*(1).

Mauro, P., & Hellebrandt, T. (2015). *China's Contribution to Reducing Global Inequality.* Retrieved from: https://www.piie.com/publications/briefings/piieb15-3.pdf#page=29.

Mauzy, D. K., & Milne, R. (2002). *Singapore Politics Under the People's Action Party* (Politics in Asia Series ed.). London: Routledge.

McCloskey, D. (2008). Mr. Max and the substantial errors of manly economics. *Econ Journal Watch, 5*(2), 199–203.

McCloskey, D. (2011). *Bourgeois Dignity: Why Economics Can't Explain the Modern World.* University of Chicago Press.

McCloskey, D. (2019). *Why Liberalism Works: How True Liberal Values Produce a Freer, More Equal, Prosperous World for All.* Yale University Press.

McCloskey, D. N. (2014). Measured, Unmeasured, Mismeasured, and Unjustified Pessimism: A Review Essay of Thomas Piketty's Capital in the Twenty-first century. *Erasmus Journal for Philosophy and Economics, 7*(2), 73–115.

Mencius. (1970). *Mencius.* (D. Lau, Trans.) London: Penguin.

Mencius. (2009). *The Essential Mengzi: Selected Passages with Traditional Commentary.* Hackett Publishing.

Mill, J. S. (2009). *On Liberty.* The Floating Press.

Min, C. Y. (2017, February 25). Carbon tax expected to lead to higher electricity prices. *The Straits Times.* Retrieved from: https://www.straitstimes.com/business/economy/carbon-tax-expected-to-lead-to-higher-electricity-prices.

Ministry of Education. (2019, March 20). Overview of compulsory education. *Ministry of Education.* Retrieved from: https://beta.moe.gov.sg/primary/compulsory-education/overview/.

Mirron, J., Sollenberger, G. M., & Nicolae, L. (2019). Overdosing on regulation: How government caused the opioid epidemic. *Cato Institute Policy Analysis,* (864).

Mises, L. v. (1990). *Economic Calculation in the Socialist Commonwealth.* Auburn: Mises Institute.

Mises, L. v. (1998). *Human Action.* Auburn: The Ludwig von Mises Institute.

Mises, L. v. (2011). *Omnipotent Government: The Rise of the Total State and Total War*. Liberty Fund.

Mitchell, M., & Debnam, J. (2010). *In the Long Run, We're All Crowded Out*. Mercatus Center.

Mokyr, J. (2016). *A Culture of Growth: The Origins of the Modern Economy*. Princeton University Press.

Moore, R. Q. (2000). Multiracialism and meritocracy: Singapore's approach to race and inequality. *Review of Social Economy, 58*(3), 339–360.

Moore, S. (2019, October 10). *Middle-Class Incomes Surging — Thanks to Trump Policies*. Retrieved from: https://www.heritage.org/markets-and-finance/commentary/middle-class-incomes-surging-thanks-trump-policies.

Mukhopadhaya, P. (2014). *Income Inequality in Singapore*. London, UK: Routledge.

Mulligan, T. (2018). What's Wrong with Libertarianism: A Meritocratic Diagnosis. In J. Brennan, B. van der Vossen, & D. Schmidtz, *The Routledge Handbook of Libertarianism* (pp. 77–91). New York: Taylor & Francis.

Munger, M. (2018). Government Failure and Market Failure. In J. Brennan, B. v. Vossen, & D. Schmidtz (Eds.), *The Routledge Handbook of Libertarianism* (pp. 342–357). New York: Taylor & Francis.

Murray, C. (2015). *Losing Ground: American Social Policy, 1950–1980*. Basic Books.

Murray, C. (2016). *In Our Hands: A Plan to Replace the Welfare State*. Washington, DC: AEI Press.

National Archives of Singapore. (1971, April 28). Address by the Prime Minister, Mr. Lee Kuan Yew, at the Seminar on Communism and Democracy. *National Archives of Singapore*. Retrieved from: https://www.nas.gov.sg/archivesonline/data/pdfdoc/lky19710428.pdf.

National Library Board. (n.d.). *"Garden City" Vision is Introduced*. Retrieved from: http://eresources.nlb.gov.sg/history/events/a7fac49f-9c96-4030-8709-ce160c58d15c#4.

Neo, B. S., & Chen, G. (2007). *Dynamic Governance: Embedding Culture, Capabilities and Change in Singapore*. Singapore: World Scientific.

Neo, H. (2007). Challenging the developmental state: Nature conservation in Singapore. *Asia Pacific Viewpoint, 48*(2), 186–199.

Nicoara, O., & Boettke, P. (2015). What Have We Learned from the Collapse of Communism? In P. Boettke, & C. Coyne, *The Oxford Handbook of Austrian Economics*. Oxford University Press.

Niemietz, K. (2016). *Universal Healthcare Without the NHS*. London: Institute for Economic Affairs.

Norberg, J. (2016). *Progress: Ten Reasons to Look Forward to the Future*. London, UK: Oneworld Publications.

Norberg, J. (Director). (2018). *Work & Happiness: The Human Cost of Welfare* [Motion Picture].

North, D. (2005). *Understanding the Process of Economic Change*. Princeton University Press.

North, D., & Denzau, A. (1994). Shared mental models: Ideologies and institutions. *Kyklos, 47*(1), 3–31.

Nozick, R. (1974). *Anarchy, State and Utopia*. Oxford: Blackwell Publishers.

O'Dempsey, T. (2014). Singapore's Changing Landscape Since c. 1800. In T. P. Barnard (Ed.), *Nature Contained: Environmental Histories of Singapore* (pp. 17–48). Singapore: NUS Press.

O'Donoghue, T., & Rabin, M. (2006). Optimal sin taxes. *Journal of Public Economics, 90*(10–11), 1825–1849.

Olson, M. (2009). *The Logic of Collective Action Vol. 124*. Harvard University Press.

Ong, P. (2012). Can Psychology Save The Planet and Improve Our Environment? In D. Low (Ed.), *Behavioral Economics and Policy Design* (pp. 69–86). Singapore: World Scientific.

Ong, Y. K. (2018, July 14). Dealing with two paradoxes of Singapore's education system. *TODAY*. Retrieved from: https://www.todayonline.com/commentary/broad-agreement-meritocracy-and-inequality-key-developing-better-education-system.

Ostrom, E. (2009). A Polycentric approach for coping with climate change. *World Bank Policy Research Working Paper Series*, (5095).

Ostrom, V. (1997). *The Meaning of Democracy and the Vulnerability of Democracies: A Response to Tocqueville's Challenge*. Michigan: The University of Michigan Press.

Othman, N. (1999). Grounding Human Rights Arguments in Non-Western Culture: Shari'a and the Citizenship Rights of Women in a Modern Islamic State. In D. Bell, & J. Bauer, *The East Asian Challenge for Human Rights* (pp. 169–192). Cambridge University Press.

Palmer, T. G. (2002). Classical Liberalism and Civil Society: Definitions, History, and Relations. In N. L. Rosenblum, & R. C. Post (Eds.), *Civil Society and Government* (pp. 48–78). New Jersey: Princeton University Press.

Pang, E. F., & Lim, L. (2016). Labour, Productivity and Singapore's Development Model. In L. Lim, *Singapore's Economic Development: Retrospection and Reflections* (pp. 135–168). Singapore: World Scientific.

Paul, R. (2007). *A Foreign Policy of Freedom: Peace, Commerce, and Honest Friendship*. Foundation for Rational Economics and Education.

Pennington, M. (2011). *Robust Political Economy: Classical Liberalism and the Future of Public Policy*. Cheltenham, U.K.: Edward Elgar Publishers.

Pennington, M. (2017). Robust political economy and the priority of markets. *Social Philosophy and Policy, 34*(1), 1–24.

Piketty, T. (2014). *Capital in the 21st century.* Harvard University Press.

Powell, B. (2015). *The Economics of Immigration.* Oxford University Press.

Preble, C. (2019). *Peace, War, and Liberty: Understanding U.S. Foreign Policy.* Cato Institute.

Prime Minister's Office Singapore. (2015, October 4). Transcript of Speech by Prime Minister Lee Hsien Loong at the OnePeople.Sg's Community Leaders' Conference at The Grassroots Club. *Prime Minister's Office Singapore.* Retrieved from: https://www.pmo.gov.sg/newsroom/transcript-speech-prime-minister-lee-hsien-loong-onepeoplesgs-community-leaders.

Quah, J. S. (2010). *Public Administration Singapore-Style.* Bingley: Emerald Group Publishing Limited.

Rabinow, P., & Sullivan, W. M. (1987). *Interpretive Social Science: A Second Look.* Berkeley, CA: University of California Press.

Rahim, L. Z., & Yeoh, L. K. (2019). Social Policy Reform and Rigidity in Singapore's Authoritarian Developmental State. In L. Z. Rahim, & M. Barr, *The Limits of Authoritarian Governance in Singapore's Developmental State* (pp. 95–130). Palgrave Macmillan.

Rajah, J. (2012). *Authoritarian Rule of Law: Legislation, Discourse and Legitimacy in Singapore.* Cambridge University Press.

Rallo, J. R. (2017). Where are the Super-rich of 1987? In J.-P. Delsol, N. Lecaussin, & E. Martin (Eds.) *Anti-Piketty: Capital for the 21st century* (pp. 31–36). Cato Institute.

Rector, R. (2014, November 17). How welfare undermines marriage and what to do about it. *The Heritage Foundation.* Retrieved from: https://www.heritage.org/welfare/report/how-welfare-undermines-marriage-and-what-do-about-it.

Redford, A. (2019). Illicit drug trade and drug misuse: The unintended consequences of well-intentioned polices. *Center for Study of Free Enterprise Issue Briefs, 2*(5).

Reporters Without Borders. (2019). *World Press Freedom Index.* Reporters Without Borders.

Reynolds, G. (2006). *An Army of Davids: How Markets and Technology Empower Ordinary People To Beat Big Media, Big Government, And Other Goliaths.* Nashville, Tennessee: Thomas Nelson.

Rizzo, M. (2017a, March 1). *Rationality — What? Misconceptions of Neoclassical and Behavioral Economics.* Retrieved from: https://papers.ssrn.com/sol3/papers.cfm?abstract_id=2927443.

Rizzo, M. (2017b, October 9). *Richard Thaler's Nobel Prize.* Retrieved from: https://thinkmarkets.wordpress.com/2017/10/09/richard-thalers-nobel-prize/.

Rizzo, M. J., & Whitman, D. G. (2009a). Little brother is watching you: New paternalism on the slippery slopes. *Arizona Law Review, 51,* 685–739.

Rizzo, M. J., & Whitman, D. G. (2009b). The knowledge problem of new paternalism. *BYU Law Review* (4), 905–968.

Rosane, O. (2019, February 22). *Climate Change is the World's Biggest Threat, According to a New Global Survey.* Retrieved from: https://www.weforum.org/agenda/2019/02/climate-change-seen-as-top-threat-in-global-survey.

Rothbard, M. (1995). Libertarianism in Ancient China. In M. Rothbard, *An Austrian Perspective on the History of Economic Thought — Economic Thought Before Adam Smith* (Vol. 1). Edward Elgar Publishing Ltd.

Rothbard, M. (2008). *The Mystery of Banking.* Ludwig von Mises Institute.

Rowley, C., Tollison, R. D., & Tullock, G. (2013). *The Political Economy of Rent-Seeking.* Springer Science & Business Media.

Rummel, R. J. (1997). *Death by Government: Genocide and Mass Murder Since 1900.* Routledge.

Sabetti, F., & Castiglion, D. (2016). *Institutional Diversity in Self-Governing Societies — The Bloomington School and Beyond.* Rowman and Littlefield.

Sai, S. M., & Huang, J. (1999). The 'Chinese-educated' Political Vanguard. In O. P. Boon, L. K. Choy, & J. Y. Thong, *Lee's Lieutenants: Singapore's Old Guard* (pp. 132–168). New South Wales: Allen & Unwin.

Salleh, N. A. (2015, May 2). Political websites creating a buzz in Singapore. *The Straits Times.* Retrieved from: https://www.straitstimes.com/singapore/political-websites-creating-a-buzz-in-singapore.

Sally, R. (2015). The Halting Progress of Capitalism in Asia. *Quadrant,* pp. 31–48.

Sanandaji, N. (2015). *Scandinavian Unexceptionalism: Culture, Markets and the Failure of Third-wave Socialism.* London, UK: Institute for Economic Affairs.

Satha-Anand, S. (1999). Looking to Buddhism to Turn Back Prostitution in Thailand. In D. Bell, & J. Bauer, *The East Asian Challenge for Human Rights* (pp. 193–211). Cambridge University Press.

Scalet, S., & Schmidtz, D. (2002). State, Civil Society, and Classical Liberalism. In N. L. Rosenblum, & R. C. Post (Eds.), *Civil Society and Government* (pp. 26–47). New Jersey: Princeton University Press.

Scarborough, B. (2015). Prospecting for Energy and the Environment. In T. L. Anderson & D. R. Leal (Eds.), *Free Market Environmentalism for the Next Generation* (pp. 67–84). New York: Palgrave Macmillan.

Schlichter, D. S. (2014). *Paper Money Collapse: The Folly of Elastic Money.* John Wiley & Sons Inc.

Schmidtz, D. (2000). Natural enemies: An anatomy of environmental conflict. *Environmental Ethics, 22,* 397–408.

Schmidtz, D. (2016). A Realistic Political Ideal. *Social Philosophy and Policy,* 33(1–2), 1–10.

Schumpeter, J. A. (2003). *Capitalism, Socialism and Democracy.* London, New York: Routledge.

Schwartz, B. I. (2009). *The World of Thought in Ancient China.* Harvard University Press.

Scruton, R. (2007). *A Political Philosophy: Arguments for Conservatism.* Bloomsbury Publishing.

Selepak, A. G. (2018). Exploring anti-science attitudes among political and Christian conservatives through an examination of American universities on Twitter. *Cogent Social Sciences,* 4(1).

SG Climate Rally. (n.d.). *Our Calls to Action.* Retrieved from: https://drive.google.com/file/d/1f7EZP85dM7v2Rn9v1ffxjpufdwxR8akL/view.

Shao, G. (2019, August 15). Social media has become a battleground in Hong Kong's protests. *CNBC.* Retrieved from: https://www.cnbc.com/2019/08/16/social-media-has-become-a-battleground-in-hong-kongs-protests.html.

Shirky, C. (2008). *Here Comes Everybody: The Power of Organising Without Organisations.* Penguin.

Shlaes, A. (2007). *The Forgotten Man: A New History of the Great Depression.* HarperCollins.

Shlaes, A. (2019). *Great Society: A New History.* HarperCollins.

Shleifer, A. (2009). The Age of Milton Friedman. *Journal of Economic Literature,* 47(1): 123–135.

Simon, H. A. (1989). *Cognitive Architectures and Rational Analysis: Comment.* Retrieved from https://apps.dtic.mil/dtic/tr/fulltext/u2/a219199.pdf.

Singapore Unbound. (2018, November 15). *My Book of the Year 2018.* Retrieved from: https://singaporeunbound.org/blog/2018/11/4/my-book-of-the-year-2018-1.

Singh, B. (2019). *Is the People's Action Party Here to Stay?* Singapore: World Scientific.

Sinha, V. (2018). *This is What Inequality Looks Like.* Retrieved from: https://www.ethosbooks.com.sg/products/this-is-what-inequality-looks-like.

Somin, I. (2013). *Democracy and Political Ignorance: Why Smaller Government Is Smarter.* California: Stanford University Press.

Soon, C., Tan, R., & Wu, P. (2015). Who Calls the Shots? Agenda Setting in Mainstream and Alternative Media. In T. H. Tan, A. Mahizhnan, & P. H. Ang (Eds.), *Battle for Hearts and Minds* (pp. 95–119). Singapore: World Scientific.

Souchère, V., King, C., Dubreuil, N., Lecomte-Morel, V., Bissonnais, Y. L., & Chalat, M. (2003). Grassland and Crop Trends: Role of the European Union Common Agricultural Policy and Consequences for Runoff and Soil Erosion. *Environmental Science & Policy, 6*(1), 7–16.

Sowell, T. (1996). *The Vision of the Anointed: Self-Congratulation as a Basis for Social Policy*. Basic Books.

Stead, E. P., & Hoo, L. C. (2014). The development of the general music programme in primary and secondary schools. In J. Zubillaga-Pow, & C. K. Ho, *Singapore Soundscape: Musical Renaissance of a Global City* (pp. 235–250). Singapore: National Library Board.

Stiglitz, J. (2002). *Globalization and its discontents*. New York: W. W. Norton & Company.

Stiglitz, J. (2003, April 9). The ruin of Russia. *The Guardian*. Retrieved from: https://www.theguardian.com/world/2003/apr/09/russia.artsandhumanities.

Storr, V. (2009). Why the Market? Markets as Social and Moral Spaces. *Grand Rapids: Journal of Markets and Morality, 12*(2), 277–296.

Storr, V. (2010). The facts of the social sciences are what people think and believe. In C. Coyne, & P. Boettke (Eds.) *Handbook of Austrian Economics* (pp. 30–42). Cheltenham, UK: Edward Elgar Publishing.

Storr, V., & Choi, G. S. (2017). Markets as moral training grounds. In *Annual Proceedings of the Wealth and Well Being of Nations*, Volume 9. Beloit College. Retrieved from: https://www.beloit.edu/upton/assets/VOL_IX.08.Choi.Storr.pdf.

Storr, V., & Choi, G. S. (2016). Can Trust, Reciprocity and Friendships Survive Contact with the Market? In J. Baker & M. White (Eds.) *Economics and the Virtues: Building a New Moral Foundation* (pp. 217–235). Oxford, UK: Oxford University Press.

Stringham, E. (2015). *Private Governance — Creating Order in Economic and Social Life*. Oxford University Press.

Sunstein, C. R. (2014). Cost-benefit analysis and the knowledge problem. Retrieved from https://papers.ssrn.com/sol3/papers.cfm?abstract_id=2508965.

Tan, K. P. (2008). Meritocracy and elitism in a global city: Ideological shifts in Singapore. *International Political Science Review, 29*(1), 7–27.

Tan, K. P. (2011a). The people's action party and political liberalization in Singapore. *Political Parties, Party Systems and Democratization in East Asia*, 107–131.

Tan, K. P. (2011b). The Transformation of Meritocracy. In T. Chong, *Management of Success: Singapore Revisited* (pp. 272–287). Singapore: ISEAS Publishing.

Tan, K. P. (2012). The ideology of pragmatism: Neo-liberal globalisation and political authoritarianism in Singapore. *Journal of Contemporary Asia, 42*(1), 67–92.

Tan, K. S., & Bhaskaran, M. (2016). The Role of the State in Singapore: Pragmatism in Pursuit of Growth. In L. Lim, *Singapore's Economic Development: Retrospection and Reflections* (pp. 51–82). World Scientific.

Tan, T. H., Das, N., Samsudin, N., & Goh, S. (2015). *Snapshots from the 2011 IPS Post-Election Media Use and Political Traits Survey.* Retrieved from: https://lkyspp.nus.edu.sg/docs/default-source/ips/snapshots-from-the-2011-ips-post-election-media-use-and-political-traits-survey.pdf.

Tan, Y. S., Lee, T. J., & Tan, K. (2016). Applying Economic Principles to Environmental Policy. In T. Y. Soon (Ed.), *50 Years of Environment: Singapore's Journey Towards Environmental Sustainability* (pp. 45–62). Singapore: World Scientific.

Tanner, M. (2013). Europe's Crisis and the Welfare State. *CATO Journal, 33*(2): 187–191.

Tanner, M., & Hughes, C. (2015). The work versus welfare trade-off: Europe. *CATO Policy Analyses.*

Taylor, P. S. (2017, October 4). *BC's Carbon Tax: Revenue Neutrality Couldn't Survive Exposure to Politics.* Retrieved from: https://www.theglobeandmail.com/report-on-business/rob-commentary/bcs-carbon-tax-revenue-neutrality-couldnt-survive-exposure-to-politics/article36488526/.

Tebble, A. (2016). *Epistemic Liberalism: A Defence.* Taylor & Francis Ltd.

Teo, J. (2018, November 6). Workfare and the Singapore approach to tackling wage inequality. *The Straits Times.* Retrieved from: https://www.straitstimes.com/opinion/workfare-and-the-singapore-approach-to-tackling-wage-inequality.

Teo, Y. Y. (2013). *Neoliberal Morality in Singapore: How Family Policies Make State and Society.* Routledge.

Teo, Y. Y. (2012). *Neoliberal Morality in Singapore: Institutionalising the Logics of Neoliberalism.* Retrieved from: https://www.isa-sociology.org/uploads/files/EBul-Teo-Jul2012.pdf.

Teo, Y. Y. (2018). *This is What Inequality Looks Like.* Singapore: Ethos Books.

Tetlock, P. (2017). *Expert Political Judgment: How Good Is It? How Can We Know?* Princeton University Press.

Thaler, R. H., & Benartzi, S. (2004). Save more tomorrow: Using behavioral economics to increase employee saving. *Journal of Political Economy, 112*(1), 164–187.

Thaler, R. H., & Sunstein, C. R. (2003a). Libertarian paternalism. *American Economic Review, 93*(2), 175–179.

Thaler, R. H., & Sunstein, C. R. (2003b). Libertarian paternalism is not an oxymoron. *The University of Chicago Law Review*, 1159–1202.

Thaler, R. H., & Sunstein, C. R. (2008). *Nudge: Improving Decisions About Health, Wealth and Happiness.* New Haven & London: Yale University Press.

The Heritage Foundation. (2019). *2019 Index of Economic Freedom: 25th Anniversary Edition.* Washington: The Heritage Foundation.

The Straits Times. (2011). *Lee Kuan Yew: Hard Truths to Keep Singapore Going.* Singapore: Straits Times Press.

The Straits Times. (2020, January 22). The will to defy the odds of history. *The Straits Times.* Retrieved from: https://www.straitstimes.com/opinion/the-will-to-defy-the-odds-of-history.

Thierer, A. (2016). *Permissionless Innovation: The Continuing Case for Comprehensive Technological Freedom.* Mercatus Center.

Thomas, M. D. (2018). Reapplying behavioral symmetry: Public choice and choice architecture. *Public Choice, 180*(1–2), 11–25.

Thornhill, J. (2017, September 4). The Big Data revolution can revive the planned economy. *Financial Times.* Retrieved from: https://www.ft.com/content/6250e4ec-8e68-11e7-9084-d0c17942ba93.

Tocqueville, A. d. ([1835], 2010). *Democracy in America: Historical-Critical Edition of De la démocratie en Amérique.* Indianapolis: Liberty Fund, Inc.

TODAY. (2015, March 23). Taking on the Western media. *TODAY.* Retrieved from: https://www.todayonline.com/rememberinglky/taking-western-media

Tomasi, J. (2014). The moral case for economic liberty. In *2014 Index of Economic Freedom*, by Heritage Foundation, 59–66. Washington, DC: Heritage Foundation & Dow Jones & Company, Inc.

Tullock, G. (1993). *Rent Seeking.* Brookfield: Edward Elgar.

Tversky, A., & Kahneman, D. (1974). Judgment under uncertainty: Heuristics and biases. *Science, 185*, 1124–1131.

Vasquez, I., & Porcnik, T. (2019). *Human Freedom Index 2019.* Massachusetts: Cato Institute.

Veryser, H. (2013). *It Didn't Have to Be This Way: Why Boom and Bust Is Unnecessary.* ISI Books.

Vincent, S. (2018). *The Naysayer's Book Club: 26 Singaporeans You Need to Know.* Singapore: Epigram Books.

Wagner, R. E. (2017). *James M. Buchanan and Liberal Political Economy.* Lanham: Lexington Books.

Walker, P. (2008, January 31). Human rights group condemns western hypocrisy. *The Guardian.* Retrieved from: https://www.theguardian.com/world/2008/jan/31/uk.usa.

Wang, B., & Li, X. (2017). Big data, platform economy and market competition: A preliminary construction of plan-oriented market economy system in the information era. *World Review of Political Economy, 8*(2), 138–161.

Wendling, Z. A., Emerson, J. W., Esty, D. C., Levy, M. A., & Sherbinin, A. d. (2018). *Environmental Performance Index*. Connecticut: Yale Center for Environmental Law & Policy.

White, J. B. (2019, August 13). *Is Big Soda winning the soft drink wars?* Retrieved from: https://www.politico.com/agenda/story/2019/08/13/soda-tax-california-public-health-000940.

Wilson, B., & Smith, V. (2019). *Humanomics: Moral Sentiments and the Wealth of Nations for the Twenty-First Century*. Cambridge University Press.

Wong, B., & Huang, X. (2010). Political legitimacy in Singapore. *Politics and Policy, 38*(3), 523–543.

Wong, K. (2019, September 21). *More than 1,700 turn up at first Singapore Climate Rally*. Retrieved from: https://www.channelnewsasia.com/news/singapore/1700-participants-sg-climate-rally-die-in-11930486.

Yahya, F. B. (2015). *Inequality in Singapore*. Singapore: World Scientific.

Yasuaki, O. (1999). Toward an Intercivilizational Approach to Human Rights. In D. Bell, *The East Asian Challenge for Human Rights* (pp. 103–123). Cambridge University Press.

Yeoh, L. K., Ho, S. C., Low, D., Bhaskaran, M., Tan, K. S., & Vadaketh, S. (2012). *Inequality and the Need for a New Social Compact*. Retrieved from: https://lkyspp.nus.edu.sg/docs/default-source/ips/singapore-perspectives-2012-background-paper.pdf.

Yip, B. (2019, April 29). Understanding the four critiques of Singapore's meritocracy. *TODAY*. Retrieved from: https://www.todayonline.com/commentary/understanding-four-critiques-singapores-meritocracy.

Yip, C. S. (2015). *Intergenerational Income Mobility in Singapore*. Retrieved from: https://www.mof.gov.sg/Portals/0/Feature%20Articles/Executive%20Summary%20-%20Intergenerational%20Income%20Mobility%20In%20Singapore.pdf.

Young, L. (1996). The tao of markets: Sima Qian and the invisible hand. *Pacific Economic Review, 1*(2), 137–145.

Yuen, B. (1996). Creating the Garden City: The Singapore experience. *Urban Studies, 33*(6), 955–970.

Zak, P. (2011). Moral markets. *Journal of Economic Behavior & Organization, 77*(2), 212–233.

Index

www.ingramcontent.com/pod-product-compliance
Lightning Source LLC
Chambersburg PA
CBHW071956260326
41914CB00004B/815